538

Norman K. Denzin is Professor of Sociology, Communications, and Humanities at the University of Illinois, Urbana-Champaign. He is the author of numerous books, including *Sociological Methods, The Research Act, Interpretive Interactionism, The Recovering Alcoholic,* and *The Alcoholic Self*, which won the Cooley Award from The Society for the Study of Symbolic Interaction in 1988. He has been the editor of *Studies in Symbolic Interaction: A Research Journal* since 1978.

Twentieth-Century Social Theory

Series Editor: Charles C. Lemert

Twentieth-Century Social Theory invites authors respected for their contributions in the prominent traditions of social theory to reflect on past and present in order to propose what comes next. Books in the series will consider critical theory, race, symbolic interactionism, functionalism, feminism, world systems theory, psychoanalysis, and Weberian social theory, among other current topics. Each will be plain to read, yet provocative to ponder. Each will gather up what has come to pass in the twentieth century in order to define the terms of social theoretical imagination in the twenty–first.

Titles in the series include:

SYMBOLIC INTERACTIONISM AND CULTURAL STUDIES

THE POLITICS
OF INTERPRETATION

NORMAN K. DENZIN

BLACKWELL
Oxford UK & Cambridge USA

Copyright © Norman K. Denzin 1992

The right of Norman K. Denzin to be identified as author of this work has been asserted in accordance with the Copyright, Designs and Patents Act 1988.

First published 1992

First published in USA 1992

Blackwell Publishers
Three Cambridge Center
Cambridge, Massachusetts 02142
USA

108 Cowley Road
Oxford OX4 1JF
UK

Library of Congress Cataloging-in-Publication Data
Denzin, Norman K.
  Symbolic Interactionism and Cultural Studies: The Politics of Interpretation/Norman K. Denzin.
    p. cm. – (Twentieth-century Social Theory)
  Includes bibliographical references and index.
  ISBN 1–55786–059–9 – ISBN 1–55786–291–5 (pbk.)
  1. Symbolic interactionism.   2. Culture.   I. Title.   II. Series.
  HM291.D454   1992   91-33020
  306–dc20   CIP

British Library Cataloguing in Publication Data

A CIP catalogue record for this book is available from the British Library.

Typeset in Sabon 10 on 12 pt by TecSet Ltd, Wallington, Surrey and printed in Great Britain by T.J. Press Ltd, Padstow, Cornwall.

This book is printed on acid-free paper

CONTENTS

SERIES EDITOR'S PREFACE

"The *fin* is coming a little early this *siècle*." Angela Carter's line is likely to become *the* line of the early years of the decade. Indeed, the twentieth century is coming to some sort of ending long before its years have run out.

In this respect, these years seem to bear comparison to those during which it was thought the nineteenth century was ending. Yet, we know that the previous century did not exactly end at any time close to its calendrical expiration date. Within the spheres of European influence, the 1890s were without question a decade of fantastic inventions in culture, politics, letters, and science. Still, the trajectory from this *fin de siècle* ferment, to the big change in Western history was long and tortuous. The nineteenth century ended some time or another in the early 1940s after two world wars, a devastating economic depression, and a holocaust somehow cleansed the older European societies of their uncomplicated faith in enlightenment progress.

If we might fairly say that the nineteenth was the century in which Europe invented itself in order to dominate the world through the extraordinary means of civilizing power, then it would be just as correct to define the twentieth century from the moment the Americans inherited, and transformed, the cunning faith of the original Europeans. In the truth of lived (as distinct from calendrical) time, our century did not meaningfully begin until about 1944 when Henry Luce declared it "the American Century."

Perhaps Angela Carter's experience is widely shared not because the *fin* of the twentieth *siècle* comes so soon, but because the *siècle* itself was so awkwardly short. It would not be preposterous, after all, to situate the distinctive character of the twentieth century within, more or less, the years of the Cold War. Such a principle would define the twentieth as the

century in which the Modern Age took its best, final shot at perfecting
the human condition with at best inconclusive results. Modernity being
what it is (an oddly sly but still naive belief in perfect progress),
uncertainty is its worst nightmare. The triumph of Communism would
have been more tolerable. Its failure, unaccompanied by proof positive of
the West's success, is somehow a much more unsettling fate. Eastern
Europe and the former Soviet republics look, in these days, to the West
for market principles and model democracies. When their heads
eventually shake the dizziness induced by strobe-like change, they will
find, instead, a series of social crises looming over the basics of human
existence. The former East hungers for freedom and economic growth;
the West for the simple need of health care, education, shelter, and clean
air. The true Good Society is nowhere to be found. The twentieth
century, thus, could be said to end, or begin its ending, upon the
disappearance of the competitive conditions in which the Americans
meant to prove the truth of their Way. What comes after is still another
question.

   Twentieth-Century Social Theory, the series of which this is the first
book, was conceived and proposed by editors at Blackwell Publishers in
1988, before the dramatic events of the last two years made clear the
likelihood that something in the world was ending. Nevertheless, the
original intent of the book's series remains powerful and useful, now
more than ever. Sociology and social theory – two related if not exactly
identical endeavors – were both born in the nineteenth century to come
of age in the twentieth. In Europe and the United States, sociology
enjoyed a golden age in the 1950s and 1960s when it was among those
social sciences counted upon to discover the scientific truths necessary to
the Good Society. Social theory, always somewhat eccentric to each and
all the social sciences, came into its own in the twentieth century just
about a half-step after sociology. It is not too far wrong to say that what
is today known as social theory was required by the obvious failure of
sociology to perfect the social world. Social theory, thus, has been
fashioned out of the varieties of marxisms, feminisms, numerous other
critical theories and, even, residual sociological ideas skeptical always of
any society's too great faith in its destiny.

   It is entirely fitting that Norman Denzin's *Symbolic Interactionism and
Cultural Studies* is the first book in the series to appear. Of all the
theoretical lines in current sociology, symbolic interactionism is one of
the few that could be said to be largely an invention of the twentieth
century (however defined). Even more to the point, it is that one enduring
line of theoretical inquiry that begins and continues almost entirely under
the influence of classical American sources and concerns. That a number

of European sources, most notably Habermas, have turned to pragmatism in order to reconstruct modernist social ideas only confirms the surprising endurance of pragmatism from which symbolic interaction took so much of its original inspiration. Just the same, symbolic interactionism in sociology, like pragmatism more generally, finds itself limited today by its weird irrelevance to the debate over the postmodern condition. Symbolic interactionism with its decided interest in language, and pragmatism, with its deep structural commitment to view knowledge as always close to the workings of the world, would seem to be the natural kin of any postmodern social theory. This has not, however, been the case (with the possible exception of Richard Rorty's peculiar resort to a pragmatist politics after having demolished the grounds for a philosophy as anything more than literary criticism).

Symbolic interactionism has certainly been limited by its confinement within the disciplinary field of sociology. To be sure, this location has produced a proud tradition of important work, one as distinctively American as any. Yet, its relations to the most dramatic and radical cultural inventions of the so-called Chicago tradition have frequently been furtive, even subterranean. That symbolic interactionism was always close to the work of Goffman, the societal reaction and labeling theories of deviance, and, generally, much of underdog sociology before the 1970s is beyond dispute. Just the same, these were always more eruptions from the tradition that would want to claim them. Thus, when Herbert Blumer in particular codified and publicized the symbolic interactionist tradition, even he did so in a fashion that sought mostly to establish its credentials as a science. The essays Blumer brought together in 1969 in *Symbolic Interactionism: Perspective and Method* (perhaps the locus classicus of SI) were notable for their surprising suppression of the art and politics in American pragmatist social theory; this in favor of a symbolic interactionism seeking the status of a reputable sociological method. 1969 was, it turned out, just exactly the wrong time to invent a sociology as method, and one wonders what would have happened to symbolic interactionism had Blumer, then, taken the other turn toward breaking open American sociological pragmatism to the broader concerns of cultural and literary studies.

The publication of Norman Denzin's *Symbolic Interactionism and Cultural Studies: The Politics of Interpretation* should bring great satisfaction and relief to those troubled by questions of what might have been. What Blumer was unable to do in the 1960s, Denzin's is doing now. Denzin makes clear why it could not have been at that earlier time. In the 1960s, when symbolic interactionism was seeking to preempt the qualitative wing of American sociological science, there were few of the many real choices available today. The dramatic changes in sociology that would occur in the 1970s were yet to come. The field was still living very much the life of the Science of the American Way, trying hard to forget C. Wright Mills and to shake off the irreverence of younger men and women just then entering graduate school. In those days, George Homans was known as a rebel. It was, therefore, still incumbent on anyone who would dare to define and establish a distinctly different line in sociology to do so as though it were the very best science to be had. This was Blumer's choice. Then as now, symbolic interactionism was a rich, productive enterprise. The questions one could put to it were those Blumer chose to answer: Was it really a science? Should it be?

It is a sign of the present time that Norman Denzin's brilliant reconsideration of symbolic interactionism is not preoccupied with these questions. They have, in a sense, lost their urgency. Sociology today, even more than before, is divided into the camps of those who hang onto its potential as a science and of those who find this hardly something to fight over. If the former camp is today nicely represented in the bizarre musings of various rational choice theorists, then the latter could well enough be symbolized by Denzin. Though he is not by any means the only available representative of this growing boldness among sociologists, his ideas in the present book provide an excellent view of just what sociologies of all kinds might need to do to rescue themselves from the shadows slowly settling over the official sociologies of Method.

Norman Denzin has, in this, taken to heart one of the great traditions of American sociology by demonstrating just exactly how it might revive, and be revived, in vital relation to the new and ubiquitous field of cultural studies. He is, thus, bold in at least two ways. For one, he refuses to restrict himself to anything like a "sociology of culture." For another, he reaches far and wide beyond any specific discipline into a loose but dynamic domain, cultural studies – known principally for being one of those activities most likely to help produce whatever will stand in the place of human sciences in the twenty-first century.

Denzin is just the person to engage sociologists in such a politics of interpretation. From the beginning of his remarkably productive career, Denzin has always sought to reach beyond what was there. He was trained in the methodologically more conservative of the two symbolic interactionist sub-traditions – at Iowa under Manford Kuhn. Yet, in his earliest writings he reached beyond the experimental cautions of his teachers to the other, more ethnographic symbolic interactionist line. Then, when ethnomethodology appeared brashly on the scene he sought, in a controversial *American Sociological Review* article, to breach the divide between it and his own tradition. Ethnomethodologists abruptly and rudely rejected this proposal of marriage. But this did not deter Denzin. In the 1970s, long before very many American sociologists thought to do so, Denzin began to read and use the ideas of what then seemed to be the impenetrable writings of the early structuralists and poststructuralists. He has, since then, labored in writing and teaching to master this other, largely European line of social theoretical work. One supposes he did so without benefit of wild applause from either his own department or those in the symbolic interactionist enclaves and associations still dominant throughout much of the Midwest. Yet, he continued. Those who know Norman Denzin know him to be a man of courage and persistence, as much in his personal as his intellectual life. These qualities of character are evident in the sensible, but provocative proposals he makes in this book.

Norman Denzin's *Symbolic Interactionism and Cultural Studies* is a book poised just at a point near the end of twentieth-century American social thought, close to the beginning of whatever will follow. It reminds us specifically of all we have been taught by a distinctive American social theory, yet leads the reader on – beyond America, beyond sociology, beyond any one social theoretical line – to what could come to be.

Charles C. Lemert

PREFACE

Cultural studies, on an American terrain, has been given its most powerful expression by John Dewey and in the tradition of symbolic interactionism, which developed out of American pragmatism generally. It was Dewey's student, Robert Park, who provided the most powerful analysis of mass culture. . . that was adapted to the circumstances of this country. (J. W. Carey 1989: 96)

This is a programmatic book about symbolic interactionism. My intentions are threefold. First, I offer my version of the history of this unique American sociological and social psychological theory. Second, I examine what I regard as key theoretical and empirical issues in this perspective. Third, I present a research agenda for those who follow this tradition.

These intentions create two problems, both of which turn on the reading of social texts and the politics of theory. Fortunately, or unfortunately, there are multiple versions (readings) of this perspective and its history (see, e.g., Blumer 1969; Stone and Farberman (eds) 1981; Manis and Meltzer (eds) 1972; Reynolds 1990; Farberman and Perinbanayagam (eds) 1985; A. Rose (ed.) 1962; Deegan and Hill (eds) 1987; *Symbolic Interaction* 1988, *Symbolic Interaction* 1989; Stryker 1987; Maines 1977, 1988; Maines and Morrione (eds) 1990; Lyman and Vidich 1988; Fisher and Strauss 1978; Joas 1987; Fine 1990; Plummer 1990, 1991). I will attempt to wrestle to the ground and make my interpretive sense of this shifting theoretical paradigm called symbolic interactionism.

The second problem involves how to recast this theory in a mold which will better allow it and its practitioners to fulfill the original promise of a critical, pragmatic, cultural, and interpretive social science (J. W. Carey

1989: 96). Such an interactionism will speak to the "terrible and magnificent world of human society" (Mills 1959: 225) in the waning years of the twentieth century. Contrary to Carey's assertion, I will argue that symbolic interactionists have failed to produce an American version of cultural studies. This failure absorbs the majority of the criticisms that have been directed at the theory (see Reynolds 1990 for a review, and below). How this failure may be overcome is my central project.

Symbolic interactionism is that unique American sociological and social psychological perspective that traces its roots to the early American pragmatists James, Dewey, Peirce, and Mead. It has been called the loyal opposition in American sociology (Mullins 1973: 98), the most sociological of social psychologies (Manis and Meltzer (eds) 1972: 557). In its canonical form (Blumer 1969) it rests on three root assumptions: first, that "human beings act toward things on the basis of the meanings that the things have for them" (p. 2); second, that the meanings of things arise out of the process of social interaction; and third, that meanings are modified through an interpretive process which involves self-reflective individuals symbolically interacting with one another.

I will examine the strains, tensions, and varieties of symbolic interaction, treating the works of interactionists as cultural texts. I assume that these works embody, as do all cultural texts, taken-for-granted understandings (Barthes 1957/72: 11). These understandings include certain theoretical, empirical, and ideological biases. When deployed, they serve a double function. They permit the construction of an "interactionist" subject, and they mark any given work as an instance of an interactionist text (see Saxton 1989; Flaherty 1989).

Symbolic interactionism comes in multiple varieties (Reynolds 1990: 3; Warshay 1975; Warshay and Warshay 1986; Martindale 1981: 348–74; Mullins 1973, 4), including pragmatic (Rochberg-Halton 1986), dramaturgical (Goffman 1959; Perinbanayagam 1985; Brissett and Edgley (eds) 1990), negotiated order (Maines 1982; Strauss 1978; P. M. Hall 1987), political (P. M. Hall 1972, 1985), feminist (Deegan and Hill (eds) 1987; Clough 1987, 1988, 1989, 1991; Richardson 1990), phenomenological (Wiley 1979, 1989; Bentz 1989; Gurevitch 1990), formal (Couch 1984b) and everyday life sociologies (Adler *et al.* 1987), existential sociologies of the absurd (Lyman and Scott 1988; Douglas and Johnson (eds) 1977; Kotarba and Fontana (eds) 1984), discourse (Stone 1962, 1981), and structural, role-identity theories (G. J. McCall and Simmons 1978; Stryker 1980, 1987), reality constructionism (Berger and Luckmann 1967), interpretive (Denzin 1989b), and contextual interactionism (Farberman 1989). Alongside these varieties rest mythical

(and real) distinctions between the Iowa and neo-Iowa (Couch *et al.*
1986a, p. x; Denzin 1986a: xiv), Chicago (Reynolds 1990: 3; Farberman
1979; Lal 1982), Minnesota (Mullins 1973: 93), and Illinois (Martindale
1981: 374) schools.

Diversity is not just theoretical. At the methodological level,
interactionists employ a variety of interpretive, qualitative approaches,
including the "new" ethnographies identified by Adler and Adler (1987);
the postmodern ethnographies of Turner and Bruner (eds) (1986); the
structural, articulative, semiotic, and practical ethnographies of Gubrium
(1988) and Manning (1987); Glaser and Strauss's grounded theory
(1967); the biographical, life history method (Plummer 1983, 1990;
Denzin 1989a; McCall and Wittner 1990); the performance science of
Becker *et al.* (1989); the feminist ethnographies of Clough (1991); the
more traditional interviewing, fieldwork, and participant observation
practices advocated by Becker (1986a), Fine (1987), Fine and Sandstrom
(1988), Warren (1988), and Jorgensen (1989); Douglas's (1985) creative
interviewing, the interpretive practices hinted at by Blumer (1969),
Athens (1984), and Maines (1989a); conversational analysis (Maynard
1987); Lofland and Lofland's (1984), Prus's (1987), and Couch's (1987)
ethnographic and laboratory searches for generic principles of social life;
and Couch's (1984a) and Lyman's (1990b) historical studies of
civilizational processes.

Substantively, interactionists have made major contributions to many
areas of sociology. An incomplete list would include the fields of
deviance (Becker 1963; Lindesmith 1968; Reese and Katovich 1989),
social problems (Spector and Kitsuse 1977), collective behavior
(J. Lofland 1981), medical sociology (Glaser and Strauss, 1965; Strauss
et al. 1985; Charmaz 1991), the emotions (Hochschild 1983; Franks and
McCarthy (eds) 1989; Ellis 1991), the arts (Becker 1982), social
organization and bureaucratic structures (P. M. Hall 1987; Altheide and
Johnson 1980), race relations and industrialization (Lyman and Vidich
1988; Maines and Morrione (eds) 1990), childhood socialization (Power
1985; Leavitt and Power 1989; Cahill 1989; Fine and Sandstrom 1988);
family violence (Ferraro and Johnson 1983; Johnson and Ferraro 1984;
J. M. Johnson 1989; Loseke 1987, 1989); criminal violence (Athens
1989); the mass media (Altheide 1985), and small groups (Couch *et al.*
1986a, b). In short, there are many styles and versions of symbolic
interactionism and these variations are displayed across the fields of
sociology and social psychology. (Too often these contributions have
been ignored by critics of the perspective.)

The *interpretive* version of the perspective (interpretive
interactionism), which I present here, attempts to make the worlds of
lived experience directly accessible to the reader. Interpretive

interactionists endeavor to capture the voices, emotions, and actions of those studied. They focus on those life experiences which radically alter and shape the meanings persons give to themselves and their experiences (Denzin 1989b: 10).

Interactionism has had a tortured history in American sociology. Many times its death has been announced and its practitioners maligned (see Flaherty 1989: 35–8; Saxton 1989: 10–13). But the perspective refuses to die. It has been nearly 30 years since Manford Kuhn, in his presidential address to the Midwest Sociological Society ("Major Trends in Symbolic Interaction Theory in the Past Twenty-Five Years," 1964a/72), presented what has become the classic reading of symbolic interactionist texts. In that essay Kuhn predicted (1964a/72) that symbolic interactionism would hold its own and gain against the competition. Eleven years later, Nicholas C. Mullins (1973: 98), in his highly influential book on theories and theory groups in American sociology, proclaimed symbolic interactionism's demise: "As a change-maker and general orientation for sociology and as the loyal opposition to structural functionalism [symbolic interactionism] has come to an end." Two years later Randall Collins, a preeminent American social theorist would argue that "Symbolic interactionists, for all their self-image as proponents of freshness and life in sociology, are themselves responsible for the feeling that sociologists give other names to what everybody already knows" (1975: 34). Collins would elaborate this interpretation in 1986 thus: "By the 1980s, the central messages [of symbolic interactionism] have become a little stagnant . . . symbolic interaction [ists] seem to be merely repeating the same general points with different empirical content" (1986: 1347–8). (He repeated these arguments, with slight variation, in 1989a.) In 1987, Hans Joas, writing on the history of symbolic interactionism, remarked on the theory's "self-isolation" and inability to oppose the "comprehensive, theoretically and historically broadly-inclusive approaches of Parsons (or of Marxism and critical theory)" (1987: 84). Prendergast and Knotternus (1990: 178) bring the following terms to bear on the theory: "quaint, unreal, ideologically biased, ahistorical, noneconomic, apolitical, fuzzy and imprecise." Lemert (1979b: 103) suggested that symbolic interactionism's version of sociological interpretivism provides " a weak metaphoric theory of social structures, such as Blumer's joint actions." These meanings echo charges raised elsewhere by Reynolds (1990) and earlier by Meltzer et al. (1975).

But symbolic interactionism will not go away. In 1992 it is alive and well, thriving in two journals (Symbolic Interaction and Studies in Symbolic Interaction), an international association (the Society for the

Study of Symbolic Interaction), annual meetings, and the annual Stone symposium.[1]

The seven chapters which follow are intended to show why this perspective will not die.[2] Chapter 1 examines the interactionist heritage. Chapter 2 presents my version of the interpretive position and offers a critical reading of the poststructuralist project as it bears on symbolic interactionism. Chapter 3 discusses the major criticisms which have been brought against the perspective. Chapter 4 moves from interpretation to cultural studies, opening the door for chapters 5–7 which take up, in turn, the relationship between symbolic interactionism and cultural studies, the communications research tradition in interactionism, interactionist cultural criticism, and the politics of cultural studies. Chapter 7 comes full circle and recapitulates the arguments of earlier chapters. Here I call for interpretive strategies which will overcome that "certain blindness" to the perspectives of others that William James (1899) located at the heart of the human condition.

This book extends the arguments presented in my *Interpretive Interactionism* (1989b), *Interpretive Biography* (1989a), and *Images of Postmodern Society: Social Theory and Contemporary Cinema* (1991d), at the same time building on the cultural-interpretive framework for reading texts utilized in my *Hollywood Shot by Shot: Alcoholism in American Cinema* (1991b).

Three biases structure my analysis. First, interactionism, if it is to thrive and grow, must incorporate elements of poststructural and postmodern theory (e.g. the works of Barthes, Derrida, Foucault, Baudrillard, etc.) into its underlying views of history, culture, and politics. Second, this growth will be best realized by merging the interactionist sociological imagination with a critical, feminist, cultural studies point of view (Balsamo 1988, 1989, 1990). Third, a politics of interactionism must be developed if the perspective is to merge the worlds of theory with the worlds of practice.

I would like to thank the following individuals for their contributions to this book: Charles Lemert for initiating the project and giving me a critical reading of earlier drafts; my editors at Blackwell Publishers, Romesh Vaitilingam and Simon Prosser, for their enthusiastic support of the project; Norbert Wiley, David Maines, Carl Couch, James W. Carey, Patricia Clough, Peter K. Maning, John Johnson and Katherine Ryan-Denzin for a lifetime of conversations about symbolic interactionism; my students, who have heard various versions of what is here in one place or another; Jean van Altena for careful copy-editing; Jill Landeryou for overseeing the editing process; Paul Benson and Richard

Louisell for proofreading. C. Wright Mills for inspiration; and finally, Manford H. Kuhn and Herbert Blumer, who introduced me to this perspective in the first place.

Norman K. Denzin
Champaign, Illinois

NOTES

1 The Stone Foundation, created by the late Gregory P. Stone, a founding father of the Society for the Study of Symbolic Interaction, supports an annual Spring symposium for symbolic interactionists. The 1991 symposium marked a decade of such annual meetings.

2 Space restrictions require that I should not deal explicitly with the interactionist conceptions of the cultural object, act, language, self, and lived experience (see Denzin 1986b, 1988, 1987a, for preliminary statements on these terms).

1 THE INTERACTIONIST HERITAGE

The term "symbolic interactionism" has come into use as a label for a rather distinctive approach to the study of human group life and conduct . . . [it] has been followed more than it has been formulated . . . [It] is a down-to-earth approach to the scientific study of human group life and human conduct. (Blumer 1969: 1, 78, 47)

It is absolutely necessary to include the relevant subjective elements in a sociological analysis of human society, yet the instruments (human documents) for getting such subjective elements do not allow us to meet the customary criteria for scientific data. (Blumer 1979: xiii)

In this chapter I will trace the development of the interactionist perspective from 1890 to 1990, noting phases of development, key works in each phase, and the recurring problems which interactionists have addressed. It will be necessary to offer an outline of the theory, even though detailed histories are available elsewhere (e.g. Blumer 1969; Fisher and Strauss 1978; Stryker 1981; Lyman and Vidich 1988; Maines 1977; Rock 1979; Maines and Morrione (eds) 1990; Joas 1987; Fine 1990; Plummer 1991). I will present capsule summaries of the views of particular interactionists (e.g. Cooley, James, Mead, Dewey, and Blumer). More in-depth overviews can be found in Strauss 1956; Farberman and Perinbanayagam 1985; Fisher and Strauss 1978; Lyman and Vidich 1988; Martindale 1981; Joas 1985; and Becker and McCall (eds) 1990. Besides, there is no substitute for reading the original texts.

The heritage

Interactionists are cultural romantics (see Shalin 1984). They are pre-occupied with Promethean human powers. They valorize villains and outsiders as heroes and side with the downtrodden little people. They believe in the contingency of self and society and conceive of social reality from the vantage point of change and transformations which produce emancipatory ideals "for which one lives and dies" (West 1989: 215). Often tragic (and ironic), their romantic vision of self and society stands in a direct line with the left romanticism of Ralph Waldo Emerson, Karl Marx, William James, John Dewey, Antonio Gramsci, Martin Luther King, Jr, and Roberto Unger (see West 1989, ch. 6).

From its birth, symbolic interactionism – which I arbitrarily date with the publication of William James's *Principles of Psychology* (1890), John Dewey's seminal article "The Reflex Arc Concept in Psychology" (1896), Charles Horton Cooley's *Human Nature and the Social Order* (1902), and G. H. Mead's 1910 essay "What Social Objects must Psychology Presuppose?" – has been haunted by a double-edged specter. On the one hand, its founding theorists argued for the interpretive, subjective study of human experience. On the other hand, they sought to build an objective science of human conduct, a science which would conform to criteria borrowed from the natural sciences. Through each phase of historical development (see Table 1) interactionists have been plagued by an inability to merge these two problematics. This inability, I shall argue below, stems directly from the pragmatic tradition which contemporary interactionists have inherited from their founding fathers.

The interactionist subject

Interactionists have persisted in believing in the presence of a concrete, real subject (see Lemert 1979b: 103–4). This subject's presence in the world is given through subjective and objective reports about personal experience and the interaction process. Language (and the verbal reports it permits) has been taken as the window into the inner life of the person. A behavioristic theory of the sign, symbol, and language (C. Morris 1938), unresponsive to Peirce's (1934, 1958) semiotic of the sign, has given interactionists a weak theory of the symbolic (Gottdiener 1985; Rochberg-Halton 1986). This behaviorist theory fails to accord with the more radical semiotics of language which traces its roots to Saussure (1959) and ends with Baudrillard (1981), after passing through Peirce's phenomenological treatment of the interpretant (Manning 1988b). Such a theory also fails to treat language and its relationship to cultural objects and the political economy of everyday life (Farberman 1980). A metaphysics of presence, predicated on a simplistic theory of language, thus structures the interactionist tradition.

Early (and contemporary) interactionists were (and are) preoccupied with the stream of consciousness of the subject (James 1890), the experience of temporality in the organization of social acts (Mead 1910; Reese and Katovich 1989; Katovich 1987), blocked acts (Dewey 1896), joint acts (Blumer 1969; Couch 1989), interior self-conversations (Mead 1934), the place of the other in the act (Mead 1934) and experience and its organization (Goffman 1974). Always seeking a unit of analysis, they wavered between acts and experience. This preoccupation led to the continual search for a method of analysis that would incorporate the subjective (and interactional) features of human conduct into valid scientific documents about human society (Blumer 1969; Couch 1987).

This has created an interpretive heritage that relies on the "soft," qualitative methodologies outlined in the Preface. Assuming that the subject is (and was) the final authority in subjective experience, interactionists seek a method that will produce unimpeachable scientific data.

A product of functional psychology (James and Dewey), and Darwinian naturalism (Blumer 1969), interactionism (in its many forms) is anti-behaviorism (Mead), both pro- and anti-psychoanalysis, Marxism, and utopianism (Mead; Blumer 1969, 1980; Clough 1987), pro-democracy and social reform (James, Dewey, Mead, Park, and Blumer), pro-instrumental experimentalism (Mead and Dewey), pro-ethnology (Goffman 1971), Durkheimian structuralism (Goffman 1974), dramaturgical frameworks (Goffman 1959; Perinbanayagam 1985), conversational studies (Molseed 1989), negotiated order theories (Strauss 1978; Maines 1977, 1982), role-identity theories (McCall and Simmons 1978; Stryker 1980), formal theories of social processes (Couch 1989; Prus 1987), performance science (Becker et al. 1989), and interpretive, critical, contextual formulations (Denzin 1989b; Farberman 1989). Simultaneously interpretive and analytic, structural and interactional, interactionism is both a theory of experience and a theory of social structure. A brief review of the theories of James, Cooley, Mead, and Blumer will establish this point.

In the beginning: Cooley, James, Mead, Dewey, Park, and Blumer

Cooley regarded the individual and society as opposite sides of the same coin. The self of the person is a reflected appraisal of the reactions of others. It is based on self-feeling and the imagined judgments of others. It arises out of the individual's experiences in primary groups, especially the family. Modern societies are shaped by the communication process, public opinion, competition, conflict, and economic exchange. Human nature is social in nature, nourished by primary groups whose values are mediated by social institutions, especially the economy. Governmentally regulated competition was regarded as the best mechanism for maintaining the democratic values of a society like the United States (Jacobs 1979: 41).

James could be called a phenomenologist. Three terms are central to his perspective: consciousness, self, and reality. For him the state of consciousness was all that the field of psychology needed to posit (1890/1950: 226). The stream of experience is continuous, albeit fragmented, immediate, unique to each person, selective in content, with moving horizons and fringes of shifting awareness. The self, in its principal form of knower, or subject (the "I"), is at the center of the person's state of consciousness. In experience the "I" interacts with the "me," or the self as object. For James persons have as many selves as they have social relationships. States of consciousness are known through the process of introspection, or reflection on our thoughts, bodies, and perceptions. Reality ("Any object which remains uncontradicted is ipso facto believed and posited as absolute reality"; 1890/1950: 289, emphasis original) comes in multiple forms: the worlds of the senses, science, metaphysics, illusions and prejudices, religion, individual opinion, madness, and practical reality (1890/1950 : 292–3). Emotion and feeling are central to the belief in any one of these forms of reality, an emotion being an embodied state which ratifies an experience with the world.

Mead turns Cooley and James on their heads. For him the self is not mentalistic. It is a social object which lies in the field of experience. It is structured by the principle of sociality, or the taking of the attitude of the other in a social situation. The self can be scientifically studied, like an object in the physical sciences (1910/64: 108). Rejecting introspection because it is not scientific, he argued for a view of self and society which joins these two terms in a reciprocal process of interaction. His key term was the act, which replaces James's concept of stream of experience. The self, in its "I" and "me" phases, begins as an impulse, moves through a phase of manipulation, and culminates in a consummation phase. With Mead, as with Blumer's extension of Mead, the interaction tradition decisively moves away from the interpretive and phenomenological suggestions of Cooley and James. It enters a confused phase which, as noted above, attempts, but never succeeds in becoming naturalistic, subjective, and scientific. (In 1974 Goffman will attempt to reclaim and then reject the neglected James [and phenomenological] tradition.)

Dewey. Mead could not have rewritten James's psychology without having first absorbed Dewey's 1896 article "The Reflex Arc Concept in Psychology." In that article Dewey attacked the use of the stimulus–response unit as the building block of psychological theory. He argued that the organism is not a passive receiver of stimuli, but an active perceiver of the situations it confronts. Thus behavior must be seen as a constant adaptation to the environment. It is continuous, present to the organism as a constant flow of sequenced acts with beginnings, middles, and ends.

Park styled a self-conscious, reflective cultural sociology which drew on Sumner's evolutionism, Dewey's concept of society-as-communication, and James's belief that human beings hide behind masks and are never able to understand one another fully (see Fisher and Strauss 1978: 474; Lyman 1991). Unlike Thomas (see Wiley 1986), who believed that history was progressive, Park held to a conflict-assimilation model of social change. He stressed the importance of the newspapers and the schools in the emerging American democratic community. For Park, race was the greatest problem confronting American society.

Blumer (1969) molds Mead into a sociologist. Offering a view of society that derives from Mead's picture of the social act, he introduced the concepts of joint action and acting unit to describe the interactions that extend from dyads to complex institutions. His self is an interpretive process, and his society (after Park, Thomas, and E. Hughes) is one built on the play of power, interest, group position, collective action, and social protest. He applied Mead and Park to the study of fashion, film, racial prejudice, collective behavior, and the industrialization process (Lyman and Vidich 1988; Maines and Morrione [eds] 1990).

Pragmatism

As a theory of knowing, truth, science, and meaning, pragmatism in its several forms (James, Mead, Peirce, and Dewey) is central to the interactionist heritage. Mead (1929–30/64: 386) rejected James's pragmatic theory for its failure to separate in advance the values of the individual from the situation being studied. Aligning himself with Dewey's instrumentalism (or experimentalism), Mead argued that truth involves the solution to a problem which is resolved through the use of the scientific method (a method he found lacking in James). James (like Mead) defined truth in terms of its consequences for ongoing action. What is true is what works, what can be verified, and what satisfies. Peirce's pragmaticism (1934), contrary to James's, defines this method independent of personal experience. For Peirce (1934: 248) the "meaning of a concept lies in the manner in which it could conceivably modify purposive action." A clear idea is one whose consequences are clearly spelled out in action. Truth is what is known in a community of (scientific) knowers. Dewey's pragmatic instrumentalism (1922, 1938) holds that truth and meaning lie in the consequences of an action that receives confirmation or verification in practical, or experimentally controlled, situations. The needs or desires which truth must satisfy are not personal, as they are for James. They are public goods, defined by the political ideals of a social democracy (see Rorty 1989, ch. 3). Dewey's pragmatism celebrated critical intelligence, implemented through the scientific method, as the proper mode of scientific inquiry.

The early pragmatists may be divided into two political camps, one critical, the other more neutral and meliorative. In the hands of James and Dewey, pragmatism was a form of cultural criticism. It located politics in the everyday experiences of ordinary people (see West 1989: 213). For James, this led to a focus on the individual and a distrust of big institutions and groups. He envisioned a moral heroism "in which each ameliorative step forward is a kind of victory, each minute battle won a sign that the war is not over, hence still winnable" (West 1989: 227). Dewey went even further, arguing for a kind of democratic socialism which viewed supertheories (e.g. Marxism) as instruments or weapons "we use when they serve our purposes . . . and criticize and discard when they utterly fail us" (West 1989: 221).[1] Dewey's cultural criticism promoted pedagogy, dialogue, and open communication as the means for creating the Great Society (Dewey 1927: 184; see also Novack 1975). The political pragmatism of Mead, by contrast with that of Dewey and James, was less critical of contemporary cultural formations, but more aligned with a politics which sustained a liberal-minded version of the status quo. This often translated into a conservative cultural romanticism which turned the modern self and its interactional experiences into a moral hero. However, there were two versions of this hero: the man who leads the masses and the ordinary, working man, who is led by his informed moral leader (the man best able to take the attitudes of the group (see, e.g., Cooley 1902/1922/1956, ch. 25; and Dykhuizen 1973: 101–4 on Mead and Dewey and their relations to the Chicago unions). The Chicago pragmatists were pro-labor until it threatened the capitalists like Rockefeller (Dykhuizen 1973: 101).

This pragmatic tradition, in its several forms, continues to the present day. (This is the case in part because Mead's pragmatism defined Blumer's methodology, and his interpretations of the pragmatic tradition (see Wellman 1988; Tucker 1988; Morrione and Farberman 1981a, b; Morrione 1988: 8–9; see also Krug and Graham 1989). The pragmatists' search for a method that would separate the observer from the observed, so that valid, scientific observations could be made, has persisted in the participant observation, ethnographic, and controlled video studies of subsequent phases (see Table 1.1). More recently Habermas (1987) has aligned himself with the Mead–Dewey versions of pragmatism in the reformulations of his theory of communicative conduct (see below, also Rochberg-Halton 1989; Frank 1989; Rorty 1989: 66–9; Antonio 1989). This has coincided with a renewal of discussions of pragmatism, Blumer, Mead, and the methods of interactionism (*Symbolic Interaction*, 1988; *Symbolic Interaction*, 1989; Plummer 1991; Denzin 1989a, b; Shalin 1986, 1987a, b, 1991). At the same time, philosophers like West (1989) and Rorty (1989) have taken up the pragmatic tradition within American philosophy (see chapter 6 for extended discussions of West and Rorty).

Politically, the pragmatists (and Chicago School sociologists) who followed Mead were main- (and side-) street liberals. They had bonds to the status quo and the business community (Farberman 1979; Dykhuizen 1973: 101–4) and commitments to social change engineered from within, through the politics of a democratically informed public. This version of pragmatism did not produce a radical politics of reform or revolution (J. T. Carey 1975, ch. 3 and 5). The ideology of the Chicago pragmatic social reformers clung to the values and beliefs of America's middle and upper classes (Mills 1964).

Mead is typical in this regard. He criticized the press and the movies (1925–6/64: 300–5) because they promoted forms of reverie and day-dreaming that "answer to the so-called inferiority complexes" (p. 300) by creating enjoyable imagery which "may hardly rise above unsatisfied animal impulses of gain, sex, or hate" (p. 302). These modern forms of communication (especially the movies) do not lend themselves to shared experience: "The movie has no creative audience . . . what the average film brings to light is that the hidden unsatisfied longings of the average man and woman are very immediate, rather simple and fairly primitive" (p. 303). Predictably, Mead compared popular culture unfavorably with fine art, "which has never been the dominant language of men's hearts"

(p. 299). Fine art is healthy and normal and elevates men's existence to new moral planes (pp. 298–9). Popular art brings out man's debased, animal characteristics. Herbert Blumer would repeat these arguments in 1933.[2] Now the history of the perspective.

Interactionism's history

Table 1 provides a historical overview of the main currents and theoretical formations in symbolic interactionism over the last 100 years. It divides this history into six phases, starting with the emergence of the canonical texts in the late 1800s and ending with 1990. A brief discussion of each phase is required.[3] The *canonical phase* (1890–1932) describes the period when pragmatism emerged as a distinct philosophical formation in America. It references two bodies of work, that of the founding philosophical fathers – Dewey, James, Mead, and Peirce – and that of those American sociologists, including Cooley, who drew upon Mead (and Dewey) in their sociological work. Here I include Thomas and Znaniecki's *The Polish Peasant*, Park and Burgess's *Introduction to the Science of Sociology* textbook, the early Chicago school ethnographies (Zorbaugh 1929; Shaw 1930), the discussion of Chicago methodology in Rice (1931), the emergence of a discourse around personal documents (Dollard 1935), and Blumer's early criticisms of the concept in social psychology (1931).

The *empirical/theoretical period* of 1933–50 covers the appearance of Mead's works published after his death (1932, 1934, 1936, 1938), early textbooks (Karpf 1932; Krueger and Reckless 1930) identifying the "Chicago-interactionist" tradition in social psychology, Blumer's coining of the term in 1937, Blumer's 1933 *Movies and Conduct*, his 1939 critique of *The Polish Peasant*, The Second World War, new analytic ethnographies using Mead (Lindesmith 1947), and a new textbook explicitly identified with the tradition (Lindesmith and Strauss 1949). The 1933–50 period solidifies "Chicago" sociology around two poles: Mead's heritage, through Blumer and Faris, and the ecology-urban sociology of Park, Burgess, Wirth, E. Hughes, and others.

What would later be called "Chicago sociology" was developed and institutionalized in this period. E. Hughes (and his students) moved to connect the concepts of role and status to self, moral careers, social structure, work, and deviance. They saw society as collective action, not as a structure. They saw work as being the key to the contemporary self. The professions (e.g. medicine) were seen as instances of collective

Table 1 Historical overview of symbolic interaction. Phases and time periods

The canon 1890–1932	Empirical/theoretical 1933–50	Transition/new texts 1951–62	Criticism/ferment 1963–70	Ethnography 1971–80	Diversity/new theory 1981–90
		Representative Texts			
James 1890; Cooley 1902; Mead 1910; Dewey 1922; Thomas & Znaniecki 1918–20; Simmel 1908;[a] Park & Burgess 1921; Payne Fund 1928; Zorbaugh 1929; Shaw 1930; Rice (ed.) 1931; Blumer 1931	Mead 1934, 1936, 1938; Blumer 1933, 1937, 1939; Peirce 1934; Karpf 1932; Krueger and Reckless 1930; Lindesmith 1947; Second World War; Lindesmith & Strauss, 1949; Conwell and Sutherland 1937; Lee 1949; Dollard 1935	Gerth & Mills 1953; Faris 1952; Park 1950; E. Hughes 1958; Goffman 1959; Strauss 1959; Shibutani 1961; Hickman & Kuhn 1956; Martindale 1960; Rose (ed.) 1962; Blumer 1962; Stone 1962; Strauss (ed.) 1956; Pfeutze 1954; Reck 1964; Shils 1961; Becker et al. 1961; Mills 1959; Natanson 1956; Ames 1956	Becker 1963; Aldine series; Blumer 1966; Faris 1970; Manis & Meltzer (eds) 1967; Glaser & Strauss 1967; Becker 1967; Garfinkel 1967b, Goffman 1963 a, b; Vaughan & Reynolds 1968; Blumer 1969; Gouldner 1970; Matza 1969; Blumer-Hughes 1969, 1970 (discussed in L. Lofland 1980); Shibutani (ed.) 1970; Stone & Farberman (eds) 1970; Vietnam War; Becker 1970	Douglas (ed.) 1971; Hughes 1971; *Urban Life* started, 1972; Manis & Meltzer (eds) 1972; Mullins 1973; Goffman 1974 1979; Strauss 1978; SSSI formed, 1974; Couch & Hintz (eds) 1975; Meltzer et al. 1975; J. T. Carey 1975; Douglas 1976; *Symbolic Interaction* started, 1977; Rock 1979; Douglas & Johnson (eds) 1977	Stone & Farberman (eds) 1981; Maines, 1982; Goffman 1981; Bulmer 1984; Couch et al. 1986b; Emotions Section started 1987; Lyman & Vidich 1988; Mall, 1987; Manning 1988b; Perinbanayagam 1985; Habermas 1987; Becker & McCall (eds) 1990; Reynolds 1990

[a]Between 1893 and 1910 a number of Simmel's writings, translated by Albion W. Small, appeared first in the *American Journal of Sociology* and then in Park and Burgess's *Introduction to the Science of Sociology* (1921). See Wolff 1950: xxiv.

struggles to gain power and to define and control the nature of work and the self-identities and authority that flow from the professionalized occupations (E. Hughes 1958: 8). They studied experience firsthand (Becker 1970: xi). The sociologists (and social psychologists) who would be the main carriers of this tradition (Lindesmith, A. Rose, Strauss, Becker, Goffman, and Stone) received their Ph.D.s during this time, or early in the next period. This period also saw limited attempts to merge Mead's theories with French and German phenomenology (e.g. Sartre, Husserl, and M. Buber; see Ames 1956; Natanson 1956; and Pfuetze 1954). Alfred Schütz, the Austrian phenomenologist, also began, after his arrival in America in 1939, to write essays on the pragmatists (see Wagner 1983). His work would not be incorporated into the Chicago tradition, even though he published in the *American Journal of Sociology*.

The *transition/new texts period* of 1951–62 saw the emergence of new texts articulating symbolic interaction and its relation to Freud and European social theory (Gerth and Mills 1953; Shibutani 1961); new social psychology texts (Faris 1952; Shibutani 1961); collections of papers by Park (1950) and E. Hughes (1958); A. Rose's 1962 reader *Human Behavior and Social Processes*, which contains statements by Chicago-trained interactionists; major theoretical statements expanding the base of the perspective by Goffman (1959), Strauss (1959), and Stone (1962); Martindale's (1960) formalization of the school in his theory text (see also Shils 1961); two new collections of Mead's works (Strauss (ed.) 1956; Reck (ed.) 1964); and a major empirical study, *Boys in White* (Becker *et al.* 1961), which evidenced a rigorous concern for method when applied to participant observation.

The third generation: Goffman, Strauss, Stone, and Becker

Goffman, Strauss, Stone, and Becker radically altered the perspective. As third-generation interactionists, their work grounded the theory in mid-century empirical work, which spoke simultaneously to the Chicago tradition, Mead's social psychology, and the increasing presence of symbolic interactionism as a counter-theory to structural functionalism. Goffman (1959), barely taking note of Mead or Blumer, forged a dramaturgical framework for the reading of the man in the "grey flannel suit" who would go to work in the new white-collar occupations. Such labor, he suggested, demanded a concern for manners, ritual, secrecy, deference, proper demeanor, the presentation of the right self, team work, backstage collusions, and consensual performances before hostile audiences. Not a "death of the salesman," *The Presentation of Self in Everyday Life* presented a sociology boldly at ease with itself and its society, ironically distant but not overtly critical.

Mirrors and Masks, subtitled "The Search for Identity," expressed a concern for the fusion of symbolic interaction and organizational perspectives into a workable social psychology (Strauss 1959: 11). It reworked Mead's theory of the symbol into a linguistic model not unlike that of Wittgenstein. It stressed, in existential fashion, the place of indeterminacy and danger in everyday life, even as it pointed the way to a more structured treatment of the interaction process. It also offered a model of identity transformations, connecting turning-point experiences to personal and group history. In the next decade Strauss would study American cities and their images, death and dying in the modern hospital, and status passages in complex, industrialized societies, while formulating a new Chicago method, called "grounded theory" (Glaser and Strauss 1967).

Stone (1962) offered a fundamental reanalysis of Mead's model of the act and the self. Stressing the importance of appearance, discourse, and meaning in interaction, Stone (and his many students), like Strauss, used the concept of identity to encompass Mead's self, which he located in structural and interpersonal relationships. Value (instrumentality) and mood (affect) provide two axes along which the qualifications of identity are formed. Identities are activated through appearance (clothing). This involves the placement of identities and the appraisal of values and moods.

Becker's work during this period involved problems of sociological method (see 1970, part 1), educational organizations, and occupational careers, personal change in adult life (1970, part 3), and the study of deviance. He implemented a Hughes- and Strauss-like model of identity change, while developing (with Geer) the logic of participant observation.

Odd man out: Manford Kuhn

The odd man out in this period was Manford Kuhn, who, in 1956, offered symbolic interactionists (with C. Addison Hickman) *Individuals, Groups, and Economic Behavior*. Employing a post-Veblen-like institutional model of economics, this work expressed Kuhn's commitment to a valid, testable, empirical, symbolic interactionist theory of human behavior, called "self" theory. Chapter 1 of the book presents a powerful, empirically based critique of Freudian psychoanalysis, Field theory and Gestalt psychology, and Learning theory (Pavlov, Hull, Miller, and Dollard). Kuhn's "self theory" is then presented and distinguished from the Cooley–Dewey–Mead (and Blumer) version of symbolic interactionism, which Kuhn calls an orientation, not a theory (Hickman and Kuhn 1956: 22). Defining the self as a set of attitudes (verbal plans of action), Kuhn introduced the "Twenty Statements" or "Who AM I?" test (TST) as a valid and reliable measure of the self. This work would later become the center of what Reynolds and others would call the "Iowa school" of symbolic interactionism. It contained no hints of what would come later in Kuhn's work, including the interpretive reading of interviews as interaction (1962) and lectures and unpublished manuscripts suggestive of an alignment with the Hughes–Blumer–Strauss versions of symbolic interactionism.

1963–1970: A fourth generation emerges

The 1963–70 period (criticism/ferment) gave rise to a flourishing of interactionist work in the area of deviance (e.g. Becker 1963), continued publications by Goffman (e.g. 1963 a, b), Becker's observations series with Aldine, which would publish dissertations by Blumer-and Goffman-trained students (e.g. Cavan and Scott), two new collections of interactionist work (Manis and Meltzer (eds) 1967; Stone and Farberman (eds) 1970), essays in honor of Blumer (Shibutani (ed.) 1970), Glaser and Strauss's grounded theory book (1967), Blumer's collected papers (1969), Vaughn and Reynolds' (1968) argument that there was an Iowa and a Chicago tradition in symbolic interactionism, and Gouldner's criticisms of Becker and Goffman (1968, 1970).

As the decade came to a close, the Vietnam War was everywhere present. In 1969, alongside these political currents, Blumer and Hughes met with a group called the "Chicago Irregulars" at the San Francisco American Sociological Association meetings and shared memories of the "Chicago" years (J. Lofland, 1987: 31). Lyn Lofland (1980: 253) describes this (1969) as a time of "creative ferment – scholarly and political. The San Francisco meetings witnessed not simply the Blumer–Hughes event but a 'counter revolution' . . . a group first came together to . . . talk about the problems of being a sociologist and a female . . . the discipline seemed literally to be bursting with new . . . ideas: labelling theory, ethnomethodology, conflict theory, phenomenology, dramaturgical analysis." Matza's (1969) book on Chicago-style naturalism attempted to capture the subjective spirit of Becker's deviance studies, while Gouldner charged that the Chicago sociologists were partisans of the welfare state.

The *ethnography period* of 1971–80 saw the appearance of four new journals devoted to qualitative research: *Urban Life, Qualitative Sociology, Symbolic Interaction*, and *Studies in Symbolic Interaction*. Paradigms for formalizing interaction theory and research were put forward (e.g. J. Lofland 1971, 1976, 1977). This search for generic social processes would continue into the 1980s (e.g. Prus 1987; Couch 1987, 1989). Manis and Meltzer offered another collection of interaction work (1972); Mullins (1973) predicted the death of the perspective; while Meltzer *et al.* presented a collection of criticisms of the theory (1975). Role-identity theories (Stryker 1980; McCall and Simmons 1978) continued to be popular. J. T. Carey (1975) formalized the Chicago school and traced its history; Rock (1979) attempted a history of the movement; and Douglas and Johnson (eds, 1977) offered an existential sociology which encompassed the interactionist tradition. Goffman's major work, *Frame Analysis* (1974), appeared, as did his studies of gender advertisements (1979) and the gender-stratification process (1977). The beginnings of a new Iowa school (Couch and Hintz (eds) 1975) were announced, but went unnoticed. By the end of the decade, the Society for the Study of Symbolic Interaction had its own journal and a large international membership.

1981–1990: The greying of interactionism

I call the contemporary period (1981–1990) *diversity/new theory*. Several currents are going on at the same time. Practitioners in the perspective are getting older, and the decline of new students is perceived by some as problematic (Saxton 1989: 20). There is a resurgence of interest in dramaturgy (Perinbanayagam 1985, 1991; Brissett and Edgley (eds) 1990), phenomenology (Gurevitch 1990; Bentz 1989), the emotions (Franks and McCarthy (eds) 1989), the sociology of the absurd (Lyman and Scott 1989), feminism (Deegan and Hill (eds) 1987; Clough 1987), social organizational problems (P. M. Hall 1987; Maines and Morrione (eds) 1990), information technologies and the study of communication (connecting back to Cooley and Park's early interest in the mass media (Couch 1990; Maines and Couch (eds) 1988; J. W. Carey 1989), everyday life sociologies (Douglas *et al.* (eds) 1980; Adler *et al.*

1987), and ethnographies (Adler and Adler 1987), semiotics and ethnography (Manning 1987), returns to the canonical texts (Farberman and Perinbanayagam (eds) 1985; Becker and McCall (eds) 1990), including Blumer (Maines and Morrione (eds) 1990; Lyman and Vidich 1988), a formalization of the neo-Iowa (Couch et al. (eds) 1986 a, b) and Chicago (Bulmer 1984) schools, and a concern for the "new" European social theories (Barthes, Derrida, Foucault, Althusser, Baudrillard, and Lacan), including postmodernism (Dickens and Fontana (eds) 1991; Richardson 1990), postmodern ethnography (Clifford and Marcus (eds) 1986; Turner and Bruner (eds) 1986; Marcus and Fischer 1986), and the production of social texts (Brown 1989; Van Maanen 1988; Richardson 1990). Much of this work appeared in *Studies in Symbolic Interaction* (vols 9–12). This period also saw critical reassessments of mainstream social psychology by symbolic interactionists (*Studies in Symbolic Interaction*, vol. 8, 1987), as well as assessments of the tradition itself (*Studies in Symbolic Interaction*, vol. 10, 1989). Interactionists were taking the lead in their own self-criticisms. They, of all American theory groups, seemed the most receptive (with certain exceptions) to new theory formulations and the problems of communication in a postmodern media-defined world (see Fine 1990).[4]

Two new schools emerged in the 1980s: the California school and the new Iowa school.

The California school

A group of students (including J. Johnson, D. Altheide, A. Fontana, J. Kotarba, and the Adlers) under the leadership of Jack Douglas (in the early to middle 1970s through the mid-1980s) emerged to secure a middle ground between phenomenology, ethnomethodology, existentialism, and symbolic interactionism (see Douglas and Johnson (eds) 1977; Kotarba and Fontana (eds) 1984). In texts and monographs and as journal and series editors, they have advanced the sociology of everyday life perspective (see Adler et al. 1987; also Lyman and Scott 1989). Their concerns have focused on the mass media, family violence, sports, deviance, ageing, and the AIDS crisis. This group continued and built upon the earlier work of Goffman, Garfinkel, and Blumer, who had developed California versions of the Chicago school in their emphasis on the emerging postwar California society and its multiple worlds of experience (Vidich and Lyman 1985: 274). The *Urban Life* project of John Lofland (and his associates) was another variant of this school.

The new Iowa school

From the mid-1960s to the present, Carl Couch, with several cohorts of students at the University of Iowa, has reworked Kuhn's Iowa school program (see Couch et al. (eds) 1986 a, b). This has involved laboratory studies of dyadic and triadic interactional structures, investigations of tyranny, authoritarian power relations, partisan groups, intergroup negotiations, and constituent relationships. Explicitly based on Simmel and Mead, this body of work builds on Kuhn and Blumer through the use of a naturalistic methodology which utilizes audiovisual recordings. It reconceptualizes such traditional, taken-for-granted interactionist (and Mead) terms as "self," "other," "role-taking," "social object," "initiating act," "response," and "alignment," replacing them by the terms "reciprocally acknowledged attention," "acknowledged attention," "mutual responsiveness," "congruent functional identity," "shared focus," and "social objective" (Couch et al. (eds) 1986a: xxiii). These terms are then fitted to a processual theory of sociation (Simmel), which stresses temporality (shared pasts, projected futures), emotionality, and power. Simmel, Mead, Blumer, Goffman, Stone, and Strauss are reworked to fit an interactionist social psychology of the 1980s. This work returns to the original Mead and Simmel proposals concerning a naturalistic, valid science of social forms (see Flaherty 1989).

Key texts

If one stands back a step from each of these six key periods, it is possible to locate a key interactionist text or texts for each moment: for 1890–1932, Thomas and Znaniecki's The Polish Peasant; for 1933–50, Mead's Mind, Self and Society (1934) and Blumer's 1939 critique of The Polish Peasant; for 1951–62, Goffman's The Presentation of Self in Everyday Life (1959), Strauss's Mirrors and Masks (1959), G. P. Stone's "Appearance and the Self" (1962), and Becker et al.'s Boys in White (1961); for 1963–70, Becker's The Outsiders (1963), Glaser and Strauss's The Discovery of Grounded Theory (1967), Blumer's Symbolic Interactionism (1969), and Gouldner's The Coming Crisis in Western Sociology (1970); for 1971–80, Goffman's Frame Analysis (1974) and Strauss's Negotiations (1978); and for 1981–90, Perinbanayagam's

Signifying Acts (1985), Couch's *Constructing Civilizations* (1984a), P. M. Hall's "Interactionism and the Study of Social Organization" (1987), and Habermas's *The Theory of Communicative Action* (1987). This is an admittedly biased reading of the six historical moments of symbolic interactionism. It reflects an analysis of those texts which have either attracted the greatest amount of attention in the interactionist literature (Blumer 1979, 1969: 1; Saxton 1989; Flaherty 1989) or (by my reading) signalled radical turns in theorizing, research method, or substantive contribution in each period.

The Polish Peasant created an interpretive base for the Chicago ethnographies, just as it defined a unique American sociology (Wiley 1986). It was, in Blumer's words, the most significant sociological work in the first third of the twentieth century (Blumer 1979: vi–vii). Blumer's critique of this work in the empirical/theoretical period boldly stated the pragmatic view of methods when applied to a classic text. *Mind, Self and Society* quickly became the major work of Mead as far as sociologists were concerned. In the 1951–62 period, the Goffman, Strauss, and Stone texts drastically rewrote Mead's self theory, creating new avenues of empirical work and introducing new metaphors into the interactionist tradition. The works spoke, in part, to the everyday life experienced by the new middle classes. *Boys in White* showed that interactionists could study a powerful profession in American sociology and do so with irony. Becker's *Outsiders*, Glaser and Strauss's grounded theory, and Blumer's collected works defined the decade of ferment. Interactionists had a method to study deviance (or anything else) which was scientific but not positivistic. Gouldner's critique shattered this picture and complemented other criticisms of the perspective. *Frame Analysis* and *Negotiations* are pivotal statements for the period 1971–80. They extended the theories of their authors in new, phenomenological and structural directions and inspired considerable research in the next decade. Perinbanayagam's *Signifying Acts* attempted to join dramaturgy with the new structuralisms. Couch's *Constructing Civilizations* applied his theory of temporality and action to the problem of how societies emerged and disappeared throughout human history. P. M. Hall (1987) offered a comprehensive framework for interactionist-organizational-societal studies of power, politics, and ideology, while Habermas (1987) challenged interactionists to take back their theory and develop their own pragmatic politics of action.

Who got the SSSI awards?

To complicate matters further, it is necessary to consider the decade of the 1980s in greater detail. In 1978 the Society for the Study of Symbolic Interaction (SSSI) created three committees to give what came to be termed the annual Cooley, Mead, and Blumer awards. The Charles Horton Cooley Award is presented annually in recognition of the most outstanding recent contribution to the study of symbolic interaction. The George Herbert Mead Award is presented annually to an individual whose career contributions to the advancement of the study of human behavior and social life best exemplify the tradition and spirit of George Herbert Mead's work. The Herbert Blumer Award is given annually for a graduate student paper in the tradition of symbolic interaction. Table 2 presents the Cooley and Mead award winners from 1978 to 1990.

The Mead awards first. It is clear that the members of the Society desired, in a ritualistic fashion, to call attention to those members who

Table 2. Winners of the Society for the Study of Symbolic Interaction awards, 1978–1990

Year	Cooley Award	Mead Award
1978	R. Turner	I. Misumi & H. Blumer
1979	A. Strauss	A. Lindesmith
1980	H. Becker	G. Stone
1981	P. Conrad & J. Schneider	E. Hughes
1982	No award given	K. Burke
1983	J. Gusfield	E. Goffman
1984	A. Hochschild	S. Lyman
1985	K. Luker	A. Strauss
1986	D. Altheide	T. Shibutani
1987	P. Biernacki	H. Becker
1988	N. Denzin	L. Zurcher
1989	J. Katz	J. Wiseman
1990	J. Hewitt & P. Manning[a]	R. Turner

[a]In 1990 the Cooley Award Committee decided to recognize an "In Special Recognitions" Award, to be given to the work which was more than a runner-up for the Cooley Award. Such works had not been recognized previously. Manning (1988b) received this award in 1990. I would like to thank Mark Hutter who supplied much of the above information.

had kept alive the idea of "The Chicago School" and its connections to the early canon – hence the awards to the key figures from the 1951–62 period. The Cooley Awards[5] are more difficult to read, although they signal works which have focused on self and society (Turner 1978; Hewitt 1990); classic empirical studies (thus Becker's 1980 award was in part for *Boys in White*, but also for his work on photography and his studies of arts and crafts); new work in the classic interactionist area of deviance (Conrad and Schneider 1980); social problems (drunk driving, abortion, drug addiction, alcoholism, crime; e.g. Gusfield 1981; Luker 1985; Biernacki 1987; Denzin 1988; Katz 1988); the emotions (Hochschild 1983 1984); and the mass media and communications (Altheide 1985; Manning 1990). The Blumer awards, with few exceptions, have mirrored this preoccupation with deviance and ethnography.

In their awards the interactionists keep alive the idea that they identify with underdogs (Gouldner 1970) and study the intersection of self and society, doing so from a qualitative, interpretive, ethnographic point of view. Furthermore, they continue to value theory that sustains some commitment to the canonical texts of Cooley and Mead. (What happened to Simmel and Park?)

A *biased reading*

Three factors stand out from the above lists. First, in the 1981–90 period the canonical texts have shifted from Mead to Blumer, while Goffman attracts the greatest empirical interest and Becker continues as the symbolic representative of the Chicago tradition (e.g. Clough 1988). Second, the Chicago tradition has become synonymous (Reynolds 1990: 3) with symbolic interactionism (or one version of the theory), even though there are at least four Chicago traditions (Fisher and Strauss 1978: 458; Adler and Adler 1987: 8–20; Manning 1987: 14–16): Mead's social psychology (through Blumer), Thomas and Park's urban sociology (through Hughes and Becker), Warner's Durkheimian structuralism (through Goffman), and the statistical Chicago school (Stouffer, Hauser, etc.). There is no single Chicago school of sociology. In the same vein the concept of an "Iowa school" (Vaughn and Reynolds 1968) persists (Reynolds 1990). As with the readings of Blumer (the supposed founder of the Chicago interactionist school), the interpretations of Kuhn (the Iowa founder) remain superficial (e.g. Kuhn's methodological and theoretical diversity; see Tucker 1966), just as the differences between Kuhn's work and that of Couch and his students remain unrecognized. The perpetuation of the myth of the Iowa and the Chicago schools serves to give a center and focus to interactionism that it does not (and never did) have.

Third, the major theoretical and empirical developments of the last 30 years have primarily involved incremental additions to the perspective, with occasional (and quite recent) bursts of activity in the area of the "new social theory" from Europe. Earlier criticisms concerning the astructural, apolitical, acultural, ahistorical, and overly rational (non-emotional), commonsense biases in the theory (Reynolds 1990, ch. 8–10) have been addressed (P. M. Hall 1987). There has been a return to Simmel through the neo-Iowa school, which has resulted in a quasi-formal theory of social interaction and social structure. Interactionist ethnographers (e.g. Ramos, Kotarba, the two Schmitts and J. M. Johnson) have kept abreast of key social issues (e.g. AIDS and family violence). Connections between the early pragmatists and recent critical theory (e.g. that of Habermas) have been explored (Shalin 1991; Antonio 1989). Links between structuralism, interactionism, pragmatism, and semiotics have been built (Manning 1988b; Fine 1990). A phenomenological turn is developing (Gurevitch 1990; Denzin 1984b; Bentz 1989), as is an incipient cultural studies perspective (Denzin 1991b, e, 1990d, f; J. W. Carey 1989). Social structure, power, and politics are no longer ignored (P. M. Hall 1985, 1987; Farberman 1975; Denzin 1978, 1977b; Couch et al. (eds) 1986b). A feminist interactionism (Deegan and Hill (eds) 1987) is now available, and it merges with poststructural, psychoanalytic, and Marxist theory (Clough 1987; Denzin 1991e). An interactionist conception of emotionality is firmly in place (Franks and McCarthy (eds) 1989). A postmodern interactionism is also taking shape (Dickens and Fontana (eds) 1991). Challenges to the meanings of key texts have occurred (McPhail and Rexroat 1979; Lewis and Smith 1980; Fine and Kleinman 1986; Rawls 1987), but there is now less concern with what Mead (or Blumer) meant (but see *Symbolic Interaction* 1988, 1989).

However, the canonical empirical work in the perspective occurred in the 1951–62 transition period (or just after), when Mead's works were either consolidated into empirical texts or bold, new social psychological theories were put forth (Strauss, Goffman, and Stone). The empirical studies of the ferment and diversity periods (1971–90) have yet to find their way into the canon. When this occurs, it will become apparent that the theory is ready to enter its next phase, which will be the merger with cultural studies (on leads, see Fisher and Strauss, 1978: 485–7). For this to occur, interactionists will need to attach themselves to a new body of theory wherein a new grouping of canonical texts (Barthes, Lacan, Althusser, Derrida, Foucault, and Baudrillard) will be seen as supplementing – but not replacing – the works of Dewey, Cooley, Mead, James, Peirce, Simmel, Park, Thomas, Blumer, Hughes, Strauss, Becker, and Goffman.

Conclusion: the interactionist framework

This version of the interactionist story can now be summarized. The interactionists cling to a pragmatism which produces a crippling commitment to an interpretive sociology too often caught in the trappings of positivist and postpositivist terms (e.g. validity, proposition, and theory). This pragmatism leads to a humanistic politics of action which is ingrained in the liberal traditions of American democracy. It produces a romantic preoccupation with the interactionist subject and the ethnographic (and audiovisual) representations of this subject's experiences in empirical texts.

The following assertions are central to what interactionists do. They study the intersections of interaction, biography, and social structure in particular historical moments. Interactional experience is assumed to be organized in terms of the motives and accounts that persons give themselves for acting. These accounts are learned from others, as well as from the popular culture. These motives, gendered and nongendered, explain past behavior and are used to predict future behavior. They are ideological constructions which create specific forms of interactional subjectivity in concrete situations (see chapter 2). Power, emotionality, and force are basic features of everyday life. Intersubjectivity – the shared knowledge that exists between two persons regarding one another's conscious mental states – is basic to shared, human group life. Intersubjectivity is established through shared emotional experiences which are temporally constituted (Denzin 1984b).

Constantly preoccupied with the daily, ritual, and enforced performances of stigmatized identities (race and gender), the interactionists speak always to those persons who occupy powerless positions in contemporary society. These interests set interactionism apart from other points of view. This includes those perspectives which stress attribute-like properties of systems, persons, their identities and actions, rational choice, exchange, structural, ritual chain, role-guided, and lifeworld/system theories of communicative competence.

In the next chapter I present an interpretive and poststructural picture of interactionism, while examining what interactionists don't like to do. This will lay the groundwork for chapter 3, in which I start to examine in detail the criticisms of the perspective.

Notes

1 According to West (1989: 221), Dewey "accepted much of the validity of Marxist theory and simply limited its explanatory scope and rejected its imperial, monistic, and dogmatic versions" (but see Novack 1975, ch. 1). West's neo-prophetic pragmatism represents a re-doing of Dewey within a contemporary, critical, cultural studies Marxism (e.g. S. Hall 1988a).

2 It is tempting here to see some overlap with the Frankfurt school's early criticisms of popular culture (see Jameson 1990, ch. 1). However, unlike Adorno and Horkheimer, who saw the culture industries under capitalism as engaged in mass deception, neither Mead nor Blumer nor Dewey offered similar economically and politically motivated critiques of capitalism. Indeed, they seemed to be calling for a form of aesthetic social realism that would endow industrial work with higher moral meaning (Mead 1925–6/64: 300, 305). Of interest is the fact that both the Chicago and the Frankfurt schools reacted negatively to this new information technology and art form.

3 This division differs from earlier classifications including those of: Kuhn (oral tradition and age of inquiry distinction (Kuhn 1964a); Mullins (normal science (to 1931), network (1931–45), cluster (1945–52), and speciality (1952– (Mullins 1973: 77); Meltzer *et al.* (genesis [James to Mead] and varieties [Chicago and Iowa] (1975: v); and Reynold's (antecedents, early interactionists, and contemporary varieties [Chicago, Iowa, Dramaturgical, Ethnomethodology] (1990). Historically, my scheme, with its emphasis on the post-1960 developments, supersedes the Kuhn, Mullins' and Meltzer *et al.* frameworks, which basically stopped with the 1960s. Farberman's (1979: 17) distinction between the pre-Chicago, Chicago, and post-Chicago schools is closer to my framework.

4 Reflecting this concern, the publishing house of Aldine de Gruyter, in 1988, began a new monograph series called *Communication and Social Order*. The series editor is David R. Maines.

5 Here I present the year of the award, not the date of the publication associated with the award. Strauss's 1979 award was not connected to a specific work.

2 THE INTERPRETIVE HERITAGE

Symbolic interactionism provides the essentials for a provocative philosophical scheme that is peculiarly attuned to social experience. (Blumer 1969: 21)

In this chapter I sketch a working, interpretive version of symbolic interactionism, stressing connections between interactionism, recent feminist theory (Denzin 1990a, 1989a, b; Clough 1987), poststructuralism (Foucault 1982), postmodernism (Denzin 1991d), and cultural studies (J. W. Carey 1989). I begin, though, with a discussion of what interactionists (and poststructuralists) do not do. Then I discuss what they like to do, moving quickly to the analysis of gender and to feminist contributions to interaction theory. I conclude with a critical reading of a classic interactionist test *The Jack-Roller* (Shaw 1930/66). Not all interactionists will agree with what I say, however.

What interactionists think they should not do

Interpretive (and symbolic) interactionists don't think that general theories are useful. They do not write, like their functional counterparts, grand or global theories of societies (Blumer 1981: 162; 1990: 113–14). They take this position because they believe that "society" is an abstract term which refers to something that sociologists have invented in order to have a subject matter. They understand society to be something that is lived in the here and now, in the face-to-face and mediated interactions that connect persons to one another. Society, as it is lived, known, felt, and written about, goes on behind people's backs (Marx 1852/1983). Interactionists believe they should write about how people are constrained by the constructions they build and inherit from the past. Society, like interaction, is an emergent phenomenon (Blumer 1981: 153), a framework for the construction of diverse forms of social action (Blumer 1990: 133). It makes no sense to write a grand theory of something that is always changing. Interactionists, accordingly, study how people produce their situated versions of society. They see these situated versions of the social everywhere, from encounters to friendships to interactions in small groups to economic exchanges in the marketplace to the interactions that occur when a television viewer argues with a President's speech.

Rejecting totalizing, grand theories of the social, interactionists, like many poststructural (Foucault 1980) and postmodern theorists (Lyotard 1979/84) believe in writing local narratives about how people do things together (Becker 1986a; Richardson 1990). These narratives take the form of small-scale ethnographies, life stories, in-depth interviews, laboratory studies, historical analyses, and textual readings of bits and pieces of popular culture as given in films, novels, and popular music.

Interactionists do not believe in *Sociology* with a capital S. They believe in a *sociology* which is anti-sociology (Couch 1987). They believe that the best hope for sociology is not to practice *Sociology*. Interactionists think that *Sociology* has outlived its usefulness. Sociology for them simply means studying how social things hang together (see Rorty 1982: xiv–xv). They do not believe in using complex sociological terms which refer to things that cannot be immediately observed in the interactions of individuals. This means that they rework concepts like culture and institution to describe the recurring meanings and practices which persons produce when they do things together. Interactionists like to use the ordinary language and interpretive theories that everyday people use. They don't like to use theories that only make sense to other sociologists. They don't like theories which are built around terms like "social and functional integration," "pattern variables," "system complexity," "ego development," and "sociocultural lifeworlds."

Interactionists don't like theories that are imported from other disciplines, such as the natural sciences, psychology, or economics (Blumer 1981: 155). Such models have not been fitted to the actual, lived, emotional experiences of interacting human beings. Aligning themselves more with the humanities than the natural sciences, interactionists approach their materials from a narrative, textual position, understanding that their texts create the subject matter they write about (Brown 1989; Richardson 1990: 15). They don't like overly rational, cognitive theories of human behavior (Denzin 1990b, e). They don't like mono-causal theories which stress single factors like exchange, reward, or sexual desire as the causes of human behavior. They believe that the human being is active from the moment of birth to death. The important question becomes one of understanding how humans develop their own accounts and motives for explaining their actions to one another. Mono-causal motivational theories are rejected.

Interactionists don't like theories which ignore history, but they are not historical determinists (Maines *et al.* 1983). They believe that persons, not history, make history; but they understand that the histories that individuals make are not always of their own making. In that case any individual's or group's history becomes the history of other people. Symbolic and interpretive interactionists attempt to speak to the nuances, realities, and fabrics of these two kinds of history which shape one another (Denzin 1983: 130). This is how they study power, which they also call "force" and "violence." This means they study the micro-power relations that structure the daily performances of race, ethnicity, gender, and class in interactional situations.

Interpretive interactionists are skeptical of those who call themselves scientists (Couch 1987). They believe that science too often gets confused with ideology and the powers of the state (Foucault 1980). They think that the findings of science are often used to manipulate people in the name of some societal good or goal which is always defined in political terms. They are fearful of those who would build a totalizing science of the social. They are anti-science; at least, they like to see themselves as cultural subversives who undermine the repressive workings of science in everyday life.

Interactionists don't like theories which ignore the biographies and lived experiences of interacting individuals. They believe that the bio-graphies of individuals articulate specific historical moments. Each individual is a universal singular (Sartre 1981), who expresses in his or her lifetime the general and specific features of a historical epoch. Hence interactionists don't like Sociologies which ignore the stories people tell one another about their life experiences.

Interactionists don't believe in asking "why" questions. They ask, instead, "how" questions. How, for example, is a given strip of experience structured, lived, and given meaning?

Interactionists don't like theories that objectify and quantify human experience (Blumer 1969: 57). They assume that the important human processes cannot be quantified; mind cannot be measured, and the human body is not a behavioral machine whose actions can be meaning-fully understood through procedures that count activity. Interactionists don't like theorists who pontificate about human conduct, who write as if they understand what a given experience means to an individual or the members of a group. They prefer, instead, to write texts which remain close to the actual experiences of the people they are writing about. They like texts which do not place a wedge between themselves and what they are writing about. They like texts which express an immediacy of experience, unmediated by sociologists' interpretations (see Richardson 1990). This means that interactionist narratives often convey pathos, sentimentalism, and a romantic identification with the persons being written about. Interactionists write about people who struggle to make sense of themselves and their life experiences. But all too often, these people find that personal, biographical, and structural factors make them and their lives less than they could be. Interactionists study the marked, deviant, stigmatized, lonely, unhappy, alienated, powerful, and power-less people in everyday life.

Because of the things interactionists don't like to do, they are often criticized for not doing what other people think they should be doing like making macro-studies of power structures, or not having clearly defined concepts and terms, or being overly cognitive, or having emergent theories, or being ahistorical and astructural (see Reynolds 1990: 135–57; Smelser 1988; Coser 1976; Alexander 1987). Too often these criticisms (see chapter 3) reflect a failure to understand what the interactionist agenda is, or the critics have not read what interactionists have written (e.g. Collins 1986; see Denzin 1987b; also Fisher and Strauss 1978: 485–7; Maines and Morrione (eds) 1990; Maines 1988).

What symbolic interactionism is

Here are the assumptions that guide what interpretive, symbolic interac-tionists think they do. As indicated in the Preface, interactionists assume that human beings create the worlds of experience they live in. They do this by acting on things in terms of the meanings things have for them (Blumer 1969: 2). These meanings come from interaction, and they are shaped by the self-reflections persons bring to their situations. Such self-interaction "is interwoven with social interaction and influences that social interaction" (Blumer 1981: 153). Symbolic interaction (the merger of self and social interaction) is the chief means "by which human beings are able to form social or joint acts" (p. 153). Joint acts, their formation, dissolution, conflict, and merger, constitute "the social life of a human society" (p. 153). A society consists of the joint or social acts "which are formed and carried out by the members" (p. 153).

The self of persons connected in part to their identities (below), is a multilayered phenomenon and comes in several forms. The *phenomenological self* describes the inner stream of consciousness of the person in the social situation. The *interactional self* refers to the self that is presented and displayed to another in a concrete sequence of action (e.g. as a customer). Self is also a linguistic, emotional, and symbolic process. The *linguistic self* refers to the person filling in the empty personal pronouns (I, me) with personal, biographical, and emotional meanings. The self also involves material possessions. The *material self*, or the self as a material object, consists of all the person calls his or hers at a particular moment in time (Denzin 1989a: 32). The material self is also commodified in the exchange relations that the person enters into. The *ideological self* is given in the broader cultural and historical meanings that surround the definition of the individual in a particular group or social situation (e.g. tourist, husband, wife). (Ideology refers to the "imaginary relations of individuals to the real relations in which they 'live' and which govern their existence. . . Ideology constitutes concrete individuals as subjects" (Althusser 1971: 165, 171). The *self as desire* refers to that mode of self-experience which desires its own fulfillment through the flesh, sexuality, and the bodily presence of the other (Denzin 1989a: 32). These forms of the self (phenomenological, interactional, linguistic, material, ideological, as desire) are enacted in the interactional situation and become part of the biography of the person.

The interaction order (Goffman 1983b) is shaped by negotiated, situated, temporal, biographical, emergent, and taken-for-granted processes (Garfinkel 1967b). The central object to be negotiated in interaction is personal identity, or the self-meanings of the person (Stone 1962; Strauss 1959; Couch *et al.* (eds) 1986a, b: xxiii). These identities, which are personal (names), circumstantial (age, gender), and social or structural (professor, student) range across the modes of self-identification just described. The meanings of identity lie in the interaction process and emerge and shift as persons establish and negotiate the task at hand (Couch *et al.* (eds) 1986 b: xxiii). The situations of interaction may be routinized, ritualized, or highly problematic. In them consequential experience occurs. Epiphanic experiences rupture routines and lives and provoke radical redefinitions of the self. In moments of epiphany, people redefine themselves. Epiphanies are connected to turning-point experiences (Strauss 1959). Interpretive interactionists study epiphanic experiences. The interactionist locates epiphanies in those interactional situations in which personal troubles become public issues (Denzin

1989b: 18). In this way the personal is connected to the structural, through biographical and interactional experiences.

Communication as culture

The personal and the structural are mediated through the process of communication.[1] This process is connected to the world of cultural meanings. These meanings are defined, in part, by the systems of ideology and power in a particular social order. They circulate through specific communication systems (oral, print, electronic). The messages they convey are structured and contained within a narrative and a semiological code which invests all "newsworthy" events with an "aura" of political, social, and historical meaning. This code short-circuits receivers and interlocutors. The messages come already interpreted; they overflow with meaning (see Baudrillard 1981: 175–9). They enter into and define the structures of everyday life (Lefebvre 1971/84). In the contemporary, postmodern world (post-Second World War), these communication systems reflect a preoccupation with the real and its representations in video images (Baudrillard 1983a, b; Ulmer 1989).

The phrase "communication as culture" points to the relationship between information structures, systems of communication, the popular cultures of a particular time, and the lived experiences of interacting individuals (see Cooley 1902/22/56; Park 1938/50; Dewey 1927; Couch 1990; Maines and Couch (eds) 1988: 12–13; P. M. Hall 1988; Gronbeck 1988).[2] Communication is indispensable to the processes which articulate cultural meanings. (Park 1938/50: 39; J. W. Carey 1989: 64–5). These meanings are symbolic, never singular, always multiple, and always carried through the processes of direct and mediated communication (Carey 1989: 64–5).

Social structure and social relationships

Everyday and problematic interaction exhibit a situated, constraining structuredness based on ritual, routine, and taken-for-granted meanings. These constraining features are woven through the structures of the social relationships and ensembles of action (Sartre 1976) that connect individuals with one another in differentially coercive ways. As interactional structures, ensembles are reified, patterned regularities of thought, action, and interpretation. They are often embodied in laws and official codes. They provide the bare outlines of lived experience; they are forms of interaction, whose contents must be filled in by the interactions, intentions, and experiences of interacting individuals (Simmel 1950: 11, 14, 385–6, in Wolff (ed.) 1950). They include relationships of love, hate, and competition, and ensembles of individual and collective action. These collective structures (ensembles) range from the series (unconnected persons) to gatherings and encounters to fused, pledged, and organized groups to complex institutional structures (made up of series, groups, and sovereign leaders) and social classes which synthesize institutional groups and series into emerging structures of collective, social, moral, political, and economic awareness and protest. Midway between class structures and gatherings stand the incipient forms of collective behavior (crowds, fashion, protest movements, etc.) which interactionists have traditionally studied (J. Lofland 1981; Blumer 1978; McPhail 1991).

A person's location in the world of experience is organized into a body of localized, interactional practices which reify these relational-structural forms. Such practices include doing work and gender, making love, and being entertained. These practices are connected to the projects that persons pursue. Practices and projects personalize social structure. They are always emergent productions which draw upon local knowledge structures (Geertz 1983), while reflecting the micro-power relations that impinge in the specific situation at hand. These practices are often staged and executed so as to deliberately alter the specific fate of one ensemble of individuals, often at the expense (moral, symbolic, economic, legal) of another group, or interactional collectivity.

If, as interactionists argue, societies exist only in the interactions between persons, then structures – linguistic, gender, kinship, political, economic, religious, cultural, scientific, moral – provide, as Simmel contended, the horizons of experience against which the actual contents of human experience are sketched and lived (Denzin 1983: 136). In this sense all structures, if they are to affect the fate of individuals, even in unintended, unanticipated, or unconscious ways, must be realized interactionally. Gender is a specific structure which all human beings must confront.

Gendered identities

Every human being in any culture belongs to a specific sex class, male or female, and this assignment is made immediately upon birth, if not before

(Cahill 1989: 282).[3] Femininity and masculinity are socially defined terms that are added to the biologically determined sex class of the individual (Garfinkel 1967a: 116–17, 122–4; Mitchell 1982: 2). Gender defines the social and cultural meanings brought to each anatomical sex class; children learn, that is, how to "pass as" and "act as" members of their assigned sexual category. Gender, however, is more than learning masculine and feminine behavior (Deegan 1987: 4).

Gender also involves sexuality, sexual desire, and being sexual – that is, enacting a gendered sexual identity with another. As Mitchell (1982: 2) argues, the "person is formed through their sexuality" and their sexual desires, which become part of their personal sexual identity. Sexuality (being sexual) is culturally shaped (e.g. being sexually alluring or sexually dominant), and these cultural understandings are fitted to the sexual biography of the individual.

Emotional codes, specific to each gender, are learned as language is acquired. These codes interact with the sexual selves and sexual identities that circulate in the various arenas of popular culture in everyday life. The masculine code in our society represses emotionality, whereas the feminine code expresses vulnerable and nurturant forms of emotionality. Each code speaks to a body culture which stresses health, beauty, and erotic attraction. Two gender-specific sexual and emotional cultures thus exist side by side, with females taught to do the emotional labor work (Hochschild 1983) that males avoid, yet expect.

The gendered identity is an interactional production. It is embedded in those interactional places (home and work) that give recurring meaning to ordinary experience. These are places where emotional experiences, including sexual practices, occur. In them concrete individuals are constituted as gendered subjects with emotions, beliefs, and social relationships with others (see Althusser 1971: 165). In these sites, ideology and beliefs about the way the world is and ought to be intertwine with taken-for-granted cultural understandings about love, intimacy, sexuality, the value of work and family, money, prestige, status, and the meaning of the "good life."

Ideology, which works at the level of language and the symbolic (e.g. everyday conversation), also exists as a set of material (economic), interactional practices (i.e. inscriptions by social sciences, popular music and film, etc.) which "*hail or interpellate concrete individuals as concrete subjects*" (Althusser 1971: 173; emphasis original). Ideology consists of the myths, beliefs, desires, and ideas people have about the way things are and should be. At the material level, ideology works through the interactional structures that bring people together. In this way ideology recruits sexually gendered subjects. Through this process of interpellation, of hailing (e.g. "Hey, girl, come here!"), individuals are called to their sexually gendered identities. In Althusser's words (1971: 174): "The hailed individual [when called] will turn around. By this mere one-hundred-and-eighty-degree physical conversion, he becomes a *subject*. Why? Because he has recognized that the hail was 'really' to him, and that 'it was *really him* who was hailed'" (emphasis original). Daily greetings, requests, and conversational exchanges ("Honey, I need a cup of coffee"; "Hey, big fella, give me a hand here") cast individuals in gendered identities. These activities constitute individuals as concrete, gendered subjects in the gender stratification order.

It must be understood that an interactional, dialectical relationship connects these material practices to the worlds of experience in which gendered identities are produced. Specific systems of discourse and meaning operate within specific places to create particular sexually gendered versions of the human being. These systems cohere during particular periods of time (e.g. the Victorian era or post-Second World War America) to create coherent, consistent images of the gender stratification order (e.g. the return of women to the home after the Second World War). During other historical moments, these systems fall apart or enter interregnums during which competing images of sexuality, gender, family, marriage, and work conflict (e.g. the 1970s and 1980s in the United States), only to be brought back together again during another historical moment (e.g. the 1990s, which has seen the return of the "traditional mother and woman," as promoted by such magazines as *Good Housekeeping*).

The above terms and their meanings are culturally and historically specific. The sexually gendered human being in late twentieth-century America is a social, economic, and historical construction, built up out of the patriarchal cultural myths which have been articulated in American popular culture for the last 200 years.

The interactionist/poststructural perspective

A "feminist," interactionist sociological imagination (Balsamo 1990) takes up the problematics of sexuality, desire, language, gendered selves and identities, and the cultural narratives which work to create the worlds of gendered emotional experience in contemporary society. Gender and sexuality (as indicated above) arise out of the complex interactions that connect the texts, meanings, and experiences that circulate in everyday life with the things the members of our culture tell one another about what it is to be a man or a woman. Stories in the daily newspaper, in social science articles, comic books, daytime TV soap operas, night-time family comedies, and melodramas, and in large box-office-drawing films like *When Harry Met Sally, Sex, Lies and Videotape, Blue Velvet, Driving Miss Daisy, Working Girl, Biloxi Blues,* and *Everybody's All-American* reproduce the gender stratification order.

Sexuality and gender are situated in and interactional accomplishments are shaped by a surrounding patriarchal culture (Garfinkel 1967a; Denzin 1989a; West and Zimmerman 1987). Woven through this culture are the myths and beliefs surrounding romantic love, the beautiful woman, the handsome man, the all-American family, and erotic sexuality contained within a monogamous marriage structure (Fiedler 1966: 339). The performances of sexuality and gender, like those of race and class, constitute experiences "which shape the emergent political conditions that we refer to as the postmodern world" (Downing 1987: 80). These performances, when captured in social texts, constitute what we know about these phenomena.

Symbolic interactionism and gender studies

A great deal of caution is necessary when addressing the question, "What is the relationship between symbolic interactionism, poststructuralism and the study of gender and gender inequality?" I want to avoid the path which suggests that the topics of women and gender can easily be fitted under the rubrics of standard, conventional symbolic interactionist thought (e.g. Reynolds 1990; Deegan and Hill (eds) 1987). Rather, with Clough (1987: 4), I want to "emphasize the historical moment at which feminist theory challenges the function of [symbolic interactionism] in the production of" texts on and about sexuality and gender. This challenge to interactionism has occurred as a result of the work of theorists like Levi-Strauss, Lacan, Althusser, Barthes, Derrida, and Foucault and the reading of this work by feminist theorists (see Clough 1987 for a review) who have taken up Freud's challenge to forge their own theory of sexuality, meaning, and existence within a patriarchal culture. (Recent developments by feminist theorists (M. Morris 1988b, c) have attempted to move poststructural-postmodern theory into the field of cultural studies, as discussed above.)

It has been the traditional function of symbolic interactionism (see below), along with the other subjective, interpretive social psychologies (phenomenology, ethnomethodology, everyday life sociology, etc.), to offer a theory of self, interaction, and socialization which speaks to the question of how the human being is formed out of the interaction order (see Denzin 1977a; Lindesmith *et al.* 1991, ch. 1). For the symbolic interactionist gender and sexuality are social constructions (Deegan 1987: 4–5), which emerge under a patriarchal regime in which women are exchanged between male and male, as currencies of exchange (Clough 1987: 10). Although gender and sexuality entered interactionist thought quite early (e.g. G. S. Hall 1898: 360; Cooley 1902/22/56), Mead's (1934) theory of self, like Blumer's later (1969) theory, was gender-free and scarcely took notice of sexuality. The classic textbooks in the tradition (Lindesmith and Strauss 1949) and the revisions of the perspective in the 1960s and 1970s by such authors as Stone (1962) and Goffman (1974, 1979) either treated gender from the perspective of psychoanalysis (Freud and H. S. Sullivan) or applied a structural reading to the sexual stratification order in American society. By the late 1970s and throughout the 1980s interactionists increasingly turned to the socialization of gender and the acquisition of gender identities in a variety of settings. These studies mined the inner, developmental side of gender, arguing, in a manner consistent with the origins of the perspective, that society is in interaction and that the meanings of terms like "gender," "sexuality," "male," and "female," must be found in the meanings persons bring to these categories of experience (see Denzin 1977a; Joffe 1977; Cahill 1989; Power 1985; N. Williams 1990; Ferraro and Johnson 1983; Cho 1990; Bentz 1989; and the readings in Deegan and Hill (eds) 1987).

Poststructuralism

Poststructuralism is that theoretical position which asks how the human subject is constructed in and through the structures of language and ideology. Two key terms, "text" and "deconstruction," organize this perspective. A "text" (see also below) is any printed, visual, oral, or auditory production that is available for reading, viewing, or hearing (e.g. an article, a film, a painting, a song). Readers create texts as they interpret and interact with them. The meaning of a text is always indeterminate, open-ended, and interactional. "Deconstruction" is the critical analysis of texts. It is a process which explores how a text is constructed and given meaning by its author or producer. Poststructuralists argue that "there is only the text" – that is, that the objective reality of social facts (e.g. gender) is a social accomplishment. This accomplishment is documented through the production of texts about the topic at hand – e.g. gender and sexuality. Deconstructionism analyses how a text produces its subject matter.

Commonly called poststructural, post-Marxist, and postmodern, this work (e.g. Foucault 1982) argues that the micro-relations of power in late capitalist societies continually reproduce situated systems of discourse (i.e. social science articles, the law, religion, art, literature, film) which create particular versions of the human subject (male, female, and child), the family, the state, science, and social control. These systems of discourse have reduced women to the status of socializing agents in society and have treated the family as the site of madness.

Women's sexuality, their relationships to children, to their own bodies, and to men have been systematically excluded from this discourse, which until the early 1970s was primarily written by men. A number of feminists have appropriated this theoretical position for their own purposes. Under this new view, power displaces the traditional Marxist conception of base-superstructure and is located in a "disciplinary society" which continually transfers individuals from one disciplinary system of discourse to another (from schools to colleges, work, family, the courts, mental hospitals, prisons, etc.). The intervention of the state in the economy and the family under late capitalism erases the distinction between the private and public spheres in everyday life. There is a dialectical relationship "between women's oppression in the home and in her exploitation in the work force" (Clough 1987: 20). In both spheres she does unpaid emotional labor (Hochschild 1983), which further increases her oppression and alienation. These subjective states are seen as being produced by the social practices and discourses of patriarchal and bourgeois ideologies which reproduce the hegemonic order (Clough 1987: 20).

Feminism thus becomes a way of reading how sexuality, gender, and subjectivity have been constructed under a bourgeois power structure. This system of power and the orders of knowledge (Foucault 1966/70) which it has constructed (the human disciplines) have incorporated a psychoanalytic view of sexuality into a theory of science, narration, and representation. This theory of representation presumes the ability to "realistically" map the world out there within a positivist and postpositivist theory of knowledge (D. E. Smith 1987). An Oedipal logic structures the sociological texts that are written about the individual. These texts, whether ethnographic and qualitative or quantitative, locate subjectivity back in the family, in the male–female relationship (Clough 1987: 16; 1988, 1989). The figure of woman emerges in the "patriarchal culture as a signifier of the male other, bound by a symbolic order in which man can live out his fantasies and obsessions through linguistic command, by imposing them on the silent image of woman still tied to her place as the bearer of meaning, not the maker of meaning" (Mulvey 1982: 413). The poststructuralist feminist intervention into symbolic interactionist work concludes "that a 'man's discourse' about women thoroughly saturates the discourse of the human sciences" (Clough 1987: 18). Feminist knowledge is thus both "implicated in and is an implication of this order of power/knowledge" (p. 16).

From interpretation to cultural studies

A more critical, interactionist, psychoanalytic feminism (Clough 1987, 1988, 1989, 1990) has emerged which has attempted to bridge symbolic interactionism with the poststructural theories of Lacan, Derrida, and Barthes and the more recent postmodern arguments of Lyotard (1979/ 84) and Baudrillard (1987/8) (see Denzin 1991d). The failures of traditional interactionism have been augmented by this poststructuralist feminist perspective (Richardson 1991a, b). Both symbolic interactionists and feminist poststructuralists focus on the production of cultural meanings. Recent work in cultural studies (Denzin 1991e, 1990a, 1990d) has blended these perspectives through a consideration of the economic and cultural conditions that lead to the reproduction of a gender stratification in a society like the United States. This version of cultural studies attempts to unravel the ideological meanings that are coded into the taken-for-granted meanings that circulate in everyday life, tracking down "in the decorative display of what-goes-without-saying, the ideological abuse which is hidden there" (Barthes 1957/72: 111).

Cultural studies (see chapters 4–7) examines three interrelated problems: the production of cultural meanings, the textual analysis of these meanings, and the study of lived cultures and lived experiences (R. Johnson 1986/1987: 72). Each of these problems constitutes a field of inquiry in its own right. When applied to the study of gender and sexuality, the production of cultural meanings involves issues of ideology and political economy, since these processes produce recurring meanings which are attached to the gender stratification system in postmodern society. The textual analysis of these meanings involves the implementation of a variety of reading strategies, from semiotics to hermeneutics to psychoanalysis and feminism. At the level of textuality, the question turns on how a text creates a gendered subject. At the level of lived experience, a central problem becomes the examination of how interacting individuals connect their lived experiences to the cultural representations of those experiences.

Interpretive interactionism enters the field of cultural studies and the analysis of gender at the level of lived experiences. In the field of gender studies, this strategy seeks those moments of existential crisis when a person's sexuality and gender identity are forcefully and dramatically called into question. This is a matter of extreme theoretical and methodological importance, for in these epiphanic moments the gender order is revealed in ways that are normally not seen.

Self, experience, and expression

Gendered experiences, epiphanic and routine, as just indicated, are given expression in a variety of ways, including rituals, interactional dramas, the stories people tell one another about their life crises, and the representation of such experiences in cultural texts, including myths, novels, songs, films, autobiographies, and biographies. Experiences are shaped by social texts, which both define the experience and often constitute a significant version of the experience itself (e.g. getting divorced, giving birth, entering treatment for alcoholism, etc.).

There are several levels and forms of self-experience and its expression. I term these the *worldly* (or *flesh-and-blood*), the *empirical*, the *analytic*, and the *textual* (Denzin 1990a: 212). The *worldly, flesh-and-blood subject* describes me sitting here typing these words. This is the subject as a universal singular, who expresses in his or her lifetime deeply felt emotions that may escape textual representation. The *empirical subject* is the one who appears to the sociologist in an interview, life story, or personal narrative. This is the concrete, empirical expression of a worldly person (e.g. Garfinkel's Agnes (Garfinkel 1967a) or Shaw's Stanley (Shaw 1930/66). The *analytic subject* is an ideal type (e.g. Garfinkel's intersexed Agnes and Goffman's mental patient).

The *textual subject* is a threefold construction. When Shaw's Stanley (see discussion below) described himself to Snodgrass in 1982 (p. 17) in words given to him by Shaw when he was a young man, he was using Shaw's text to describe himself. In this moment he became a second-order, textual subject. When Stanley's experiences are moved directly into Shaw's or Snodgrass's text, without interpretation, a first-order, empirical textual representation occurs. When Shaw (or Snodgrass) rewrite Stanley's experiences in sociological terms, analytic textuality results; for now Stanley has become a product of still another system of textuality. Direct experience, then, is never captured. It is only recorded in a text. How does this work?

Consider the following example, which I have analyzed in detail elsewhere (Denzin 1989a: 50–4). This is the story of Stanley, *The Jack-Roller*, perhaps sociology's most famous juvenile delinquent. "A jack-roller is a robber of drunks or sleeping men and is equivalent to today's mugger, particularly if the emphasis is on the helplessness of the victim" (Snodgrass 1982: 3). As a teenager, Stanley became acquainted with Clifford R. Shaw, a graduate-student sociologist at the University of Chicago in the late 1920s. Shaw recorded Stanley's life story. The University of Chicago Press published the autobiography, along with Shaw's introduction, in 1930. His story, told by Shaw (1930/66) and retold by Becker (1966), is one of symbolic interactionism's mythical texts (see Bennett 1981, ch 8, for a review of the major criticisms of this text). By the 1980s, the republished paperback edition of 1966 had sold over 23,000 copies. The text became a classic in the field of juvenile delinquency. It has been required reading for generations of sociologists in the field (Snodgrass 1982: 3). It is read as an instance of the kind of work sociologists did during "the Golden Age of Chicago sociology" (Becker 1966: ix).

Stanley and Clifford: Undoing an interactionist text

The life history and the case study were methods heavily promoted by the University of Chicago sociology department during the 1920s (Becker 1966: xii). *The Jack-Roller* became a model for and of this research. What would be called the "classic, natural history approach" to case studies emerged during this period. It had several characteristics. The researcher would (1) select a series of research hypotheses and problems to be answered, formulate tentative operationalizations of key concepts, and select a subject and a research site; (2) record the objective events and experiences in the subject's life that pertain to the research problem; (3) check out these events by source and point of view so that contradictions, irregularities, and discontinuities can be established; (4) obtain the subject's interpretations of these events as they occurred in their chronological, or natural order; then (5) analyze these reports in terms of their validity, truthfulness, and reliability; (6) resolve the validity of the above sources and establish the priority of the sources for testing hypotheses; (7) begin testing hypotheses, while searching for negative evidence, and (8) organizing the initial draft of the entire life history, submitting this to the subject for reactions; finally (9) rework the report in its natural sequence in light of these reactions and present the hypotheses that have been supported, concluding with a statement concerning theory and practice.

These nine steps include all the essential features of the classic, natural history approach. They were implemented over and over again in the Chicago life history, case study series (see Becker 1966: v). They build on the position that lives have natural histories that unfold over time and that these lives are marked by objective events and experiences. A life is pictured as an orderly production. The steps assume that hypotheses can be operationalized. They are preoccupied with objective events and subjective definitions of these events. They assume that accurate, truthful, valid, consistent interpretations of events can be given.

Shaw, the collector and editor of *The Jack-Roller*, describes how this record is to be obtained:

The story should be as spontaneous as possible and always follow the natural sequence of events in the life of the delinquent . . . we hoped to be able to describe . . . the natural process involved in the development of his delinquent-behavior. . . The technique . . . is that of the personal interview. . . In most . . . cases a stenographic record of the interview is made . . . thus . . . its objectivity is preserved. (1930/66:21)

Earlier in *The Jack-Roller*, Shaw (p. 2) discusses the criteria for judging these materials. He suggests that family history, medical, psychiatric, and psychological findings on the subject be collected, and, in the case of delinquents, the official record of arrest, offenses, and commitments, play-group relationships, and:

any other *verifiable* material which may throw light upon the personality and actual experiences of the delinquent . . . In the light of such supplementary material, it is possible to evaluate and interpret more accurately the personal document. It is probable that in the absence of such additional case material any interpretation of the life-history is somewhat questionable. (p. 2; emphasis added)

Lives are verifiable concerns. Interpretations should be withheld if verifications of a subject's account cannot be found. Furthermore, all aspects of a life should be examined. Only then can objective documents mapping the life be produced.

It is assumed that the "real" Stanley's life history lies somewhere in the convergences that connect these personal, family, medical, legal, psychiatric, and psychological documents. Shaw hopes to find the "real" Stanley in the verifiable materials that "throw light upon" his personality and his actual experiences. But what is the truth about Stanley? Where is he? Is he in these other materials? Is he to be found in his personality? Or is he, as Burgess (1930/66: 189) suggests, to be found in "his reactions to the events of his experience." Burgess comments:

> Granted that Stanley told the truth about himself, as he sees it, the reader will have still a further question, What were the facts as they are about Stanley's stepmother ... the House of Correction ... The absolute truth about these or other points cannot be secured by the life-history method and probably be obtained by any other method known. But in human affairs it is not the absolute truth ... that concerns us, but the way in which persons react to the events.

So Stanley is not in the documents. He is to be found in his reactions to events (also given in documents): broken homes, poverty, bad housing, bad companions, a criminal career, the discrimination of his stepmother, the patterns of stealing prevalent in his neighborhood, and "the dynamic relationship between [his] personality and his varied and stimulating experiences" (p. 189).

I have no quarrel with the position that the definitions of situations are what count. I accept W. I. Thomas's dictum ("If men define situations as real, they are real in their consequences") and Goffman's attempt to rewrite it (1974: 1). What is at issue is how these situations get into the text and become real for the reader (and the writer). However, if only definitions matter (for Shaw and Burgess), then why the preoccupation with verifiable statements? The answer is clear. In order to create Stanley, Shaw and Burgess must anchor him in a social world filled with others. Stanley exists in the oppositions that connect him to this "mythical" world of "otherness." While Burgess and Shaw disclaim the pursuit of absolute truths, they seek to uncover a center to Stanley's personality that will explain his "reactions to the events of his experience."

Uncoupling Stanley and Shaw

The classic, natural history approach fails to make problematic the set of issues considered above. It conflates the flesh-and-blood, textual, empirical, and analytic versions of the subject. It assumes that "an objective" record of a life can be given and that this objective report lies in documents and records which detail the life in question. It fails to consider the possibility that these other documents are themselves social constructions, social texts which create their own version of the subject — in this case Stanley and his life history (see Cicourel 1968). This approach sees in a life materials for the testing and development of scientific hypotheses about human behavior. By turning lives into objects of study, this approach gives scant attention to the problems involved in describing real lives with real, objective meanings.

While announcing a concern for the differences between objective experiences and their subjective, interactional meanings and expressions, the approach tells us surprisingly little about the gaps between experiences and their expression. Indeed, when confronted with these gaps, practitioners like Shaw and Burgess escape into the "definition of the situation" dictum. Dancing round the problems of truthfulness and verifiable statements, these authors, committed as they are to the canons of positivist, naturalistic science, ignore the pervasive gray area that joins their life histories with narrative fiction. Seeing themselves creating and contributing to a genre, they fail to see how the very conventions they employ create the subject matter (delinquency) they wish to analyze. They then proceed to assume the existence of knowledgeable authors, objective texts, starting points in lives, and the presence of influential others.

The classic stance pits the interactionist against the subject. It turns the subject into an object of study. It involves the production of a text that locates the subject inside a world that has been rendered understandable from the sociological point of view. Thus both Shaw and Burgess attempt to explain why this particular youth became a juvenile delinquent.

Burgess, on the basis of his reading of this and other life stories, was led to conclude that the personality is fixed in a child's early years. There are, he argued, four personality types: (1) Persons who view their lives in conventional terms, or chroniclers; (2) Self-defenders, who seek to justify their lives; (3) Confessants, who tell everything about themselves; and (4) Self-analysts, who analyze everything (Burgess 1930/66: 190).

Stanley, according to Burgess, was a self-defender. Hence his story was full of rationalizations explaining why he became a delinquent.

Nevertheless, Burgess (and Shaw) felt that Stanley had no choice but to become a delinquent. He came from a broken home and from an area of Chicago where delinquency was high. Moreover, Stanley's personality portrayed a series of traits which set him on the path to delinquency. These traits included self-pity, hypercriticalness of others, excessive need for attention, ideas of persecution, always being right, blaming others, lack of self-insight, being suspicious of others, resentments, and a tendency to moralize (Burgess 1930/66: 190–1). Burgess saw Stanley's personality traits as the "characteristic attributes of the personality pattern of the individual who is able even under the most adverse circumstances to maintain his ego against an unfriendly and even hostile social world" (p. 191).

Shaw and Burgess read these traits off and from the text of Stanley's life. They saw Stanley as a person who imposed himself on others as a way of dealing with his humiliating, threatening life situations. They found a center to Stanley's life: his personality type.

In 1982 J. Snodgrass found these same traits still present in Stanley, who, at the age of 69, in 1976, agreed to do a follow-up to his life story. Commenting on Stanley, who died in 1982 at the age of 75, Snodgrass observed:

> I have tried to outline a pattern in Stanley's behavior; that is in order to avoid feelings of inferiority he repeatedly reacts by attempting to impress his superiority on others . . . Burgess's identification of the early rise and persistence of a sense of injustice, as a "key" personality trait, is related to this theme. (Snodgrass 1982: 170)

Stanley found these same traits in himself. He states:

> I'm trying to back away from all contention . . . the tendency to react is always there. If I'm prodded I go off like a cannon. Then I want to react strongly against anything I feel is unfair . . . I agree with certain authorities that your personal make-up mentally is established in the early years. I must have had some awful experiences before I was conscious of them. (Snodgrass 1982: 171)

Here the empirical subject merges with the social scientist and becomes a first-order, analytic textual construction. At the time of his death, Stanley felt that he had overcome these negative personality traits: "The fires of passion have long since burned out and today I follow a routine that allows for rather simple requirements" (p. 173). Stanley became the man Shaw said he would be; and this man, at the age of 75, told yet another social scientist: "If anyone ever had an influence over me it was Shaw . . . He would laugh at me, you see . . . I would be inclined to say, 'Who the hell is this guy, I'd like to punch him in the nose' " (p.171).

A few months before he died, this man stated, "I am pleased also, if by this publication, I am helpful to Jon Snodgrass, his associates, and to social science" (p. 173). Stanley, the man who, after Wladek Wisniewski, made the life history (and Clifford R. Shaw) famous in sociology thanks sociology for having made him. This is what the classic, natural history, interactionist approach to life stories accomplished. It gave delinquents, prostitutes, alcoholics, drug addicts, and immigrants traits, personalities, personality flaws, and the chance to tell their stories. It transformed subjects into sociology's images of who they should be.

Shaw and Burgess conflated the flesh-and-blood subject (the real Stanley) with the empirical subject (the youth who was interviewed) and turned him into an analytic, ideal type, the classic inner-city delinquent. He then became a complex first- and second-order textual production. Stanley and Clifford Shaw became one in *The Jack-Roller*. They cannot be uncoupled, for to take Shaw (and Burgess) out of the picture is to leave only an empty story of Stanley. There is no Stanley story without the investigative tale told by these two sociological experts. The natural history, life history method permitted two illusions to be sustained: that the real Stanley, and the real Stanley's real experiences, had been captured. Once these illusions were in place, the interactionist experts could then write their objective, analytic, interpretive accounts of Stanley's life. And then he could lead that life.

The romantic tale

These accounts romanticized the subject. They turned Stanley into a sociological version of a screen hero. Not quite the "cute little mischief-maker called Andy Hardy" (Roffman and Purdy 1981: 136), he might have been the focus of any of a number of Depression and post-Depression era juvenile delinquent films starring Mickey Rooney, Jackie Cooper, Ronald Reagan, James Cagney, E. G. Robinson, Humphrey Bogart, the "Dead End" Kids, Leo Gorcey, Freddie Bartholomew, and Spencer Tracy (e.g. *Dead End*, 1937; *Tough Guys*, 1938; *Boys Town*, 1938; *Reformatory*, 1938; *Hell's Kitchen*, 1939; *Boy Slaves*, 1939;

Angels Wash their Faces, 1939; *They Made me a Criminal*, 1939; *Knock on any Door*, 1949; and *City across the River*, 1939). Such films, like the Chicago ethnography series on gangs, delinquents, and criminals, focused on the reformed delinquent's reintegration into society. They employed a social disorganization model of personality adjustment, seeing delinquents as products of bad environments. A delinquent cycle was deployed (the slum and crime or reform school and a healthy, normal life). Both alternatives taught crime; the bad child's only choice was to find a healthy adult as a role model.

These films, like *The Jack-Roller* told their stories from within a realistic, melodramatic framework which hopefully (but not always) had a happy ending. They followed the moral careers of such individuals, taking them through the three stages of the classic morality tale (Elbaz 1987, e.g.: being in a state of grace, being seduced by evil and falling, and finally being redeemed). Not all of these sociological tales took the subject through redemption, although the films did. (When redemption or the end of the moral career is not revealed, it is presumed that the sociological story itself is the end of the story.) These melodramas portrayed, in graphic, realist detail, the plight of a virtuous individual victimized by "repressive and inequitable social circumstances, particularly those involving . . . family" (Schatz 1981: 222) and neighborhood (the slum). Hopefully he grew out of his deviance. If he didn't, he had to be punished. There were no Marlon Brandos (*The Wild One*, 1954) or James Deans (*East of Eden*, 1955) here; no brooding, disillusioned individuals who turned their backs forever on a corrupt system. Hollywood's and sociology's delinquents were good boys gone bad because of the slums and the absence of a good woman (and a father) in their lives.

Realist, textual complicity

These texts were produced under the mantle of a moral social "realism," a mode of presentation which pervaded both Hollywood film and sociology during the social realist period (1945–60; see Cook 1981, ch. 11) in cinema. Social realism and "social consciousness" films drew upon literary (and scientific) naturalism, a literary form which stressed a "slice of life" approach to the human being's struggles for survival in a hostile natural and social environment (see Cowley 1950).[4] These texts, in the hands of the sociologist (also the novelist and the filmmaker), turned the researcher into a hero-as-saviour who made sense of the subject's life (Clough 1991, ch. 1), and even, as in Shaw's case, enters into the life of the deviant and supervises his recovery. As narrator of the subject's story, the sociologist is the expert on the life in question. As a result, the subject is displaced from the sociologist's text, appearing only in excerpts from transcribed interviews and field notes.

An interactionist complicity thus structured these texts. Like their filmic counterparts, they created the sympathetic illusion that a solution to the delinquency problem had been found. The solution was, of course, interactional, not one of political economy. The correct (loving, fatherly) system of discipline and punishment (Foucault 1977) could instill the proper values in the wayward youth. Such a solution placed the burden of the delinquent's problem on his (or her) family, on neighborhood, and on improperly run reform schools. If the delinquent failed to reform, it was his fault – actually the fault of his personality. Failure was not due to flaws in the system or because of an absence of loving people wishing to cure him of his "waywardness".

While society could certainly do better and while it was clear that Hollywood wasn't doing all that it could (Blumer and Hauser 1933), with a little push (Blumer 1933), films and sociology could offer proper role models for these children of America's largely unwanted immigrants. That is, the mass media, especially films, had to be directed away from the positive representations of crime and the criminal way of life on screen (Blumer 1933; Blumer and Hauser 1933). Movies caused or shaped delinquency. Thus movies had to change. In the early 1930s, Hollywood put in place a Production Code that punished criminals and rewarded law-abiding citizens (see chapter 5, also Sklar 1975: 82–5 for a discussion of this code and the Chicago sociologists' relationship to the film industry and this code). Thus sociological, social, moral realism joined forces with a new brand of realistic cinema, a cinema of American social problems. These two agendas were then blended into a meliorative, social pragmatism, with the goal of eradicating crime (and other social problems) from society. This program of social reform rested on the moral generosity of philanthropic individuals (Mead 1930/64) who had either the money and wealth (the benefactor) or the big heart (Father Flanagan) to share with these poor children of the slums. It depended for its success, in part, on the film industry's willingness to present crime and delinquents in new ways (Roffman and Purdy 1981, ch. 9). And this they did. It also required morally inclined sociologists who would study these people sympathetically with the interpretive methods of a new, scientific (pragmatic) sociology. These sociologists needed to be committed to the building of a free, open democratic American society, a society predicated on communication, informed publics, and morally responsive leadership. They could not call for revolutions or radical social reforms. The Chicago sociologists complied.

Conclusion

The Jack-Roller is not an isolated case. In 1967 Garfinkel told a similar story about Agnes (see Denzin 1990a). J. Lofland did the same in 1977 with an enlarged edition of his classic text Doomsday Cult. In 1990 Plummer reasserted the canonical status of The Jack-Roller in the interactionist tradition, as he offered a re-reading of its method and called for more texts like it. The moral is clear. The melodramatic, realist, interactionist social (problems) text reproduces a romantic overidentification with society's undesirables. This identification produces interactional and emotional reactions, not economic solutions, to social problems. It creates the comforting illusion that if one identifies with and understands another's plight, then somehow that person's sorry situation will go away. This, of course, is pure fantasy. It is romantic ideology woven through liberal and conservative political agendas which make individuals responsible for their own problems. This kind of interactionist complicity reproduces the conditions the theorist-as-moralist finds so discomforting. This is why moral realism is so hard to do away with. Without it, there would be no way for the interactionist to sympathetically project himself or herself into the moral deviant's social situation. Realism thus functions to perpetuate the status quo. It brings to the interactionist the halo of the one who identifies with the downtrodden of the world.

In this chapter I have detailed what interactionists don't do. I then outlined an interpretive, poststructural, feminist approach to the problems of structure, constraint, and social control in contemporary society. A critical reading of a classic interactionist text was then offered. In the next chapter I examine the internal and external criticisms that have been brought to the symbolic interactionist tradition. I will also continue the above line of criticism, concerning politics, texts, and pragmatism.

Notes

1 I take the heading for this section from J. W. Carey 1989.
2 As noted in chapter 1, unlike their Critical Theory counterparts in Germany (Adorno, Horkheimer, and Marcuse; see Kellner 1989), the Chicago-connected interactionists (and pragmatists) failed to develop an in-depth, critical cultural studies approach to communications and popular culture. They did, however, produce readings of the press, popular novels, and movies (see Blumer 1933; Mills 1959). These readings, with the exception of Mills's,

never assumed the critical edge of the German school. (See ch. 5–7 and below).

3   The following discussion of gender draws from Denzin 1991d.

4   According to J. T. Carey (1975: 177–83, 189), the Chicago sociologists read Sinclair Lewis, John Dos Possos, James Farrell, Dreiser, and Sherwood Anderson and used these works as models for writing up life history data.

3 CRITIQUE AND RENEWAL: LINKS TO CULTURAL STUDIES

The basic premises of symbolic interactionism have to have their empirical validity tested. If they cannot survive that test they . . . should be thrown ruthlessly aside. (Blumer 1969: 49)

'It appears that interactionists may have lost control of their own texts . . . [this] complicity . . . is an act of political self-destruction. (Maines 1988: 53–4)

As the loyal opposition in American sociology, symbolic interactionism and symbolic interactionists have been subjected, since Mead's death, to almost constant criticism. Negative evaluations have come from conflict theory (Collins 1986), functionalism and neo-functionalism (Alexander 1987; Smelser 1988), Marxism (Lichtman 1970), positivism (Huber 1973a, b), feminism (Deegan and Hill (eds) 1987), poststructuralism (Clough 1988), cultural studies (S. Hall 1980a, b), communications theory (J. W. Carey 1989), Critical Theory (Habermas 1987), and ethnomethodology (P. Atkinson 1988).[1]

These criticisms have come in three waves, which correspond, respectively, to the criticism and ferment (1963–70), ethnography (1971–80), and contemporary periods (1981–90) of development.[2] The 1963–70 criticisms focused on the politics of the theory (see Reynolds 1990: 138–54 for a review; also Shaskolsky 1970 and Gouldner 1968, 1970), omissions in Mead's framework (Meltzer 1959), an over-reliance on the oral tradition, and ambiguous definitions of key terms like "self" (Kuhn 1964a; Denzin 1969). Those in the 1970s focused on the failure of interactionists to address political issues (P. M. Hall 1972; Block 1973; D. L. Smith 1973; Ropers 1973; Maryl 1973; Lichtman 1970), the question of social organization (Reynolds and Reynolds 1973), a reluctance to build theory (J. Lofland 1970), the supposed emergent bias of the grounded theory perspective (Huber 1973a, b), and the neglect of the emotions. Others attacked Blumer's readings of Mead (McPhail and Rexroat 1979, 1980) and the perspective's obsession with a metaphysics of meaning which makes a fetish of everyday life (Brittan 1973). Critics in the 1981–90 period (see Maines 1988: 45 for a review) argue that the theory has become stagnant and commonsensical (Collins 1986), is still unable to address social structural issues adequately (Prendergast and Knotternus 1990), and that Blumer's work was subjectivistic and antistructural (Alexander 1987; Smelser 1988; Stryker 1988; Warshay and Warshay 1986). Near the end of the decade, a series of poststructuralist criticisms were brought to bear on the works of Becker, Blumer, Goffman, and Mead (Clough 1988, 1989, 1991; Denzin 1987c, 1988; also Denzin and Keller 1981).

These criticisms divide into five categories: (1) theory and method (e.g. definitions of key terms, the emergent bias, scholasticism, stagnation, the oral tradition, the preoccupation with meaning, etc.); (2) the astructural bias, including the neglect of history and macro-organizational problems; (3) politics; (4) the neglect of the emotions; and (5) textuality (e.g. readings of Mead, the production of texts, etc.)

In this chapter I examine and answer these criticisms. I take them up, not in order of their appearance, but in terms of their focus. In the process I hope to develop a more detailed picture of the interactionist project. This picture should create the space for the emergence of a cultural studies project within the interactionist tradition.

Criticisms of theory and method

Blumer's damning praise of *The Polish Peasant* (1939, 1979) anticipated most, if not all, of the methodological and theoretical criticisms that interactionism has received. His criticisms turned on five basic points: (1) the quality of the data used to test a theory, (2) the rigorous, scientific analysis of documents which purport to represent subjective human experience, (3) the researcher's place in the research act, (4) the definition of key terms, and (5) the place of theory in the interpretation of research findings. He argued that this monumental work failed to offer decisive tests of its theoretical interpretations (1939: 75). Its interpretations did not come from the documents but were present before Thomas and Znaniecki approached their research (p. 74). The interpretations were strained and were based on observations (documents) which did not offer sufficient data for the generalizations made from them or for tests of their hypotheses, which were thus not verified adequately (p. 75). The validity of their theory, he argued, could not be determined by their documents. Their data failed to meet the scientific requirements of representativeness, adequacy, reliability, and decisiveness (1939: 75; 1979; xxii–xxxviii). Blumer concluded that *The Polish Peasant* set a "series of methodological problems of the gravest import to sociology" (1979: xxxvii).

These problems were present in 1964 in Manford Kuhn's discussion of the major trends of symbolic interaction theory. Although he was analyzing another body of work (dramaturgy – e.g. Goffman, Burke, and Stone), he argued that testable generalizations could not be derived from the framework. He then applied the same criticism to the career and socialization studies of Hughes and Becker, as well as to the work of theorists who attempted to operationalize and measure the self. He stated that "the difficulties . . . seem to lie in operationalization. It is most difficult to establish generalizations valid for human behavior without methods wherewith to make precise checks on intersubjective perceptions of events" (Kuhn 1964a: 78).

Blumer and Kuhn's criticisms lie at the level of the concept (definitive, sensitizing, operational) and its relation to data on the one hand and theory on the other. In 1970 John Lofland complicated matters by attacking the general imagery of interactionist work and its relation to theory. He argued that a form of analytic interruptus structures interactionist work. This is seen in the tendency of interactionists to generate mini-concepts, but no theory. They fail, that is, to self-consciously assemble all the relevant materials on a specific topic so that a body of mini-concepts could be constructed out of the empirical variations that have been observed. Interactionists, he argued, typically list only a handful of variations on a theme. Were they to use an implicit or explicit paradigm of strategic analysis, they could articulate generic types of strategies (1970: 43), which would allow them to "build back up to the large, abstract and magnificent imageries provided by people like Blumer" (p. 44). Such a move would permit the "construction of generic and comparative theories of strategic constitution" (p. 45). Lofland then went on to offer recipes for doing fieldwork and for writing up field notes into generic typologies (1971, 1976). Such a strategy supposedly allows for the development of middle-range theories of interaction in everyday life (Lofland 1978).

The Huber logico-theoretic exchange

Analytic interruptus was not the criticism that Huber (Rytina and Loomis 1970; Huber 1973a, b, 1974) and later McPhail and Rexroat (1979, 1980) would bring to symbolic interactionism. Taking her reading of pragmatism (and Dewey) from Bertrand Russell (1945: 811–28), Huber (Rytina and Loomis 1970: 316; Huber 1973b: 276; 1973a: 800; 1974: 465–6) attacked the so-called emergent bias in symbolic interaction theory, connecting this bias to Dewey's pragmatism. Her argument was threefold. Following Russell, she argued that Dewey's pragmatism was insensitive to power. Second, she contended that Dewey (and by implication Blumer and symbolic interactionists) were unable to determine the truth of an assertion because of their focus on the consequences, not the causes, of an action. Third, she contended that interactionists had no way of guarding against an emergent political or social bias reflective of "unstated assumptions of the researcher, the climate of opinion in the discipline, and the distribution of power in the interactive setting" (1973b: 282). She argued that interactionists lacked, but needed an a priori logico-theoretic component to their method. This method would "spell out in advance and in detail what is expected and why . . . such preliminary spadework would help to integrate the findings into a larger body of work." Such frameworks are important because they "give the researcher a chance to lose the game. A theoretical formulation forces researchers to bet on particular outcomes . . . In the absence of such a formulation, the researcher always wins" (p. 282).

For Huber, the assumptions of pragmatism and symbolic interactionism lead to research which is initiated with "the atheoretical simplicity of a blank mind" (p. 282). This initial absence of theory then lays the researcher open to the emergent biases noted above. Her attack is predicated on the following assumptions: that symbolic interactionism has always been an important perspective in American sociology (p. 274); that it is related to many other perspectives, including labelling theory, phenomenology, existentialism, participant observation, and qualitative sociology (pp. 274–5); that most of what is useful in the "SI approach has already been absorbed into the mainstreams of social psychology" (p. 274); that the problems of symbolic interactionism also apply to these other perspectives; and that many young sociologists are drawn to this perspective because it does not emphasize quantification ("Apparently the SI tradition and similar approaches answer a need in the discipline; and, whatever their inadequacies, they will probably be around a long time" [p. 275]). But beware! Symbolic interactionism is not a science. No wonder, then, that "the practitioners of SI remain nervous lest their reports be confused with mere journalism. The fear is justified" (p. 282). Yet she cites no interactionists who express this fear.

Her agenda is clear. Huber is attempting to protect sociology's young people from this sociological perspective. Although its good parts have already been absorbed into those versions of mainstream social psychology which use logico-deductive methods, it remains a seductive alternative to those who want a sociology that speaks without numbers to the lives of real people. Beware, she says, for politics can creep into the situation and make your observations unscientific, shaped by the biases of "those who do and act" (p. 282).

Thus Huber repeats, as she had done before with Rytina and Loomis (1970), her arguments against Marxism and pragmatism. Neglecting Marxism in the 1973b article, she nonetheless applies the same criticisms to interactionism as she had earlier applied to a narrow version of Marxist theory (e.g. its failure to postulate a logico-deductive system independent of social/scientific action). She thus assembles all interpretive theories under one umbrella. She then argues that they are all plagued by the same problems as symbolic interactionism. If Marxism, symbolic interactionism, and all those other approaches fail because they cannot guard against emergent biases, then only one sociology remains: mainstream American functional empiricism. Huber's intent, then, is to silence all these alternative versions of the sociological imagination.

Clearly, Huber equated science with a logical positivist version of theory, propositions, hypotheses, and data, even though she claimed that she was not a positivist (Huber 1974: 465). Her argument that Dewey did not deal with power and politics (Rytina and Loomis 1970: 316) and the scientific method, ignored his extensive writings on these very topics (see Dewey 1939, ch. 1, 5, 7, 8, 18, 19) and his desire to implement a scientific method that would promote radical social change from within social structures (West 1989: 99–100). She sides with Russell's "wrongheaded attack on Dewey" (West 1989: 99; e.g. the assertion that "Truth is not an important concept in Dr. Dewey's logic") and argues that for Dewey and the other pragmatists, truth is the "emerging consensus of the participants in an interactive situation" and scientific truth is "whatever works in a given situation" (p. 276). None of the pragmatists ever took this position. The truth of an assertion rests in its consequences for action, which are determined by the methods and protocols of scientific inquiry. Truth for Dewey is not reducible to "warranted assertibility . . . [or] in terms of correspondence with Reality or coherence with other sentences" (West 1989: 100). Truth for Dewey is defined in terms of the public good, which is conceptualized from the standpoint of democratic socialism (Dewey, in West 1989: 103).

Huber never spells out what the logico-theoretic method means in inquiry, except to state that it is a "deductive system, including the logical relations between its propositions, the formulae by which they can be expressed, and the rules governing their use" (1974: 463). She holds to a belief that there is a reality out there that can be studied scientifically, independent of the values and biases of the observer. Science thus becomes an objective mirror to nature, which reflects back the real in undistorted ways. There is no a priori test or rule for the determination of the operations which define ideas. This belief was, of course, heavily attacked by the pragmatists (Dewey 1939: 334) and more recently by interactionists (Blumer 1969; Denzin 1989a, b, e), postpositivists (Guba and Lincoln 1989), poststructuralists (Foucault 1980), narrative-rhetorical theorists (Brown 1989), feminists (Clough 1990, Richardson 1991a, b), ethnomethodologists (Garfinkel et al. 1981), and those working in the sociology of science (Ashmore 1989). She ignores the fact that science is a form of ideology shaped by particular beliefs and biases. She also ignores the question of who in society has the power to define what is a problem worthy of being funded by the state for purposes of research. Contemporary theorizing on the problem of truth, science, knowledge, and power makes the simplistic positivist view of an objective scientific method highly questionable, if not obsolete.

Several interactionists critically responded to Huber's attack, including Blumer (1973), R. L. Schmitt (1974), and Stone et al. (1974). Unfortunately the reactions to Huber all shared a commitment to a form of naturalistic science that would allow interactionists to do defensible scientific work. That is, they countered her scientific arguments with another set of scientific arguments which were also predicated on a realist epistemology – that there is a world out there that can be studied scientifically. Blumer argued that she reduced science to the "logico-theoretic component" (1973: 797) and misunderstood how a naturalistic science (after Darwin) actually worked. No scientist works with a blank mind, and for Blumer the real source of bias "lies in the procedure by which the scientific problem is constructed" (p. 798). Huber countered that Blumer offered no way of picking one interpretation over another when he argued that the best interpretation is the one that fits the world that is being studied.

R. L. Schmitt (1974) reduced Huber's complaints to four issues: (1) her equating participant observation with the methodology of interactionism; (2) her failure to distinguish the Iowa school Twenty Statements studies (and more traditional hypothesis testing interactionism) from the Blumer, emergent school variety; (3) her glib treatment of the meanings of theory and concept for interactionists (e.g. sensitizing concepts and grounded theory); and (4) her predictions that the perspective would die, of interest only to those who have a "love for the underdog" (Huber 1973b: 274). Stone *et al.* (1974) attacked Huber on methodological and ontological grounds, on her narrow conception of field methods, on her depiction of the "logico-theoretic component," and her craftsmanship. They, like Schmitt and Blumer, contended that she misread the use of field methods and the naturalistic method of analysis. They argued that, over time, valid interpretations can be developed in a field setting. They disputed her treatment of pragmatism, especially the relevance of the past and the future for conduct in the present (e.g. her argument that the "past cannot be affected by what we do" (Huber 1973b: 276). They concluded that Huber's article was "actually a revival of the old debate about the merits of positivism . . . [and] there is no avoidance that the logico-theoretic component neutralizes the influence of power arrangements on the research enterprise" (1974: 461).

Huber refused to address the issues in the responses to her article. She persisted in her blank mind theory of interactionist research ("The SI recipe for doing sociology is dangerously close to radical subjectivism"; 1974: 466), praised the virtues of the logico-theoretic component, and defended her scholarship against charges of sloppy craftsmanship. The exchanges ended in a stand-off. They reinforced, as Schmitt had observed, the general tendency to read symbolic interactionism simplistically. He observes, "The Huber portrayal of SI is particularly damaging within this context" (R. L. Schmitt 1974: 453).

More important, the exchanges solidified the general understanding that in the periods of criticism, ferment, and ethnography (1963–80), interactionists were committed to building a naturalistic science of the social world. Furthermore, they would go to considerable lengths to defend this program against attacks from the sociological establishment and those committed to a positivist program of research. Interactionists had a science too, and it was better than the one their critics advocated. (Paradoxically the interactionists did not take up Mills's (1964) criticisms of pragmatism.)

The McPhail–Rexroat–Blumer exchange

Huber's call for a rigorous symbolic interactionist methodology was repeated, with important variations, by McPhail and Rexroat in 1979. Here, as with Huber, Blumer was the main object of attack. McPhail and Rexroat argued that there were significant epistemological and ontological differences between Mead's social behaviorism and Blumer's symbolic interactionism. They charged that Blumer had misread Mead, producing a position that vacillated between idealism and realism, contrary to Mead's pragmatism (1979: 459). They further argued that Blumer's methodology is "at best an improvident [not prudent, thoughtless] vehicle for the systematic investigation of Mead's social behaviorist ideas and may, in fact, have thwarted such an investigation" (p. 460). They then cite several examples of "behavioristic" research which exemplify the "proper" nature of social investigation. (The McPhail–Rexroat argument was subsequently elaborated in controversial detail by Lewis and Smith in 1980; for reactions, see Blumer 1977, 1983; Denzin 1984a; Athens 1984; Fine and Kleinman 1986.)

Like the Huber critique, this analysis keeps the focus on Blumer. It offers a methodological variant of the Huber logico-theoretic model of inquiry, which shifts to a more behavioristic methodology that studies overt, short-term, easily definable, quantifiable behavior that is open to direct observation (Blumer 1980: 418). Like Huber, McPhail and Rexroat offer textual re-readings of key interactionist works. Like Huber, they contend that Blumer has misread Mead and that their reading is better. They also argue that Blumer's method contradicts his theory of human action; that actors construct meaning, while investigators discover meaning (p. 459). They then, like Lewis and Smith (1980), align Blumer with the pragmatism of James and Dewey, not that of Peirce and Mead. (This, of course, confuses the major differences between James, Dewey, and Mead, as discussed in chapter 1.)

Blumer responded by refuting the above charges and repeating his version of Mead's pragmatism: to wit, that there is a world of reality out there that stands over and against the human being; that this reality becomes known and changes through the actions of human beings on and towards it; and that the resistance of that world to perceptions of it "is the test of the validity of the perceptions [of it]" (Blumer 1980: 410). He then repeated his 1969 discussion of exploration and inspection as the major forms of naturalistic inquiry, forms which are distinctly different from the logico-theoretic methods of positivistic scientists.

McPhail and Rexroat (1980) called their reply "Ex Cathedra Blumer or Ex Libris Mead?", implying that they see themselves as liberating Mead from Blumer's rigid, orthodox, doctrinaire (Catholic?) reading. They charge him with failure to document his judgment that they have misread Mead (and him), concluding that "theoretical hypotheses . . . must be stated in such a way that they can be subjected to test against observed facts and, thereby, accepted, rejected, or revised" (p. 429).

A text is always a site of multiple interpretations. There can be no essential, true, or correct reading of a work; there are potentially as many readings as there are readers. As Derrida (1967/76) argues, any text can be deconstructed, unhinged, taken apart, and be shown to overflow with ambiguous, unclear meanings. These points of ambiguity relate to language, which is itself a process always in motion. Hence, any given reading of a text can itself be undone. This is what the above exchanges reveal.

Another stand-off. The McPhail–Rexroat–Blumer debate, like the one with Huber, simply brings two versions of a realist epistemology up against the interactionist (social behaviorist) project. But more is involved; for now the authors charge that they have each arrived at the correct reading of Mead. So these two readings, each put forth on the assumption that there is one correct interpretation of what Mead said or should have said, clash (Stewart 1981; Tucker 1988; Fine and Kleinman 1986). The pity is that neither side understood this basic point about texts and their multiple meanings.

The new Iowa school turn

The new Iowa school (Buban 1986: 34) brought a different set of problems to the interactionist project and to Blumer's formulations. Couch and his associates were concerned with the study of "structured process" and with the development of generic sociological principles (Couch 1984b) based on a research method that provided a complete record of social events. This led to videotape research of interactions in the laboratory. Not wishing to "downgrade the importance" (Buban 1986: 33; Couch 1984b) of the naturalistic, participant observation methods advocated by Blumer, they nonetheless argued that such methods hindered the development of generic concepts. These methods lacked precision, presumed a passive, spectatorial attitude on the part of the researcher (Kohout 1975: 17), failed to indicate how social processes were (and are) actually structured, and stopped short of ever writing theory (Buban 1986: 32; Couch 1984b).

Here the Iowa school turned J. Lofland's criticisms of the Chicago school against Blumer (and Becker). What was needed, they argued, was a total method of observation which would produce records of social processes, not just field notes for analysis (Buban 1986: 37). They wanted to study interaction *per se*, with data that were sharable, processual, researchable, naturalistic, and obtained from stable standpoints (e.g. cameras and microphones in "locked positions"; Couch 1986: 51; Katovich *et al.* 1986; see also Prus 1987: 262). Blumer's naturalistic method does not permit the maintenance of a stable standpoint in the field setting. By "making themselves vulnerable to the impingement of others, participant observers surrender considerable control over their ability to maintain a stable standpoint" (Couch 1986: 51). Who located the camera when and where and how these processual tapes were to be interpreted raised other problems (see Denzin 1985b).

The ethnography debate

As if Blumer had not been debated enough, in 1989 he again became a topic of discourse, this time in the context of what his work implied for ethnographic research. Hammersley (1989) extended Athens's 1984 critical appraisal of Blumer's naturalistic method, which contended that Blumer's method was not universally applicable to all phenomena. Hammersley argued that Blumer's notion of the definitive concept may not be achievable in sociology. Furthermore, he found problems with Blumer's argument that sociological concepts must match those of common sense. He then charged that Blumer's strategies of exploration and inspection failed to show how these problems could be resolved (p. 156). Thus Hammersley saw Blumer as treating "symbolic interactionism as a fixed body of doctrine in which its validity is obvious from our everyday experience of the world" (p. 149). (He also argued that Blumer was against quantification (p. 144).) Maines's (1989a) response argued, paradoxically, that Blumer was not opposed to quantification, that his research methods went beyond ethnographic research, and that he believed in definitive concepts that transcended common sense. Prus (1987: 263–75) thickened the above discourse by offering an elegant outline of a generic, processual ethnographic sociology which stressed the reflective, negotiable, relational, interactional, emergent features of human group life. (His proposal synthesized the Chicago and Iowa schools.) Thus, where Hammersley saw confusion and ambiguity in Blumer and Maines saw a multi-method, empirical science, Prus saw a clarity grounded in the original interpretive premises of Blumer's project. Blumer is truly a man for all seasons and all people.

The Blumer circle

The above discourse takes the form of a circle. Like two squirrels chasing each other around a tree, it is impossible to see who is chasing whom. It is as if everything that Blumer wrote in 1939 had come home to haunt him (and his ghost) in 1989 (see Baugh 1990 for the most recent example). The very criticisms (and more) that he launched against Thomas and Znaniecki in 1939 had, by 1989, been turned back on him. Blumer set in motion a methodological project which assumed the following:

1 a natural social world that could be studied scientifically
2 a realist epistemology; that is, that this empirical world could be mapped, reproduced, and made sense of through the careful work of the naturalistic researcher who got close to the phenomenon under investigation (Clough 1988)
3 the possibility of finding a processual, interpretive social science that would utilize sensitizing concepts grounded in subjective human experience
4 that the empirical materials of this science would be valid and reliable and permit the testing of hypotheses and the formulation of theoretical generalizations
5 the possibility of an interpretive theory that would confront the obdurate features of human group life and be shaped around the above kinds of materials.

The failure to produce a science that conformed to the above criteria opened the door for the criticisms just discussed. Blumer himself wrote the criticisms that would later be applied to his project: namely, that it had failed to produce (to the satisfaction of his critics) either a model for, or instances of, an empirically valid science grounded in the actual doings of the social world. Fifty years after the critique of *The Polish Peasant*, he was criticizing himself, although now in the words of others. It is not clear what, if any, progress has been achieved over this half-century period.

Politics and the astructural bias

I turn now to the next set of criticisms, those involving the so-called astructural bias in interactionist work. This criticism, which charges that interactionists are unable to deal with macro-structural issues, absorbs other criticisms as well, including the charges that the perspective avoids historical, economic, institutional, and political issues (Gouldner 1968, 1970; Block 1973; D. L. Smith 1973; Ropers 1973; Wagner 1964;

Vaughn and Reynolds 1968; Day and Day 1977; A. Rose (ed.) 1962; Zeitlin 1973). For some, the perspective "is destined to be profoundly apolitical [and its practitioners] may well wind up depicting (or constructing) a social reality that is overly quaint or exotic" (Reynolds 1990: 137). Interactionists have apparently not been able to convince "a Marxist, World-Systems theorist, or any other macroscopically included sociologist that social structure [has] been given its due" (p. 157).

In its most succinct form, the astructural bias argument claims that interactionism fails to deal with social organization and social structure. "All of this is to say that symbolic interactionism manifests a marked astructural, or microscopic bias, and any framework with such a bias is bound to be ahistorical and noneconomic . . . and profoundly apolitical" (Reynolds 1990: 137). This bias thus produces interactionism's supposed idealist bias (Huber), which "distorts its view of reality while preventing it from providing a sound, sociological analysis of the social world (Reynolds 1990: 137). Prendergast and Knotternus (1990: 161) underscore Reynolds's interpretation thus: "Everyone in sociology implicitly knows what the astructural bias refers to – the predominance of small-scale descriptive and phenomenological studies that try to put the reader 'in the scene' through colorful language, often provided by the actors themselves. Any SI journal or annual will have a sample."

Specific charges follow from this general criticism. Kanter (1972: 88) argues that interactionists can only handle power in circumstances in which power relations are roughly equal. Shaskolsky (1970: 16) contends that interactionists uncritically accept American society's pronouncements about freedom and democracy. This turns the perspective into commonsense, subjectivistic sociology which best operates in a "benignly liberal climate of opinion" (Huber 1973b: 275). For Reynolds, interactionism is "utopian thinking written in the present tense" (1990: 140), whereas Lichtman (1970: 75) charges that the idealist bent (his reading of Blumer) ignores how the interpreted meanings of individuals are "shaped and channeled by society's dominant institutions; those institutions . . . reflect a particular class structure and are class-dominated. Idealism conveniently forgets this point."

Gouldner (1968, 1970) elaborated this argument in his readings of Goffman and Becker, wherein he argued that their sociology produces an overidentification with the powerless underdogs in society. Why, he asks, don't interactionists study men (and women?) in power, instead of mental patients, sexual nonconformists, prison inmates, and small-time criminals? He goes on – this is 1970 – to allege an emerging alliance between structural functionalism, the welfare state, and interactionism (Gouldner 1968). (In 1989 Sciulli extended this alliance in his attempt to connect Blumer and Parsons.)

Mills's critique

There is little that is new in the above criticisms. They had all been formulated, in one way or another, by C. Wright Mills in his 1942 dissertation published in 1964 as *Sociology and Pragmatism: The Higher Learning in America*. In this work Mills criticized the pragmatists, especially Dewey, for their uncritical celebration of science and technology, their neglect of Marx and Weber, their overly biological model of action and the social, and their neglect of America's class structure and the power elite. At the same time he attempted to keep alive Dewey's project of a radical democracy guided, in part, by the intellectual man of action, the man of reason who directs his work *"at* kings, as well as *to* publics" (1959: 181). His trilogy – *The New Men of Power* (1948), *White Collar* (1951), and *The Power Elite* (1956) – is "essentially an attempt to highlight the dynamics of power, both sources and effects, in corporate liberal America" (West 1989: 128). Mills "resisted the conspiratorial theories of vulgar Marxists" (West 1989: 129), placing his emphasis on the psychological and cultural effects of power. He unmasked the projects and dubious moralities of the labor leaders, the waning old middle class, and the expanding new middle class who were hungry for professional status and prestige. He predicted the coming of a new cultural moment, which he called the postmodern (1959: 166), and predicted new forms of moral drift and alienation for the postmodern person.

With Hans Gerth in 1953, he outlined the essential structures of his brand of interactionist, Weberian sociology. Their *Character and Social Structure: The Psychology of Social Institutions* attempted an integration of Mead and Freud through the concepts of role, institution, and character.[3] It presented Mills's Dewey-like theory of motives and motivation and offered a theory of social structure, based in part on Marx and Weber, involving the concept of institutional order or sphere. A complex institutional picture of a social structure thus emerged. Gerth and Mills then attempted to fit specific vocabularies of motives to specific phases of capitalism and economic development in Western societies, especially the United States.

Mills's project embodied the Enlightenment ideas of self-determination and the rational exercise of human powers. It linked the personal with the political. In *The Sociological Imagination* (1959) he outlined a political project for the sociologist who wanted to shape society in terms of the values of radical democracy. With Dewey, he affirmed the importance of critical intelligence in social change; but he focused on intellectual elites as the primary historical agents of change (West 1989: 131). The sociologist's task was clear for Mills: "Deliberately present controversial theory and facts, and actively encourage controversy" (1959: 191). Like Dewey, he held out hope for a democratic society in which men and women would reason freely over the vital topics which define personal troubles and public issues.

Mills was not blind to the problems of a social structure undermined by a postwar corporate economy guided by a power elite which had fused its interests with the military machine. He did not anticipate the transformations that late capitalism would bring (the electronic revolution and the commodification of experience). He did not see that a new technocratic elite would come to challenge the place held by the old plutocracy (see Carey and Quirk 1989: 193). He did not anticipate that knowledge would become a commodity "monopolized like any other commodity" (p. 193). Nor did he see how these new arrangements would further atomize society, to the point where the masses-transformed-into-publics would find it increasingly difficult to have a voice or be represented, or how these conditions would erode any sense of political or social community in America (p. 193).

Nonetheless, Mills held out for a kind of radical democratic politics that has certain similarities with the hegemonic social strategies of Laclau and Mouffe (1985). His call for the creation of publics organized around troubles and issues has parallels with Laclau and Mouffe's emphasis on "the creation of the discursive conditions for the emergence of a collective action" (p. 153) "which emphasizes the positivity of the social and the articulation of the diverse democratic demands" (p. 189) – within " a radical and plural democracy" (p. 176).

Peter M. Hall's project

No American interactionist or critic of interactionism has succeeded in outdoing Mills. His project, despite certain basic misgivings (see Denzin 1990c), stands as a challenge to all sociologists, including interactionists and their "Marxist" critics. However, this is not the entire story. The astructural critics, with the exception of Prendergast and Knotternus (1990) and Meltzer and Herman (1990), have ignored a large interactionist literature which addresses head on the questions of social structure, social organization (P. M. Hall 1987; Strauss 1978; E. Hughes 1971; Maines 1977, 1982; Fine 1983b; Fine and Kleinman 1983; Couch 1984a, 1990), power (P. M. Hall 1985), the economy and capitalism (Farberman 1975, 1980; Denzin 1977b, 1978; Hochschild 1983, 1989;

Blumer 1990), history (Lyman 1990b), the class structure (Wolf 1986), race (Shibutani and Kwan 1965; Lyman 1990b), Blumer 1958/1988; Killian 1985), and gender (Deegan and Hill (eds) 1987; Clough 1987: Richardson 1991b).

These works indicate that interactionists do not neglect structural issues. Indeed, since the mid-1970s, "a body of substantive research and metatheoretical commentary devoted to solving the astructural bias problem began to appear in SI journals and annuals" (Prendergast and Knottnerus 1990: 177). This has led some observers (Fine 1983b: 69) to argue that the systematic examination of structure has become "one of the new frontiers of symbolic interaction and has put the perspective on the 'cutting edge' of sociology." Meltzer and Herman (1990: 223), concur, claiming that "interactionists . . . have contributed significantly to the understanding of social structure." This leads them to call for "a reformulation of the entire issue of the astructural bias" (p. 224).

In certain respects the most comprehensive presentation of the interactionist position on the above issues is given in Peter M. Hall's 1986 presidential address to the Midwest Sociological Society. Responding to Shalin's 1986 challenge to interactionists to develop a unified theory of social structure which "would bridge the macro-micro gap and seriously tackle issues of class, power and inequality," Hall contends that the materials, tools, and infrastructure for such an endeavor are already in place (1987: 1). He then examines recent scholarship on concerted action and related social processes (Becker 1982; Faulkner 1983; Farberman 1975; Denzin 1977a; Strauss 1978; Hall and Spencer-Hall 1982; Busch 1982; Wiener 1981; and Couch 1984a). Hall defines social organization as recurrent networks of collective activity. He next presents six major categories, including "collective activity, network, convention-practices, resources, temporality-processuality, and grounding" (1987: 2), as the tools for framing an interactionist theory of social organization. Hall then uses Maines's (1982) concept of mesostructure – "how societal and institutional forces mesh with human activity" (p. 10) – as a framework for incorporating the six major categories of social organization into empirical research. According to Prendergast and Knotternus (1990: 160), if interactionists accepted this paradigm, "many of the complaints about the astructural bias would cease to exist."

The Prendergast–Knottnerus Noninteractionist critique

However, Prendergast and Knotternus (1990) are not content to let Hall's paradigm stand. They state: "SI metatheory remains wedded to a three-fold dualism in which the only viable alternatives to objectivism, determinism and materialism appear to be subjectivism, humanism and idealism . . . when SI metatheory has legitimated new, system-centered instructions, the astructural bias will be no more" (p. 178).

What are these system-centered instructions? Prendergast and Knott-nerus offer what they call a "paradigm-neutral and robust" model for evaluating the astructural bias in interactionist work. While never applying the model to theories which apparently do not suffer from this bias (e.g. functionalism, conflict, structuration, and micro-ritual chain theory), they define a theory of social structure thus: as "a set of interrelated definitions and propositions, not yet axiomatically ordered, which attempts to map out a domain of phenomena consisting of social relationships, opportunities for the constraints on joint action they entail, and their coalescence into complex systems of different types, which may be represented diagrammatically and described in models" (p. 160). (Shades of Huber's logico-theoretic model?)

They then define the astructural problem more concisely: "We mean the absence of underdevelopment of a coherent set of definitions and propositions describing, and accounting for, the interdependence of units of analysis beyond the person-to-person interaction" (p. 165). Units of structural analysis become status positions, collectivities, and social classes. Interactionist research which addresses the astructural bias is then judged to make a "contribution, however humble" to the theory of social structure, "either as microstructural or macrostructural analysis" (p. 166).

Essentially reviewing the same studies as Hall, they argue that interactionist structural research suffers from the problem of telescoping macro-processes into micro-processes (p. 162). This leads to three approaches to structure: as context, as meaning, and as activity. These strategies fail to show how the units and levels of social structure fit together (p. 164). In order to answer this question, a system-centered focus – that is, "an observer's standpoint outside the context of interaction" (p. 165) – is needed. (Yet they never present a theory with a system-centered focus.)

Only one interactionist-based study (Faulkner 1983) has met these requirements (p. 176). This work, on their reading, examines a whole system of relationships from top to bottom, uses various methodologies (not just ethnography), blends micro- and macro-analysis "without a trace of voluntarism or determinism," mixes symbolic interactionism with other theories (bounded rationality theory), recognizes constraints stemming from resource contingencies, produces a causal analysis, and formalizes the relationships using "the techniques of network analysis"

(p. 176). They approvingly observe that "with Faulkner the astructural bias is completely extinguished' (p. 177).

Structure as process

To return to the discussion in chapter 2, interactionists do not like general theories. They do not like to reify their terms (like "society"). They do not borrow interpretive models from other disciplines (e.g. rational choice theory). They examine history and power in terms of the effects these have in the actual lives of interacting individuals. They don't like macro-theories. Committed to a processual, pragmatic perspective, they look at how structures, ideology, and power interact in concrete interactional sites and locales to produce specific forms of subjectivity, emotionality, and lived experience. This produces a focus on micro-power relations (Foucault 1980), systems of discourse (Barthes 1957/72), hegemonic patterns of communication (J. W. Carey 1989; P. M. Hall 1988; Mills 1963), state structures (Couch 1990), and gender, class, and racial ideologies (Althusser 1971; S. Hall 1986a) as the sites (meso-domains) where situated activity, history, and structures converge (P. M. Hall 1987).

It is an error, then, to insist, as many have (Alexander 1987: 214–17; Smelser 1988: 121–2), that interactionists have ignored social structure. Such a myth (Maines 1988) permanently exiles interactionism from structural discourse. It allows functionalist critics (e.g. Munch and Smelser 1987: 366; Alexander and Giesen 1987: 9; Habermas 1987) either to rewrite the theory to suit their own purposes (e.g. Habermas and Alexander) or to dispense with it entirely (e.g. Smelser and Collins).

The other alternative, that of asking interactionists to re-do their theory in terms of a systems-centered model, is no more desirable. As Meltzer and Herman (1990: 225) observe:

> To recommend . . . that symbolic interactionism deal with social structure by abandoning such "presuppositions" . . . as voluntarism and supplementing such "presuppositions" . . . represents, in our view, a gratuitous counsel of despair. If such advice were to be followed it would be tantamount to eviscerating the interactionist perspective . . . transforming it in fundamental ways. This would be comparable to discarding the assumption of class struggle from Marxist sociology.

This ignores the considerable interactionist literature on social structure, including the recently published Blumer (1990) text on industrialization (see Maines and Morrione (eds) 1990), the Lyman (1990b) macro-civilizational study of race, culture, and history within the interaction framework, and Peter Hall's (1987) paradigm for organizational analysis. It also ignores the recent alliances between interactionism, feminism, and cultural studies (Denzin 1990c; Clough 1991), as well as Couch's (1990) work on mass communications and state structures. The problem of the astructural bias in symbolic interactionism is a dead issue.[4]

The emotions

Critics of interactionism (Meltzer 1959; Meltzer *et al.* 1975: 92–3, 100; Brittan 1973; Reynolds 1990: 181; Hochschild 1983) have persisted in arguing that the perspective suffers from an overly cognitive, rationalistic bias that has led to a neglect of the emotions and emotional factors as they influence the interaction process. However, as Meltzer and Herman (1990: 182–99) observe, this charge, like the astructural bias charge, is without foundation. Starting in the late 1970s and early 1980s, a number of interactionists, including Scheff, Hochschild, Denzin, J. Lofland, and Gordon, began to write about the emotions. By the mid-1980s an American Sociological Association section on the emotions was started, through the efforts of Candace Clark and Carolyn Ellis. Many of the members of the section are symbolic interactionists. By the end of the 1980s, two journals devoted special issues to the emotions (*Symbolic Interaction*, 8 (Fall 1985); *Social Psychology Quarterly*, 52, no. 1 (1989), and two edited volumes *The Sociology of Emotions* (Franks and McCarthy (eds) 1989) and *Research Agenda in the Sociology of Emotions* (Kemper (ed.) 1990) had appeared; interactionists were major contributors to these works. No other theory group has contributed more to the study of the emotions.

Textual studies

The above criticisms, with few exceptions, purported to offer new, corrective readings of classic interactionist texts. Using Blumer as their point of reference, the critics sought to find in Mead positions which contradicted Blumer's interpretations. Lewis and Smith's *American Sociology and Pragmatism: Mead, Chicago Sociology, and Symbolic Interaction* (1980) exemplified this tradition. Much like Huber and McPhail and Rexroat, Lewis and Smith sought to shatter a number of interactionist myths, including (1) that pragmatism is a unified philosophical system, (2) that Mead was not the heart of Chicago-style sociology, (3) that Mead was a behaviorist, not a symbolic interactionist, and (4) that Blumer had misread Mead (see Denzin 1984a for a discussion of this book).

This strategy of searching for the true meaning of Mead and Blumer's works continued through the early and mid-1980s. Criticisms of the "objectivist" readings of Mead (e.g. Lewis and Smith 1980) were offered (Johnson and Shifflet 1981). Some wrote about "What George Herbert Mead should have Said" (Stewart 1981); others offered re-readings of Mead's theory of mind (see *Symbolic Interaction* 1981, 1989) and his (and Blumer's) pragmatism (Tucker 1988; Tucker and Stewart 1989); and some reinterpreted Blumer's project (see *Symbolic Interaction* 1988).

These works suffered from a number of problems. They were "objectivist," revisionist interpretations (Johnson and Shifflet 1981: 143). They sought to discover the "true" meanings of the works in question. They assumed that a text's meaning was clear and could be given by an objective reading. They failed to grasp the fact that the act of reading is itself an intentional act, shaped by conventions, including what one looks for when one examines a text. In many instances there was an attempt to "get it right" by establishing what Mead or Blumer really meant. (Woelfel, for example, charged that interactionists "should pay more attention to what Mead could have said, and should have said" (1967: 409). Blumer replied: "It makes no sense at all to discover what Mead 'really said' or 'really meant' . . . The task . . . is not that of trying to unearth some 'intrinsic nature' or 'inner essence' of Mead's scheme of thought" (1967: 411). Critics also committed the intentionalist fallacy of assuming that they had privileged access to the mind (and the intended meanings) of the author(s) in question. Criticisms were often "presentist" in orientation; they re-read the past through the meanings of the present, often criticizing an author for not doing what he said he would not do.

The literary turn

This commitment to an objective text was challenged in 1986 by Fine and Kleinman ("Interpreting the Sociological Classics: Can there be a

'True' Meaning of Mead?"). Arguing from a literary criticism (Derrida) and interactionist perspective, they suggested that readers construct the meaning of a text, employing conventions of interpretation (see Fish 1981) which shape the perspectives and meanings brought to a text. Texts themselves are open to multiple readings, are often rhetorical in nature, and are filled with ambiguous passages, contradictions, and gaps. Hence there can never be a "true" reading or "true" meaning of a classic. There are only multiple interpretations; the "best" interpretation is simply the one that is the most persuasive, given current conventions (Fish 1981). A weak or bad interpretation is one that fails to convince. (Hence the dialogue between Blumer and his critics was a battle over which interpretation was the most convincing.)

Clough's project

In three articles ("The Movies and Social Observation: Reading Blumer's *Movies and Conduct*" (1988); "Letters from Pamela: Reading Howard S. Becker's *Writing(s) for Social Scientists*" (1989); "Erving Goffman: Writing the End of Ethnography" (1991) Patricia T. Clough (1991) proposed nothing less than a radical re-reading of the three leading symbolic interactionists of the twentieth century.[5] These readings examined the underlying scientific interpretive apparatus, including the theories of writing, textuality, observation, and gender that structured the works of Blumer, Becker, and Goffman.

Clough argued that the works of these key interactionists could be read in terms of how they represent and position the subject within a realist epistemology which uses language as a means of revealing subjective experience. Her ironic readings build on feminist, semiotic, poststructural, and postmodernist arguments concerning the death of the author as the sole producer of the text. She asks how the interactionist text, with its focus on the "interior qualities of the person," reproduces a system of realist discourse or emotional realism that creates the impression that the reader can see and feel what the writer has seen. She connects this form of sociological writing to the nineteenth-century novel and autobiography.

These writing forms championed the individual's experience. They presented experience with an immediacy (first-person accounts) that made nearness to an event a measure of a text's truth. Such texts increasingly erased the boundaries between public and private life. They contributed to a discourse on individuality which valued individual uniqueness and subjective consciousness (Clough 1989: 160). They furthered the efforts of late capitalism. They contributed to the transformation of the private domain into a public space subject to greater state domination and a site of greater commodity consumption. Under late capitalism and postmodernism, the discourse of "individualism becomes the dominant social discourse" (p. 160). The texts of Goffman, Blumer, and Becker taught interactionally inclined students how to read, write, and value works which captured lived experience. Interactionists taught their students to produce works which spoke with the authority of one who had been out in the field and seen events at first hand.

These fully fictionalized forms of discourse claimed to be true when they were realistic. They created a new social subject, the self-reflective, fully gendered middle-class (at times lower-class) individual who wrote a life story. These texts had an Oedipal logic, for they presumed that full self-hood could only be realized by the final location of the individual in a proper sexual (family) relationship. By the end of the nineteenth century, the novel and the social sciences had become distinguished as separate systems of discourse (the humanities and the social sciences). However, the Chicago school, with its emphasis on the life story and the "slice-of-life" approach to ethnographic materials (see chapter 2, note 4), sought to develop an interpretive methodology that maintained the centrality of the narrated life history (autobiographical) approach. This led to the production of texts which gave the sociologist-as-author the power to represent the subject's life story.

These texts, Clough contends, were written under the mantle of a straightforward, sentiment-free realism. They often used the language of ordinary people or just plain folks. This writing strategy had a double effect. Often ironic in tone, interactionist texts created the effect of having lifted the veils of secrecy that surrounded a group's and an individual's central, sacred, and private life stories. (The interactionist had seen what others had not seen, because he or she had lifted these veils of secrecy.) Secondly, this strategy had the important function of creating the belief that the interactionist had in fact discovered important, generic truths about human group life.

This is the view Clough so powerfully brings to the works of Blumer, Becker, and Goffman. In each author Clough finds a methodology predicated in the look and the gaze (see also Lemert 1979b: 115; 1979a, 1986). Blumer's interactionism "grounds sociological discourse on the production of 'the look'" (Clough 1991, Blumer chapter). Becker's texts shift from a form "of cinematic and ethnographic realism, to the emotional realism of TV melodrama" (1991, Becker chapter). Here the look or gaze is reframed in terms of a form of reflective, self-conscious writing which has the writer looking over his or her own shoulder while a text written in plain prose is produced. Goffman, whom she describes as the last great ethnographer, produces a prose which parallels the writing technology of computer simulation. "The little examples which Goffman piles up in his texts demand that the reader submit to a flow of information . . . Like the displays of a computerized program, the little examples simulate interaction and dialogue, but not as examples of reality. The little examples illustrate the working of the protocol to produce a reality effect" (1991, Goffman chapter). Blumer, Goffman, and Becker carry on the idea of the interactionist ethnographer as voyeur, the outsider who looks in on society's hidden doings. Their texts differentially privilege cinematic realism (Blumer), the emotional realism of melodrama (Becker), and the technological realism of the computer text (Goffman).

Clough finds in Blumer's *Movies and Conduct* (1933) the beginnings of a cinematic observational sociology. Blumer's interpretive methods and narrative imagery ("lifting the veils," the world "talks back," the "world exists in the form of human pictures"; 1969: 22) imply a cinematic realism wherein the "imagery inheres" (Clough 1988: 95) in the world. The "objectivity of the observer is only maintained by his studying many perspectives of the world in order to immunize himself against the seduction of any one" (p. 95) "simulation of that world of a . . . preset model of . . . or . . . a picture of that world" (Blumer 1969: 48).

Clough sees parallels between Blumer and recent feminist film theory, especially in their overlapping criticisms of narrative cinema and cinematic realism (e.g. the real and its representations, the viewer's consciousness, and the positioning of the viewer in the narrative). But where Blumer turns his back on gender, sexuality, and ideology, feminist theorists (Mulvey, Doane, Silverman, A. Kuhn, de Lauretis) have offered theories of the cinematic experience which stress the problems of spectatorship, the masculine gaze, voyeurism, and the passive representation of women in cinematic texts. Blumer's realist epistemology creates a posture of sexlessness. His observer "guards against the seduction of what is merely seen, and, on the other hand, against 'going soft,' terrified by what he imagines he sees" (Clough 1988: 95).

Becker's *Writing for Social Scientists* presumes another form of realism, in this case the emotional realism and dramatic urgency found in the melodramatic novel, the TV soap opera, and the life story text. Becker seeks, Clough argues, a writing technology which is connected to "a new sensibility of compulsive self-revelation," which serves "to shape a realism for representing social reality which no longer needs to oppose fact and fiction" (1991, Becker chapter). Becker's texts become "the site for managing sentiment and sympathy" (p. 23), and this emotional balance comes to "constitute the context of scientific rationality" (p. 24).

Goffman's writings are simulated displays which trivialize the distinction between fact and fiction (1991, Goffman chapter). His look shifts from the perspective of the empirical ethnographer to the gaze promoted by commercial realism (advertisements). He thus reads these texts as protocols of experience, which is organized in terms of frames, or scenes. His texts are intended to promote a form of engrossment which disconnects meaning from empirical reality. Like computer displays, "his texts by examples push narrative to the level of the program, no longer addressable by the reader, of whom is demanded and to whom is offered immediate, instantaneous response, that is engrossment". Goffman's texts are judged by their holding power.

Clough's readings deconstruct and unravel the three main forms of realism that have structured interactionist work in the twentieth century. They present a twofold challenge. First, they call for writing experiments which reconceptualize the relationship between the writer, his or her mystory (Ulmer 1989), and the three ages (and forms) of realism (cinematic, emotional, computer) which now compete with one another in scholarly and popular discourse. Second, there is a compelling need, in the age of videocy (visual imagery and literacy; Ulmer 1989), to produce works which, with an Oedipal vengeance (de Lauretis 1987), interrogate the technologies of gender and the ideologies of realism which operate in and through the new visual-computer-video texts. Clough and Ulmer show us how to move in this direction.

Conclusions

A theory grows when its practitioners confront conflict. The successive waves of conflict and criticism (both internal and external) that interactionists have confronted in the 1963–90 period have led to developments and refinements in the perspective. Retrenchments have also occurred. Some have resisted the contemporary interpretive turn which has drawn on recent European social theory. They have argued that the answers to interactionism's problems lie in the works of Mead and the pragmatic tradition. On occasion, lines were drawn which produced a "them" (those positivists, those structural functionalists, etc.) versus "us" orientation, with interactionists adopting the view that they have been misunderstood, misrepresented, and unappreciated.

The specific criticisms that have focused on the theory – method issue, the astructural bias problem, the politics of the theory, and the neglect of the emotions have now been cast in a different light, given the "new" textual readings of the last five years. These interpretations presuppose, as indicated above, a specific approach to the analysis of a text. They reject the ideas of intentionalist, presentist, and objective readings. They seek to locate a text, its author, and its subject matter within a historical moment and to show how a text reinscribes the dominant ideological and epistemological themes of its historical period (e.g. realism; the objective, knowing author; gendered conceptions of the individual; language as a mirror to reality; etc.). These ironic readings focus on "how social discourse negotiates new constructions of the individual and social organization" (Clough 1989: 161).[6]

In the next decade it is likely (and to be hoped) that interactionist texts will be re-read in light of the above considerations. The era of the "objective" reading of Mead and Blumer is on the wane. The interpretive problems that arise from the various types of epistemological realism, including the cinematic, emotional, ethnographic, and electronic forms, must continue to be examined. At the same time, interactionists must learn to study how the technological apparatuses of information production (including television and computer technology) shape the cognitions and emotions of interacting individuals in the current historical moment (see Clough 1988: 96). Such moves will naturally take interactionists into the terrains of cultural studies and communications, the topics of the next four chapters.

Notes

1 Some of these negative evaluations were written by interactionists (e.g. Kuhn 1964a, b); but most, until quite recently, were written by noninteractionists.

2 I am focusing on the period from 1963 to the present because these criticisms tend, in the main, to absorb, in one way or another, those from the earlier periods (see, e.g., Meltzer et al. 1975 for a summary of earlier criticisms.)

3 This work was clearly influenced by Mills's contact with the Frankfurt school (see the discussion of Mills and this school in ch. 5).

4 I will, however, return to this issue in chapter 7.

5 Clough's Goffman essay is a chapter in her forthcoming book (Clough 1991), The End(s) of Ethnography in which she also reworks the earlier Blumer and Becker essays.

6 To summarize, a deconstructive reading engages four paired terms: (1) the real and its representations in a text; (2) text and author; (3) presence and lived experience; (4) subjects and their intentional meanings. All writing is a narrative production (Richardson 1990) and is structured by a logic that

presumes a separation among writer, text, and subject matter. This logic can be undone (as I did with Shaw's story of Stanley and Clough has done with Blumer, Becker, and Goffman) to show that there is no firm dividing line between these terms. A text creates its versions of the real, through the reproduction of excerpts from lived experience reported by the subject in interviews and then interpreted by the fieldworker-as-author. A reading engages the above problematics, showing how the author in question has produced a particular written (narrative) version of a text.

4 ENTER CULTURAL STUDIES

David Riesman, C. Wright Mills, Harold Innis, and Kenneth Burke, a tradition that is simultaneously historic and interpretive, and critical. Cultural studies, in an American context, is an attempt to reclaim and reconstruct this tradition.

(J. W. Carey 1989: 96)

We are losing control of the very means of cultural production itself . . . More and more culture becomes an adjunct of marketing, or of the bureaucratic ethos, or of both.

(Mills 1963: 226)

The first rule for understanding the human condition is that men live in a second-hand world. The consciousness of men does not determine their existence; nor does their existence determine their consciousness. Between the human consciousness and material existence stand communications and designs, patterns and values which influence decisively such consciousness as they have.

(Ibid. 375)

With the words of the last of the epigraphs above, C. Wright Mills laid the foundations for an American cultural studies program founded on the principles of symbolic interactionism, pragmatism, and Marxism. Central to that program would be the study of communications and culture in the current historical moment (see the earlier discussion of Mills's project in chapter 3). In Mills's framework communication is culture (see also J. W. Carey 1989). The culture we live in, he argued, is one that is already second-hand, preformed in the commercial marketplaces and communicated daily through the various mass media.

Mills envisioned a critical cultural studies which would critique, as the Frankfurt school had done earlier (see Kellner 1989 and chapter 6), this fourth historical epoch, which he called the "postmodern" period (Mills 1959: 166).

Recall James Carey's words cited as the epigraph to the Preface: "Cultural studies, on an American terrain, has been given its most powerful expression . . . in the tradition of symbolic interactionism, which developed out of American pragmatism generally" (1989: 96). In this and the next three chapters I take up Mills's legacy and the challenge of Carey's remarks. The interactionist tradition, for a variety of reasons, turned its back on the cultural studies approach embodied in the mid-century work of Mills, Riesman, Burke, and Innis.

I shape, then (as I began to do in chapter 2), a critical, feminist cultural studies for symbolic interactionism, addressing the field of cultural studies, its key terms, and its traditions in America and England, including recent transformations and resistances to this new field and its contemporary turn within interactionism. This will involve an excursion into the cultural logics of the postmodern moment and the beginning of an agenda for an interactionist-shaped cultural studies. But first some texts to work with.

Texts

Consider the following statement, taken from Blumer and Hauser's (1933) study of movies and conduct. It is reported by a *22-year-old black male*. Convicted of burglary, he is an inmate in a reformatory. He is describing how movies affected his conduct.

> I had never pulled a job until I saw —— in ——. I saw how he broke into a store and robbed a safe and how he picked people's pockets. When we came out of the show a couple of the boys suggested that we try to rob a store, the way we had seen in the picture. We went to a five-and-ten-cent store and bought a crowbar and a screw driver and the tools Mr. —— used. Then we went to a store . . . I put the crowbar a little beneath the lock and bent it back. The other boy put the screw driver in the lock and sprung the lock . . . We went in and took as many clothes as we could carry.
> (Blumer and Hauser 1933: 19)

A white 16-year-old female sexual delinquent reports:

> When I was on the outside I went to the movies almost every night, but only about twice in two months to a dance. I didn't like dances as well as movies. A movie would get me so passionate after it was over that I just had to have satisfaction. You know what I mean. If you don't I tell you in plain English and that is, to have sexual relations.
>
> (Blumer and Hauser 1933: 84)

And a *38-year-old male alcoholic*:

> How do I get to one of those A.A. meetings? What do I say? I seen them in movies. That Michael Keaton (*Clean and Sober* 1988) just stood up and said he was an alcoholic. Do I have to do that? I ain't even sure I am one, but I drank a fifth of Beam last night and I started up again this mornin'. I'm scared and I don't know what to do.
>
> (Field interview, 2 November 1990)

Accounts such as these are the stuff of an interactionist cultural studies. These emotional experiences connect persons to others (a delinquent with other delinquents, a woman with a man, an ordinary alcoholic male with a Hollywood star), yet they are filtered through preexisting cultural meanings and representations (see Clough 1988 for a critical feminist reading of Blumer's materials and Sklar 1975 for criticisms of the politics involved in Blumer's project). These accounts are shaped by the culture-making institutions of a society (e.g. the movies, the family, gangs), by the gender stratification system, and by the political economy of everyday life. They are located within the broader structural and cultural contexts of modern and postmodern (pre- and post-Second World War) American society. An interactionist cultural studies aims to make sense of such experiences.

Enter cultural studies

Culture refers to the taken-for-granted and problematic webs of significance and meaning that human beings produce and act on when they do things together (Becker 1986a: 13; Geertz 1973: 5; Carey 1989: 56). These meanings are shaped and molded by the larger culture- and meaning-making institutions of society-at-large, including the mass media, film, social science, art, religion, and politics. Culture, at this level, becomes the "endless production of myth that has no reference to the real world" (R. Hughes 1989: 29). As Barthes (1957/72: 11) observes, "Newspapers, art and common sense constantly dress up a reality which, even though it is the one we live in, is undoubtedly determined by history ... Nature and History ... [are] confused at every turn." Viewing human experience as a social text (Carey 1989: 60), cultural studies attempts to deconstruct and unravel the ideological meanings that are coded into the taken-for-granted meanings that circulate in everyday life.

For present purposes I shall define cultural studies as that inter-disciplinary project (R. Johnson 1986/7) which takes the above problem-atics as its subject matter.[1] Cultural studies directs itself always to the problem of how the history that human beings make and live sponta-neously is determined by structures of meaning that they have not chosen for themselves (Marx 1852/1983: 287). Culture, in its meaning-making and interactional forms, becomes a site of political struggle (Johnson 1986/7: 38). A central problem becomes the examination of how interacting individuals connect their lived experiences to the cultural representations of those experiences (Denzin 1989b: 13; Johnson 1986/7: 70–1).[2]

The field of cultural studies

The field of cultural studies has a long, rich history which moves from Europe to the United States and extends through the writings of the members of the Frankfurt school (Adorno, Horkheimer, Marcuse, and Habermas) to the literary humanism of Hoggart (1957), R. Williams (1958, 1965), and E. P. Thompson (1963) in England, to the transforma-tions of this mid-century British tradition in the work of Stuart Hall and associates at the Birmingham Centre (1980a; 1986b; 1988a, b),[3] to recent international developments in contemporary Marxism and cul-tural studies (Nelson and Grossberg (eds) 1988),[4] to a cultural, pragma-tic approach to communication studies in the United States (Carey 1989, ch. 4), to contemporary critiques and readings of postmodern, late capitalist societies by Baudrillard (1987/8), Lyotard (1979/84), Agger

(1989), Jameson (1984, 1991), to an emerging feminist cultural studies position (Morris 1988c), which runs alongside the deconstructive, subversive approach to cultural texts represented by Derrida's project (see Ulmer 1985).

The American and British cultural studies projects, as Carey (1989: 98–9) notes, exhibit certain similarities and differences. Both schools experienced a founding moment in the 1950s, and each was influenced by the debate over mass culture and the mass media's place in contemporary cultural life. In both cases symbolic interactionism was extensively drawn upon. In Britain it was used for the analysis of subcultures and the study of deviance (Cagel 1989), whereas in the United States it provided a model of social action (e.g. Mills). Both traditions, Carey argues, were influenced by Weber, especially his thoughts on power, legitimation, class, and status, although the British tended to ignore the Weber of class, status, and power. Finally, the British, more than the Americans, struggled with the meanings of ideology; in the works of Stuart Hall this involved a re-reading of Gramsci. British cultural studies, unlike its American counterpart, struggled with structural, poststructural, and then postmodern theories of meaning, the subject, structure, communication, and ideology.

The resistance to cultural studies

On the American scene cultural studies has met with considerable resistance. On the one side the positivists and the structural-functionalists have attempted to either dispense with the perspective or absorb it into their own framework. On the other side the interactionists have ignored the perspective or attempted to fit a weak version of it into their preexisting Mead–Blumer–Hughes framework (Becker and McCall (eds) 1990). Institutionally, cultural studies represents a threat to existing disciplinary formations. The traditional departments of English, sociology, communications, and anthropology, which have historically studied the topics that cultural studies now claims as its own, find their control over such domains as mass communications, social problems, the family, and the cultural text increasingly challenged. At the same time, new areas of study – for example, the popular film, popular music, pornography, and pulp literature – have emerged, which appear, on the surface, to have no place in a scholarly curriculum.

Still, the last decade has witnessed a revival of interest in the study of culture within American sociology.[5] Indeed, it has become a growth industry (Wuthnow and Witten 1988: 49) characterized by several strands and positions, few of which direct themselves to the above problematics. The works of Gans (1974), Becker (1982), Mukerji and Schudson (1986), DiMaggio (1977), Peterson (ed.) (1976), Swidler (1986), Griswold (1987), Lamont (1987), Wuthnow (1988), and Wuthnow and Witten (1988) are associated with this new interpretive turn, which has taken as its subject matter the study of artworks, popular music, popular literature, the news, television, and the mass media.

The empiricist American tradition

Either uninformed by or insensitive to the kinds of controversies and problems that have structured the European traditions in cultural studies, the American empiricist project glosses the complex issues involved in Marxist, interpretive, structural, and poststructural discourse.[6] There is recourse, instead, to the theories and methods that have been in place for decades in American sociology.[7] Wuthnow and Witten (1988: 49–50) provide a convenient overview of the new American sociological studies of culture. This subfield, they argue, is divided between those practitioners who view culture as implicit in social life (i.e. as built into everything) and those who see it as an explicit social product (i.e. as a commodity). They delineate three dominant theoretical positions which organize the field: that of the neo-Parsonians (e.g. Alexander), classic attitude–behavior social psychology, and the *Annales* school of France, which has (they claim) been implemented by Geertz and his followers. The methods that are utilized range, they argue, from the subjective to the structural, the dramaturgic, and the institutional. These methods are then applied to four main areas of cultural analysis: public moral discourse, science, organizational culture, and ideology. The works they cite as representative of these theoretical positions, methods, and areas include Griswold's (1987) study of book reviewers' reviews of novels and DiMaggio's (1977) study of market structures.

Elsewhere (Denzin 1989d: 11–14) I have called these the textbook, the functionalist, and the materialist approaches to culture and its study. They ignore the processual, conflictual, Marxist, feminist, deconstructive, postmodern positions noted above. They locate culture within the institutional fabric of society and often view it as performing integrative functions for the social system. Those theorists who take the explicit commodity view seek to discover a version of society in which cultural objects and commodities reside. They ignore the "writing culture" project of Clifford and Marcus (eds) (1986) and pursue a kind of "provisional, provincial positivism" (Griswold 1990) as they study these objects and their meanings. Their work empirically commodifies cultural representations, turning them into "countable" objects which can be studied with the statistical procedures utilized in the mass media studies of the 1950s and 1960s. They reduce culture, in both its popular and its high forms, to component features of mass, pluralistic societies and their local "taste cultures" (see Gans 1974). They view culture as a vessel which contains social values. Through this vessel pass meanings which are conferred by producers and conveyed to consumers. Analysts read meanings off the surfaces of these cultural objects and then argue that these meanings are given in the culture and expressed in the lives of interacting individuals. Politics dissolves into statistics, and the communication-as-culture approach to cultural studies becomes a mechanical operation fitted to the functional (micro-macro) picture of contemporary postmodern societies.

The Becker and McCall project

In *Symbolic Interaction and Cultural Studies* (1990) Becker and McCall (eds) promise more than they deliver. What they promise to develop is a general approach to cultural studies. Arguing that symbolic interactionism is not very well understood by scholars in other disciplines, they propose to show how this perspective has informed the sociologies of art, science, religion, and knowledge. They define cultural studies as "the classically humanistic disciplines which have lately come to use their philosophical, literary and historical approaches to study the social construction of meaning and other topics traditionally of interest to symbolic interactionists" (p. 4). Acknowledging the Frankfurt school and the work of Stuart Hall and his colleagues, they suggest that interactionism can inform this tradition. They suggest that this can occur through the interactionist commitment to Mead and Blumer's theory of mind, self, and society. This will involve a reworking of feminist, institutional ethnography and the study of everyday discourse systems as they pertain to social worlds, the self, the body, and situated systems of subjectivity.

Their volume presents individual essays on history, life history, religion, philosophy, art, science, the body, and language. Entirely absent is any mention of politics and the pragmatic cultural studies communications tradition which extends from Dewey through Blumer to Mills, McLuhan, Innis, Duncan, Altheide, Carey, Couch, and Cornel West.

Where is the popular in their cultural studies? There is a similar neglect of communications, history, and the information technologies of the current age. It is clear that interactionism cannot be brought into cultural studies through a noncritical, institutional analysis of art, science, and religion.

The cultural logics of postmodernism

The postmodern epoch is characterized by the following cultural configurations and cultural logics. We are now in the third stage of the sign. The sign has become reality, or the hyperreal (see Baudrillard 1983b: 11). The sign, that is, masks the fact that there is no basic reality.[8] Each stage of the sign has been (and is) surrounded by a particular epistemological regime concerning reality and its representations. These regimes correspond to the three forms of realism earlier identified as textual, cinematic, and simulational.

In each epistemic phase, capitalism has called forth and produced particular consumer ideologies regarding the cultural object. (This logic has valued the otium-sexual-prestige meanings of objects.) From the first to the third stage of the sign, ideology has shifted from consumers as users of objects to consumers as subjects who consume objects for their status and prestige values. Consumption has become a dominant cultural logic (Lefebvre 1971/84), even as consumers, through their everyday practices, attempt to show their resistance to this consumer culture (Certeau 1984).

Each ideological moment has hailed a particular type of individuality or a favored cultural type, from the class-centered subject of the Middle Ages to the labor- and family-centered individual of the Industrial Revolution to the media-centered, consumption-oriented individual of the present time. Each cultural type has been constructed around the family system and the containment of sexuality and desire within the family structure.

The cool communication forms (satellite and cable TV, telex, fax machines, instant electronic communication [electronic mail]) have produced a global village predicated not on a shared humanness, but on marginality and cultural and racial differences. Controlled by multinational and state corporate structures, a satellite communications system connects the First and Third Worlds (McLuhan's "hot" and "cold" countries). This system articulates a set of popular culture ideologies which value family, sexuality, work, and leisure. These are pro-Oedipal stories (Barthes 1975) which are marketed, distributed, sold to, and consumed by Third World, Soviet, and European audiences. These narratives and myths are communicated through (and in) the popular press (*National Inquirer, Reader's Digest*, etc.), advertisements, popular cinema, and neo- (or recycled) popular American television, including sit coms, crime dramas, family melodramas, and soap operas. They involve the telling and retelling of a very small number of stories, contained and re-contained within the above genre forms.

The meaning systems of everyday life divide between the personal and the biographical, the technical knowledge discourses of the physical and human sciences, the practical knowledge of local and popular culture, and the emancipatory, populist discourses of protest (see Habermas 1987: 374–403; Ulmer 1989). These four structures of meaning occasionally merge and then conflict with one another (science fiction). They complement each other in official state ideology. In populist discourse they openly clash (e.g. in anti-nuclear protest documents).

These discourse structures are increasingly communicated through the electronic media, producing a new "videocy," or language of the visual video image. This language displaces the earlier forms of literacy based on orality and the print media (Ulmer 1989). It introduces a new set of media logics and media formats (Altheide 1988). These new formats alter the person's relationships to the "real" and the technologies of the real. They maintain a narrative and epistemological commitment to the simulational logic of the third stage of the sign. They serve to turn the individual into a new cultural object; an object who produces cultural knowledge and cultural texts via the new informational formats. At the same time they become new vehicles for the prodution and reproduction of official ideology. In the hands of the powerful they become tools for "the perfection of a utilitarian attitude and the indefinite expansion of the administrative mentality and imperial politics" (Carey 1989: 171). (The data banks are now controlled by the state (Lyotard 1979/84).)

The new information technologies turn everyday life into a theatrical spectacle; into sites where the dramas that surround the decisive performances of race, ethnicity, gender, sexuality, and age are staged. These dramas are staged against the backdrop of compelling, newsworthy events which are shaped by uncertainty, unpredictability, and natural disaster (e.g. a tidal wave in Pakistan). The *faits divers*, or the diverse fact connected by the bizarre, is also a favorite news story (e.g. a wounded reindeer in Alaska tripped a railroad turn signal, causing the mayor of Anchorage to miss his daughter's wedding; see Baudrillard 1981: 175 on such stories). Such stories tell heroic tales of life and death, courage and survival. They reaffirm the cherished values of community, family, and individuality.

These events and their meanings are coded within a system which allows nothing to escape interpretation. The interpretive code of the media contains everything, including the message and the receiver (Baudrillard 1981: 179). The code excludes all communicators except those frozen within the communicative frame itself. The result is an overabundance of meaning, an ecstasy of communication (Baudrillard 1988) which delights in the spectacle itself and finds pleasure in the pornography of excess which flows from the media's desire to tell everything.

To summarize, a complex set of cultural logics define postmodernism. These logics turn on the meanings brought to five terms: the "cultural object," the "individual," the "family," "sexuality," and "work." Conservative, consumer-oriented, cinematic and visual to the core, postmodern culture, in its many contradictory forms, is a masculinized culture of eros, love, desire, femininity, youth, and beauty. The postmodern person is a voyeur, someone who sits and gazes (often mesmerized and bored) at the movie or TV screen. This is a looking culture, organized in terms of a variety of gazes, or looks (e.g. tourist, investigatory – medical, social science, television, religious, political – artistic, photographic, etc.; see Urry 1990: 135).

The myth of Oedipus is alive and well and continues to argue that the path to happiness and fulfillment is sexual and lies in the marital, family bond. The contemporary Yuppie family has become a valorized consumer purchasing unit, and its consumption needs now drive the political economies of everyday life. The raw racial and sexual edges of contemporary life produce anxiety, alienation, madness, homelessness, resentment, and anhedonia (Lyman 1990a). Large cultural groupings (the young, women, the elderly, racial and ethnic minorities, gays, and lesbians) are unable to live out their ideological versions of the American dream or to experience personal happiness.

The project called "cultural studies"

An effective, interpretive interactionist cultural studies attempts to make sense of the above conditions. It asks, after Mills, "How are the personal troubles of the postmodern individual transformed into public issues?"

Such an approach examines three interrelated problems: the production, distribution, consumption, and exchange of cultural objects and their meanings; the textual analysis of these objects, their meanings, and the practices that surround them; and the study of lived cultures and lived experiences which are shaped by the cultural meanings that circulate in everyday life (R. Johnson 1986/7: 72). Each of these problems constitutes a field of inquiry in its own right.

The production of cultural objects

The production, distribution, consumption, and exchange of cultural objects involves issues of ideology and the political economy (semiosis) of signs, including how these signs are worded or photographed, where they circulate, who buys them, and so forth. The systems of discourse that shape the meanings brought to any cultural object must also be examined. These systems will draw from the four meaning systems discussed above (biographical, popular culture, scholarly/scientific, populist/protest discourse).

The cinematic creation of the alcoholic subject

In a recently completed study of mainstream Hollywood cinema and the alcoholic (Denzin 1991b), covering the years 1932 to 1990, I analyzed eight systems of discourse which shaped the presentation of the alcoholic. These systems were: prohibition and the temperance legacy, the emerging presence of Alcoholics Anonymous in American society after 1934, the public statements of the National Council on Alcoholism and the public health movement concerning alcoholism as a treatable disease, the American Medical Society's statements on alcoholism as a disease, a change in the Hollywood production code to permit drinking on screen, the shifting gender stratification system in American society, existing film genres (comedy, family melodrama, crime thrillers, sports dramas, women's films) which could absorb stories about alcoholics, and pre-sold stories and plays about alcoholics (e.g. plays on Broadway, best-selling autobiographies, etc.). These eight discursive systems took shape in the preclassic period (1932–45) and cohered during the 1945–62 time period to present what I called the "classic" picture of the alcoholic. During an interregnum (1962–80) this classic paradigm fell apart, to be renewed again during the late 1980s.

A complicated process structures the production of a cultural subject at the level of the cultural text. As the alcoholism films indicate, at every level of textual production, there is an interaction between public, private, and scholarly (also ideological) systems of discourse.[9]

Textual readings

The textual analysis of meanings requires the implementation of a variety of reading strategies (feminist, semiotic, hermeneutic, deconstructive, psychoanalytic) which examine how a text constitutes (hails) an individual as a subject in a particular ideological moment and site (Althusser 1971). As argued in chapter 3, such textual readings attempt to show how specific texts create their particular images of subjects and their experiences. These readings attempt to examine the narrative-writing strategies that structure the texts' treatment of text and author, presence and lived experience, the real and its representations, and the subject and intentionality. These are explicitly critical readings; that is, they criticize the textual formations enunciated by the text in question (see below).

Lived experience

At the level of lived experiences, a central problem, as noted above, becomes the examination of how interacting individuals connect their lives to these ideological texts and make sense of their experiences in terms of the texts' meanings. *Interpretive interactionism* (Denzin 1989b), as argued in chapter 2, enters the field of cultural studies at the level of lived experiences. As a distinctly qualitative approach to the social, interpretive interactionism attempts to make the world of lived experience directly accessible to the reader (mindful of the many problems surrounding this commitment). The focus is those life experiences, called "epiphanies," which radically alter and shape the meanings which people assign to themselves and their life projects. This existential thrust calls for an examination of those moments when the individual, in a variety of locations, comes into contact with the terror and repressive taken-for-grantedness of the postmodern (Lefebvre 1971/84: 143–4). This involves a study of the epiphany.

The epiphanic moment

The epiphanic moment leaves a mark on a person's life. There are four forms of epiphany: the *major upheaval*, which changes a life for ever (e.g. a man kills his wife); the *cumulative*, which refers to the final buildup of a crisis in a person's life (e.g. a battered woman finally leaves home); the *illuminative* moment, in which the underlying existential structures of a relationship or situation are revealed (e.g. the family holiday dinner depicted in John Huston's 1987 film *The Dead*, taken from Joyce's *The Dubliners*); and the *relived moment*, wherein the person, after an event occurs, comes to define it in consequential terms (e.g. a widowed spouse gradually comes to feel free from a loved one's presence in their life).

The epiphany occurs in those problematic interactional situations where the person confronts and experiences a crisis. A personal trouble often erupts into a public issue, thereby connecting a private trouble with a public response; a battered wife flees her husband and enters a shelter. These moments occur within those larger historical, institutional, and cultural arenas that surround the subject's life. The troubles they reflect occur within the immediate world of the subject. They are private matters. Their occurrences display how cherished personal and public values have been challenged (Mills 1959: 8).

Troubles are also biographical. The public issues which they connect are always cultural and structural. These public issues – for example, the homeless, the battered wife, or the sexually abused child – transcend, as Mills notes (p. 8), local, personal worlds of experience. They concern the organization "of many such milieux into the institutions of an historical society as a whole . . . An issue is a public matter: some value cherished by publics is felt to be threatened" (p. 8). Biography and history (structure and culture) are thus joined in the study of the epiphanic moment.

An interactional cultural studies attempts to capture these moments and their tellings and meanings. Such a strategy moves at the three levels of cultural analysis outlined above: the cultural text, its meanings, and its connections to lived experience.

Here is another example from Blumer and Hauser (1933: 13):

Male, white, Italian, 17, delinquent in high-rate delinquency area – I began to run wild. I ditched school, got caught. Father licked me, but it didn't do any good and then finally the movies finished me. The gang pictures came out and soon had our bunch standing on their heads. They took on nicknames of the characters in the pictures and it wasn't before long when we went out on raiding parties of chicken coops and small stores and getting away with ease . . . we had pulled off some 35 jobs before we were caught. By this time I had quit school and was just bumming around.

Return to the earlier examples (above). Our black burglar experienced boredom in his life and found excitement with his gang friends. They saw a movie which showed them how to be burglars. They put what they had learned into practice. The 16-year-old sexual delinquent went to the movies to be sexually aroused. The alcoholic who saw Michael Keaton admit his alcoholism at an AA meeting wondered how to do the same. The Italian delinquent broke with his father over his truancy and movie-going patterns and found in the gang pictures a way of life that was satisfying.

In each instance an epiphanic moment, of the major, cumulative, illuminative, or relived variety, was experienced. From the vantage point of prison, these young men and the young woman look back to find out what got them to where they are now. (Of course, Blumer helped them make sense of this pattern.)

The telling

At the level of the telling of the experience, interpretation focuses on the personal experience and self-stories (Denzin 1989a: 43–4) that people tell one another. Self-stories are told in the "context of a specific set of experiences," while personal experience narratives are "stories people tell about their personal experiences" (p. 43). Self-stories make sense, through the process of telling, of the self and its experiences. Personal experience stories frame self-stories within larger narratives that connect the self to the oral tradition of a group, family, or relationship. (George's second story in the last chapter is an example.)

Many personal experience stories enter the level of public discourse and take the form of autobiographies and biographies. Here the self becomes a commodity, bought and sold in the public marketplace. Such stories are then told in the daily press, elaborated in weekly news magazines like *Time, Newsweek*, and *People Weekly*, become the stuff of television dramas and TV talk shows, get retold in face-to-face groups, and even become mythologized in the cultural texts of certain groups (e.g. the life stories in Alcoholics Anonymous 1976). Here is how this happens.

Turning stories into cultural commodities

Weekly news magazines purport to fill out the glossed stories of the daily news (Ericson, *et al.* 1987: 2) with versions that connect and join people. Often these are about people, and they may evolve into (auto)biographical texts. Conversely, some news magazine stories are condensed from biographies and autobiographies. Such magazine accounts express valued forms of subjectivity. They circulate as commodities in the political economies and collective consciousness of the reading and viewing publics. In them the self becomes both a commodity with an exchange value (Elbaz 1987: 152–3) and a new cultural subject. These subjects become positive and negative self-models for other members of the culture. I now examine this process.

Stories creating lives: adult children of alcoholics

In 1988 *People Weekly* published a series of stories about ACOAs. I take as my subjects two adult children of alcoholics, Suzanne Somers and Chuck Norris, both of whom were featured in this issue. The cover carries a half-page photograph of Somers. "Children of Alcoholics," in capital letters, is alongside her head. A full-page picture of Somers walking on the beach, with a father and daughter photo inset, leads the story. The text: "On a beach, near her home, Suzanne Somers says of her father, above in 1978, and his drinking: "Now that I've dealt with it, I forgive him." The narrative title, "Breaking the code of silence," is elaborated by the sentence "Children of alcoholics, educated early in fear, shame and mistrust, learn to live with themselves by making peace with the past" (p. 100). The reader is informed that an estimated 28 million ACOAs are the legacy of far too many homes in America like the Somers's house, where the "gloom inside came from the shadow cast by her father's alcoholism, which almost destroyed her family's life and her own." These child adults or adult children have been deprived of love, have been forced to take on aspects of adult roles abdicated by the parent, have grown up with low self-esteem and a need for approval, and seek out troubled relationships. Their sense of normal behavior has been badly skewed. They are three and one-half times more likely than non-ACOAs to become alcoholics themselves.

"The outlook is not unrelievedly bleak," the text reads "nearly 4,000 self-help groups support families of alcoholics, including Children of

Alcoholics Foundation, the National Association for Children of Alcoholics, Al-Anon, and Alateen." Having created a subject, the adult child, the text states that victims of alcoholism need help identifying their problems, including the sense of shame they may still carry. They must reopen the door to their childhood. This will be a liberating and agonizing process, involving memories "not of cheery suppers with doting parents but of being dragged into bars; of a loving dad or mom who can turn into an emotional bully; of fights that end in violence; and constant dread that the family itself may suddenly come apart forever."

Text as ideological narrative

What are we to make of this complicated narrative which veils and hides particular meanings while it tells a story in ordinary, understandable, factual language? In Barthes's terms (1957/72: 11, 109–10), this is a myth which also presumes a reader who can identify with Somers or Norris, or who is an ACOA. The celebrities have become commodities, vehicles for both telling a story about ACOAs and selling this issue of *People Weekly*. ACOAs are also commodified in this move. The purchase of this issue of the magazine promises the ACOA reader greater self-knowledge. At the same time it may create unforeseen trouble for such persons. Now they have an explanation for problems they have been experiencing, but they may not be ready to accept this explanation; that is, they may love their alcoholic parents. Nor may they be willing to see their personal troubles as public issues which can be shared with others.

The text draws on a heretofore unrecognized layer of everyday life – the world of ACOAs. In opening up this realm, it exploits the everyday and its problems (Lefebvre 1971/84: 173). It locates political struggle in the selfhood of the person and in his or her relation to the Oedipal battles which have occurred in the alcoholic home. It is a pro-Oedipus complex, pro-"holy family" text: Daddy-Mommy-me (on such texts, see Deleuze and Guattari 1977). It also diffuses the cultural stigma attached to alcoholism and makes persons who confront a parent's alcoholism valued cultural subjects. It reifies middle-class values concerning the family and family life as it points to the problems of alcoholic homes. The photographs of Somers and her father personalize them in a favored cultural dyad: father and daughter, shoulder to shoulder, both smiling and accepting and loving one another.

However, the text must produce yet another version of the alcoholic: the alcoholic parent/father, the villainous wrecker of middle-class family dreams, a part Somers's father plays. Without him there is no ACOA;

and with him comes the destruction of the "normal" child–parent/father relationship. He produces her; she forgives him.

The reader trapped in the alcoholic family is promised release in three steps. The text first creates a set of imaginary, remembered relations (homes of gloom versus homes with cheery suppers) that govern the parent–child relationship in the American nuclear family and holds out hope that such an idealized version of the family can be regained. Ideologically, this text defines and constitutes concrete individuals (see Althusser 1971: 171) as subjects who have suffered from the family disease of alcoholism. Second, release comes through a "talking" and "story-telling" cure, with the subject as storyteller of his or her alcoholic childhood. In this move the subject's story is turned into a commodity which reifies the self into a set of culturally described experiences. This takes the story away from the subject and creates a vacuum which can only be filled by the stories others give him or her. Third, readers must share their story. They must find an ACOA group.

In order for this to happen, the reader must accept this new cultural subject which the text creates; this subject who is both an adult (celebrity) and a child. He or she must also believe that adults are who they were as children; and that children with alcoholic parents are educated in fear, shame, and mistrust and have low self-esteem, a need for approval, and no sense of what "normal" is. "The bond of silence" regarding one's childhood must be broken in order to triumph over these experiences. Based on a model of warfare and battle, four stories then depict the victories of four celebrities and four children (kids).

The text makes the apparently contradictory adult–child couplet (and identity) unproblematic by combining in each individual two adults and two children: the adult you are now, the adult alcoholic parent you had, the child educated in shame and fear, and the child who wanted something more. The two children must be released before the true adult inside each person can be found. This means that the person must deal with and forgive the adult alcoholic. In drawing on Somers's celebrity status, the text makes her like any other ACOA while at the same time holding her up as one to be admired. She has become a star in spite of her ACOA experiences. The narrative renders a version of the American myth of the individual who overcomes adversity in the pursuit (and attainment) of success. How did Suzanne (and Chuck) do what they did?

Enter the stories

The process of recovery defined, all that remains is to insert the stories of the four stars. Page 102 opens a new story, "Suzanne Somers: Growing Up was an Emotional Battlefield." After an obligatory brief history of her father's drinking career comes a story about the night he came into her room drunk and ripped up some of her pretty clothes. Then come stories of her high school marriage, how (and why) she posed for nude photographs in order to pay her son's medical bills, and finally the story of how she and all her family hit bottom and began going to AA and Al-Anon. The narrative ends: "It's not easy telling all this stuff, but I know there are little girls out there hiding in closets and adult children of alcoholics who don't know what normal is. I hope this book can help them." The message is simple: Tell your story, and if you tell it well, you will recover and help others at the same time, just like Suzanne.

Chuck Norris

Now consider the story of Chuck Norris. It is framed by these words: "Chuck Norris: A Time Came when he had to Face Down his Father." It goes on: "Chuck Norris has made a career of being a tough guy . . . [D]espite his image, in his recently published autobiography, *The Secret of My Inner Strength: My Story*, Norris says that growing up with an alcoholic father left him anything but strong and confident . . . [He] developed a debilitating shyness and was plagued by physical and psychological insecurities that dogged him into adulthood." Norris's stories follow this interpretive life overview. He tells the reader, "Writing my book was therapeutic. It lessened my resentment towards my father . . . I thought if I could explain my problems, then people in similar situations would find encouragement to rise above their own tragedies. If I can do it, anyone can." (His book describes his development of an individual system of self-improvement.)

In his narrative there are stories about his father's alcoholic drinking, his mother's many menial jobs, the time he came home and almost had a fight with his father, a drunken trip across the desert with his family, and his turning-point experiences in the Air Force in Korea, where he learned martial arts. Somers's and Norris's stories both point to the relief that comes from telling a story. But if persons become the stories they tell, then how this happens requires discussion. First, back to Suzanne and Chuck.

Finding Somers and Norris

Are the biographically real Suzanne and Chuck in these news magazine stories? No. There are only representations of them that conform to the picture of the ACOA earlier outlined in the *People Weekly* text. This text creates Somers and Norris to fill out 10 pages of the April 18 cover story. Their actual stories, given in their autobiographies, are relevant only where they serve *People Weekly*'s purpose: to invite the reader to join a social group in which stories like those told (hence, sold) on these pages are presumably shared.

Perhaps in the stories told in these groups we will find this ACOA subject. These groups and their stories create another biographical version of the subject from yet another layer of ordinary, postmodern experience. Here are the personal troubles and the epiphanal moments that give life meaning, substance, and shape. Here is the lived history Mills sought, but never found.

The stories people tell in their groups

Consider the following statement made by a man named Allen at his first ACOA meeting: "What do you people do here? I'm an alcoholic. My mother's an alcoholic. Does that mean I'm one of you? What's an adult child anyway?" Two days later he recounts his experiences at his first ACOA meeting:

> They hate alcoholics. I'm an alcoholic. How can they hate me? They hate their parents. I don't hate my parents. I feel sorry for them. They don't run their meetings like we do [at AA and Al-Anon]. Everybody either talks at the same time, or they talk about whatever's on their mind. They don't have topics. Then this one dude decided he'd be the leader. He took over and started running it like a psychotherapy group. I mean he took control. I can't find a place for myself with that bunch. Shit, I can't relate to their idea of ACOA issues. Whatever that means. Fuck, in Al-Anon they deal with the same stuff. They know how to forgive. They got the Steps, just like we do. These bastards don't have no Program.

Apparently this particular ACOA group had yet to learn Suzanne's lesson about forgiveness, but had accepted the battlefield mentality toward the alcoholic parent that structures the *People Weekly* article. Thus this man cannot realize a form of subjectivity in ACOA that is compatible with his image of himself as a recovering alcoholic and member of AA and Al-Anon. He fails to find in ACOA the context for storytelling that he has previously experienced in these other self-help groups. The *People Weekly* story does not address this issue.

Becoming the story

To become the self of the stories one tells requires learning how to be a storyteller – that is, conforming to an implicit canon concerning self-texts. This canon varies from group to group. In biographies, autobiographies, and magazine articles, it holds that selves be gendered, familied productions, grounded in class experiences, and molded by turning-point moments that can be objectively recorded. Further, as exemplified in the *People Weekly* text, it holds that persons are the best observers of their selves and can tell stories that accurately reflect their lives. It is a cultural understanding that readers can expect the above ingredients in a biography or an autobiography. These ingredients are also the narrative devices which journalists and editors of news magazines employ to assemble stories like those of Suzanne and Chuck.

Cultural groups like ACOA and AA may not adhere to these canons, or they may vary them to fit their particular needs. ACOA, unlike AA, apparently requires a familied theory of self that involves an alcoholic parent and his or her negative influences on the member's life. As a result, these two groups create different versions of the same individual.

Reading the subject in the cultural text

The subject is built up out of stories that are told, stories themselves constructed according to cultural understandings. Subjects are narrative constructions. These constructions may draw upon media or popular cultural representations and may or may not reflect actual experiences. When they do not reflect lived experience, the gap between the real and its representations becomes existentially problematic. In such moments, ideology repressively intrudes into the worlds of lived experience.

Cultural texts, such as *People Weekly*'s stories on ACOAs, are conservative productions. They appropriate, preempt, and intimidate the workings of the everyday sociological imagination. These stories have the ring of morality plays involving conversion and salvation. They depict illnesses cured through confessions and end on an upbeat note. "But what is missing . . . is what happens the morning after release [from treatment], the month after the cover story, the year after the cure"

(Goodman 1989: A-4). They use the life stories of celebrities who are ACOAs as occasions to give value to family forms which may no longer exist. They perpetuate values and meanings which may not be appropriate to the actual situations of interacting individuals. They alter and rearrange the everyday sociological imagination which contains the interpretive theories that structure the lived experiences of ordinary individuals.

Of course, there are no real biographical subjects independent of the stories told about them, and even these texts, in the telling, displace the teller. We can never get back to raw biographical experience. The closest we can ever get is when a subject, in an epiphanal moment, moves from one social world to another. In these instances the subject is between interpretive frameworks. When this happens, experience is described in words that have yet to be contaminated by the cultural understandings of a new group.

Coming full circle

We've entered an era in which nothing is hidden any longer (Baudrillard 1988: 22). The dividing line between public and private lives has dissolved; anyone's personal troubles can now serve as a front-page story couched as a banal morality tale with a happy ending. But as this erasure occurs, groups like ACOA, AA, NA, Adult Children of Sex Addicts, Child Abusers Anonymous, and Adults Recovering from Incest appear and take their place within the fractured fabrics of the American social structure. In these groups, members attempt to take back their lives and make sense of the experiences they encountered while being raised in their particular familied version of the American dream. They thus make public, in a limited way, the very secrets they felt the public order had held against them. But along with releasing talkers from an oppressive morality that had previously trapped them in a private hell, the very moment of their talking turns their stories into commodities sold in the public marketplace.

Late twentieth-century America is producing cohorts of people who no longer accept things as they used to be. But these persons risk being trapped in a space in which nothing is private or sacred. Their newfound freedom lies in a gray area in which the older moralities no longer pertain and the ground of personal existence, which has been de-centered, no longer holds firm. There is no zero point of personal meaning that readily translates into the public realm; nor is there a zero point in the public realm.

So Mills was wrong in his predictions concerning the postmodern moment. The darling little slaves, the suburban queens, and the alcoholic robots have not settled for indifference, drift, and apathy. They have turned *ressentiment* into action, even when this involves actively (and publicly) hating their parents. Their fraudulent inspirational literature, their popular films, novels, and other cultural texts have told them to seize the day and to no longer accept things the way they are. In small and large groups and in social movements, they have taken on the American family and its incestuous, violent structures. They have challenged sexism and racism, environmental pollution, and the threat of nuclear annihilation. And in these moves, which are more than symbolic, they have attempted to fit their biographies to a historical social structure which has yet to learn how to accept them. Yet, alongside these subversive social groups persists a counter-centering logic which canonizes nostalgia, pastiche, romantic beliefs in patriotism, true character, surface images, imitations, simulations, instant information, frauds, and replicas.

Back to people

Interactionists can never get back to biography, history, or society the way in which everyday people do: for as soon as we conceptualize these terms, they are already in our texts, not out there to be grasped or joined together. And once in our texts, they become our versions of what they are. Our sociological methods now dissolve into thin air, predicated on the long-standing myth that real, flesh-and-blood subjects exist out there in the 'real world,' to be objectively studied, whether through questionnaires and interviews, life histories, quasi-experiments, unobtrusive methods, participant observation, or photographs and audio-video tape (but see Couch 1986 and Manning 1987). These methods supposedly render visible the subject's attitudes, beliefs, and experiences, thereby furthering sociological writing about the inner (and outer) workings of society. But these beliefs, attitudes, and experiences, like the subjects who supposedly hold or have them, are only cultural, textual creations. They have no autonomy outside the texts that we (or they) write (see Frank 1990). How, then, do we as interactionists get back to the social?

This was the point of the ACOA texts. There are only different versions, or glosses, of biographical experience. The three levels of glossing, from the bottom up are: first-hand, lived experience glosses; second-order, printed stories that people tell others; and third-order glosses, those given in the daily news. But beneath these three textual orders exists the ever elusive subject. The man, woman, or child who cries out and sometimes goes to others for help. This subject, despite all the ambiguity that may otherwise exist, has an occasional grasp on who he or she is and where he or she is going. We seek his or her words and stories, ever mindful of the fact that, when we get hold of them, we may, like the writers for *People Weekly* simply create another laminated version of who the person is. We risk losing sight of him or her, and the person of him or herself. We've created the subject in our own eyes.

It remains to locate symbolic interactionism within a cultural studies tradition which will address the above issues. This is the topic of the next three chapters.

Notes

1 As Johnson (1986/7: 38) observes, cultural studies is now a "movement and a network. It has its own degrees in several colleges and universities and its own journals and meetings. It exercises a large influence on academic disciplines, especially English studies, sociology, media and communication studies, linguistics and history." It is also a presence in anthropology. It has become a major site of comparative theory, drawing on structuralism, semiotics, psychoanalysis, Marxism, feminism, poststructuralism, and postmodern theories. It is increasingly "committed to research on the way basic beliefs about gender, nationality, class, and race produce coherence and conflict in cultural identity" (Grossberg 1989b: 2). A number of new journals are devoted to this field, including *Cultural Studies* in England, *Cultural Critique* in the US, and the *Australian Journal of Cultural Studies*.

2 The concept of lived experience is problematic.

3 Hall's work (see also the discussion in chapters 5 and 6) reflexively turns back on the projects of Hoggart, Williams, and Thompson, while it transcends mid-century American social theory of the functional, conflictual, and interactionist varieties and attempts to come to terms with structural, poststructural, and postmodern European social theory (Saussure, Lévi-Strauss, Lacan, Barthes, Althusser, Gramsci, Foucault, Derrida, Baudrillard, Lyotard, and Habermas) and feminist theory (see Hall 1980a, 1986b). In a pivotal piece, Hall (1980b) identifies two paradigms in cultural studies: culturalism (Hoggart and Williams) and structuralism (post-Althusser and Gramsci) and locates his project within the structuralism–Marxist tradition.

4 Grossberg (1989a) complicates Hall's picture by identifying five distinct cultural studies positions: literary humanism (Hoggart and Thompson), dialectical sociology, resistance theory, conjunctural theory, and postmodern conjunctural theory.

5 New sections within the American Sociological Association and the International Sociological Association bear the title "Sociology of Culture."

6 Giddens (1987) is representative of this stance. Although he displays a "grasp" of poststructuralism and Derrida's project, he reads it as being a dead end for sociology. I obviously disagree with his interpretations which allow him to pursue his own structuration version of Weberian neo-functionalism.

7 I exclude Mukerji and Schudson (1986: 57–62) from this judgment.

8 In the first stage of the sign (the Middle Ages), signs represented concrete things in reality. In the second stage (the Industrial Revolution) signs masked reality, but still presumed a real world referenced by the sign.

9 I did not explicitly deal with the political economy of film production in my research, noting only how the star and studio systems worked to bring mainstream Hollywood stars into the role of alcoholic.

5 COMMUNICATION AS INTERACTIONIST PROBLEMATIC

In one way or another, everyone is equal before these cultural machines.
(Mills 1963: 333)

We must return the study of man in society to a study of communication, for how we communicate determines how we relate as human beings.
(Duncan 1962: 438)

In this chapter I intend to show how the study of communications can become a central part of interactionist theory and research. Such a move will open the spaces for an interactionist-based cultural studies, for, as argued in chapter 4, communication is culture. Anticipating my conclusions, I will argue that a tradition of cultural studies (and criticism) has always lurked beneath the surface in symbolic interactionism. Its presence has been given in the undertheorized term "communication." It is necessary, then, to transform the interactionist theory of communication into an interactionist theory of culture. This will involve a discussion of communication as a neglected problematic in the interactionist literature, including the interactionist tradition of communications research, especially Blumer's cinema studies and the connection between these studies and Mills and the Frankfurt school.

The interactionist problematic

A neglected term connects the words "symbolic" and "interaction." That term is "communication." It has traditionally been embedded in the word "symbolic," for all symbolic interactionists know that human beings communicate through the use of language and symbols. But, as argued in previous chapters, interactionists have neglected the symbolic side of their theory, choosing instead to build elaborate theories of interaction. Understanding that interaction creates those versions of society that they wish to study, interactionists have seldom fitted this problematic into the larger picture and the larger story which involves the study of the communication process and the communication industries which produce and shape the meanings that circulate in everyday life. Significantly, none of the major symbolic interactionist readers (A. Rose (ed.) 1962; Manis and Meltzer (eds) 1967, 1972; Stone and Farberman (eds) 1970, 1981; Farberman and Perinbanayagam (eds) 1985; Deegan and Hill (eds) 1987; Brissett and Edgley (eds) 1990; Becker and McCall (eds) [1990b] contain a section on communication, culture, or the communication process; for a partial exception see Maines and Couch (eds) 1988. Nor is this absence noted in Reynolds 1990. Instead, the readers, with variations, follow the Mead, *Mind, Self, and Society* model.

The interactionist communication's tradition

Of course, the interactionists never completely abandoned communication and its study. As noted in chapter 2 (see also Gronbeck 1988: 325–30), Cooley (1902/22/56), at the turn of the century, discussed the press and the newspaper as modern forms of communication. In the 1920s and 1930s Park and his students (see H. Hughes 1940) studied newspapers and the local, community presses which continued ethnic traditions.[1] Blumer's cinema studies of the 1930s shifted attention to film and the movies as negative carriers of new cultural values. Dewey's (1927) arguments with Walter Lippmann's *Public Opinion* and his subsequent calls for a form of public opinion fashioned out of open dialogue in a free society anticipated arguments that "were to resurface over subsequent decades with Harold Innis and Marshall McLuhan" (J. W. Carey 1989: 79). By the late 1940s and through the 1950s both Blumer (1948, 1959) and Mills (Mills and Gaudet 1946; Mills 1950/63) were questioning the "effects" research tradition and the public opinion polls and consumer surveys of the Columbia (Lazarsfeld) school of communications. (In the early 1950s Bateson and colleagues began to redefine the field of communications within a pragmatic-ethological tradition, stressing distorted, double-bind communication structures of interaction – e.g. Bateson and Ruesch 1951.)

In 1962 Hugh Duncan published his influential *Communication and Social Order*, which offered no less than a re-reading of the James, Dewey, and Mead theories of communication fitted to a dramaturgical (Kenneth Burke) theory of language, art, and social order; while Goffman's *The Presentation of Self in Everyday Life* (1959) was explicitly built upon a dramaturgical model of communication and meaning. In the 1970s Herbert Gans's *Deciding What's News* (1979) and Gaye Tuchman's (1978) *Making News: A Study in the Construction of Reality* pointed in the directions of an interactionist theory of news as a social construction (see Reisner 1990). Goffman's *Gender Advertisements* (1979) attempted an analysis of gender displays and the advertising media. Altheide and Snow's *Media Logic* (1979) offered a communication model similar to, but different from the perspective of McLuhan and Innis. Stressing the reflexive nature of symbolic communication, they examined the media logics, media formats, and forms of mediation (e.g. definition, selection, organization, interpretation, and presentation) created by specific communications technologies (see Altheide 1988: 216; Snow 1988; Altheide and Snow 1991). This emphasis continued throughout the 1980s into the 1990s, with J. W. Carey's collection of influential essays in *Communication as Culture* (1989) and his arguments that the many forms of popular culture, especially television and the press, demand study from a perspective that emphasizes myth, ritual, and narrative (1988: 15). In the mid-1980s Meyrowitz (1985) applied Goffman's dramaturgical model to the new sense of place produced by the electronic media, and Manning (1988b) articulated a sophisticated structural-pragmatic theory of organizational communications. Altheide's *Media Power* (1985), Maine and Couch's edited volume *Communication and Social Structure* (1988), and Couch's (1990) analysis of the state and information technologies attacked these problems from another perspective, that of information technologies (e.g. orality, print, one-way and interactive electronic media – telegraph, radio, cinema, computers, television). The study of other media forms, especially cinema, resurfaced in the late 1980s with Clough's (1988) and Denzin's (1991b) film studies.

Back to communication

In seeking to reorient symbolic interactionists towards a cultural studies perspective, I choose, then, to focus on this missing, undertheorized term in their perspective. There is a paradox here, of course; for communication is interaction, and for interaction to unfold, interactants must communicate. Communication is a symbolic process, whereby "reality is produced, maintained, repaired, and transformed" (Carey 1989: 23). Communication, as Mead understood, is the process which produces significant symbols. But it is more than this. With Carey (1989: 84–6) and Couch (1990), I understand communication to refer to an ensemble of social practices, social forms, social relationships, and technologies of representation which construct definitions of reality. The social practices, relationships, and technologies of communication symbolically interact. They do so in concrete historical moments, to produce particular ideological, emotional, and cultural meanings which are connected to the lived experiences of interacting individuals.

The paradox deepens. What is called "the study of culture also can be called the study of communications, for what we are studying in this context are the ways in which experience is worked into understandings and then disseminated and celebrated" (Carey 1989: 44). The apparatuses of culture – what Althusser would call ideological state apparatuses – are also the apparatuses of communication and include (1) all the organizational milieux in which artistic, intellectual, and scientific work go on; (2) the political economy which produces, distributes, and markets these goods, including information; (3) the social institutions, including "the schools, theaters, newspapers, studios, laboratories, museums, little magazines, radio networks," films, popular literature and music, and television which distribute and interpret these products; and (4) the images, meanings, and slogans that "define the worlds in which men live." Taken as a whole, this cultural apparatus is "the lens of mankind through which men see; the medium by which they interpret and report what they see. It is the semiorganized source of their very identities" (Mills 1963: 406). This apparatus guides, defines, and expropriates experience. It sets standards of acceptability and credibility and creates contemporary sensibilities and aesthetics of desire (e.g. Bourdieu's (1984) concept of taste and distinction).

The hyperreality, the simulated realities which the media now produce (Baudrillard 1983b), makes matters more complex. The communication and cultural apparatuses which define life in the postmodern moment reflect a nostalgic preoccupation with the real and its representations. The third stage of the simulacra (the reproduced sign), the stage of computer simulations and instant news, has produced an obsession with second-hand truth, objectivity, and authenticity. "There is an escalation of the true, of the lived experience . . . a panic-stricken production of the real and the referential" (Baudrillard 1983b: 12–13). Mills's second-hand reality has become Baudrillard's third order of the simulacra. The simulational logics of the electronic media (television and computers) re-format the lived and the real, making the lived experience (an early Dewey term) a production that is now larger than life.

Re-formatting lived experiences

An interactionist cultural studies approach to communication must examine how the communication technologies and cultural apparatuses of the contemporary period produce the real and its representations. Such a project must address the communication and textual logics that structure the dominant narrative-representational forms of this multimedia age. This analysis must take a form–content approach (Couch and Chen 1988: 162; Snow 1988; 201), since each "medium of communication over a period of time will to some extent determine the character of the knowledge to be communicated" (Innis 1972: 34). The form of communication (oral, writing, electronic, visual, or simulational) shapes the message and the content of the message that is carried.

Content carries ideology, and in a multimedia age it is the content of the message that must be studied. Such an analysis must be directed to the analysis of the following problematics: (1) the genre forms (action-adventure, documentary, drama, biography, melodrama, comedy, tragedy, etc.) that structure these information technologies and frame the messages they carry; (2) the narrative traditions which these forms draw on and elaborate; (3) the regimes of realism (textual, cinematic, emotional, and simulational) that order these texts; and, by way of summary, (4) the personal, popular culture, populist, and scholarly systems of discourse they deploy when they tell the stories they tell (Ulmer 1989).

Each information technology or media form re-formats the real and its representations of lived experience. Each technology works in its own way with the above problematics. Each deploys its version of realism, fits that version to a genre-driven textual form, tells stories within specific narrative traditions, and employs particular versions of the biographical, the popular, and the scholarly in the tellings it produces. It is the content of the tellings, not their form or logic, that now concerns us, for it was on content that the early interactionist communications studies focused.

Cultural studies and the Chicago pragmatists

An incipient cultural studies tradition and agenda, focused on communications, has always lurked inside interactionism. Historically (Mead, Blumer, Burgess, etc.), this has been a conservative tradition, which has often confused form with content. It has persisted in valuing a realist epistemology at the level of high art and the life story and the ethnography at the level of the sociological. At the same time it has devalued realism at the level of the cinematic or popular culture text.

When interactionists took up the problem of how to re-format lived experiences within the new information technologies ushered in by film, they became negative. They made no attempt to analyze the new media forms in terms of the dimensions outlined above (e.g. genre form, narrative traditions, regimes of realism, etc.). In the main, the early Chicago pragmatists focused not on the symbolic and communicative realms of everyday life, but on the traditional interactional/communication forms (face-to-face communication) that sustain and display the fabrics of a democratic society.

But more was going on, and this entailed a negative reading of the media and the study of media effects on the social and moral fabrics of American society. Perhaps for these reasons, a fully formed interactionist, communications studies program has never emerged, as it did in the British case, and in certain American departments and institutes of communications.[2] Return to Mead and Blumer as the founding fathers of interactionism and reconsider their comments on the movies, as discussed in chapters 1 and 2.

Mead's aesthetic theory

An implicit highbrow, lowbrow theory of the arts organized the Mead–Blumer view of popular culture. Mead and Blumer felt that the movies pandered to the needs and tastes of the masses. The fine arts, on the other hand, answered to the human being's desire to be morally elevated through the ideal aesthetic experience, which produces the "joy of elevated thoughts" and a "sense of the sublime" (Mead 1925–6/64: 298). This aesthetic attitude, which the movies do not promote, is healthy and normal and "accompanies, inspires and dedicates common action" (p. 298). The preferred aesthetic experience is creative and activates the highest ideals of the community. The works of great artists produce such experiences, and they have "permanent value because they are the language of delight into which men can translate the meaning of their own existence" (p. 299). But the "prerogative of fine art has never been the language of men's hearts"; rather, "reverie – the field of the daydream – was the ever present escape from ennui" (p. 299). The newspapers and the movies "have spread the pattern of men's reveries before our outward eyes" (p. 301). The movies externalize this reverie. What the "average film brings to light is that the hidden unsatisfied longings of the average man or woman are very immediate, rather simple, and fairly primitive" (p. 303).

For Mead, as noted in chapter 1, the movies, like newspapers, answered to the "inferiority complexes." They produced a form of reverie and daydreaming which was not conducive to creative, shared experience. Movies, Mead argued, "have no creative audience" (p. 303). They activate compensatory and escape values (p. 303), and in many of them, where the attraction is "their salaciousness [lustfulness] there can be no aesthetic effect. They are sensual rather than sensuous . . . they blot out all but the immediate response" (pp. 304–5). Mead noted that the compensatory and escape values may not be the only values that are expressed in movies, "but I think they are the dominating values, and in large measure fix the public's taste, and therefore, select the themes for most of the films" (p. 303). (For an alternative reading of Mead's aesthetics, see Duncan 1962: 82–91).

Dewey on Art and the Aesthetic Experience

Mead contended (1925–6/64: 294) that his views of the aesthetic experience were "written under the influence" of Dewey's *Experience and Nature*. It is instructive to compare Dewey and Mead on art and experience, for the movies were a new art form producing new forms of experience for the members of American society (see Joas 1987: 88–9). For Dewey (1934), the aesthetic experience yields a completeness and a wholeness that ordinary, routine experience lacks. The artistic experience confronts and interacts with an expressive, aesthetic object, the work of art. This object produces a form of resistance; it challenges our past understandings and taken-for-granted meanings. Art expresses meaning; it captures and arrests the imagination, creating an integration or interaction of the self with this aesthetic object and the environment. The individual recreates the artistic object and its meanings, by creating an experience that incorporates the object into an interaction with the self. As Dewey (1934: 108–9) notes, "It is absurd to ask what an artist 'really' meant by his product; he himself would find different meanings in it at different days and hours and in different stages of his own development."[3]

Thus, for Dewey, every aesthetic experience is different. Its meanings cannot be determined beforehand, for "the perceiver creates his own experience" (p. 54). Mead, by contrast, argues that the movies create a uniform effect that plays on base social needs. Mead's model, then, contradicts Dewey's interpretive approach to the aesthetic experience. Yet, in his comments on the movies (see below), Dewey argues that they "stimulate in unwholesome ways" (1934/86a: 188).

Cinematic realism and narrative cinema

As a new technology and art form, cinema fused three earlier artistic traditions: drama, photography, and narrative literature. It told stories visually and later with sound. It transformed the printed page into a seen and heard text. Like drama, it reenacted on screen stories that related to the dominant cultural values of the day. Hollywood has always told stories that fitted the Victorian melodramatic format to the narrative, cinema form (Roffman and Purdy 1981: 5–8). This format continued the tradition established in vaudeville and had two variants, the comedy (usually slapstick) and the melodrama. These stories were morality tales, with good and bad characters, and they typically resolved their crises by locating a good man in the arms of a good woman.

This is the narrative tradition which Dewey, Mead, and Blumer are responding to when they claim that the movies provoke unwholesome attitudes. But these unwholesome attitudes were already present in literature, and they did not react negatively to this tradition. Dewey, Mead and Blumer were reacting instead to the realism of cinema, the cinema's ability to capture realistically what had earlier been confined to the printed page. In short, they were reacting to a new regime of realism and the new social texts that this regime and its technology made available. They could take realism at the level of the printed page, but not in its cinematic form. Cinema made public what they wanted kept private. In resisting this new regime of realism, they clung to an aesthetic and epistemological stance that celebrated high art. This led to a denigration of the popular. It perpetuated the illusion that the private and public spheres of American life could be safely separated if the proper art forms were valued. This theory also assumed that only properly educated adults could have the proper aesthetic experience with an art form. It was the function of civil society and its main socializing agencies (school, family, and church) to train American citizens in these aesthetic experiences and the art forms that produced them.

The movies in Chicago: historical context

Mead's views of the movies must be placed in historical context. During the first three decades of the twentieth century, Hollywood was under constant attack from civil, religious, and state authorities concerning the moral content of its films (these attacks continue to the present day). Mast describes the situation in these words:

> Throughout the nickelodeon era the movies had been criticized as cultivators of iniquity [wickedness]; the theaters had been attacked as unsavory or unsafe . . . The movie cold war suddenly became a very hot one in the early 1920s . . . the content of films, reflecting the new materialism and moral relativism of the decade [prohibition and the jazz era], became spicier and more suggestive . . . alongside Victorian films were others suggesting that lust was indeed a human emotion . . . and that the urbane, and wealthy and lustful were not inevitably evil and unhappy. (Mast 1976: 123)

As early as 1909, Chicago police assumed the role of censors, eliminating scenes "of murder, robbery, and abduction" (Sklar 1975: 126) from films. By 1914, the Chicago Motion Picture Commission had established a censorship ordinance concerning films showing violence and male and female sexuality (p. 128). Chicago's censorship ordinance was amended in 1914, "setting up a category of films approved for showing only to persons over twenty-one" (p. 128). In 1921 a series of scandals involving Hollywood stars, including Fatty Arbuckle, William Desmond Taylor, Mabel Normand, and Mary Miles Minter, made national and international news (pp. 78–9). Thirty-two state legislatures debated censorship bills. In 1922, the Hayes Commission was established by Hollywood to confront the censors and to promote self-censorship. Reformers regarded the Hayes Commission as a sham. By the mid-1920s the Commission (and Hollywood) were again under attack.

In 1928, University of Wisconsin sociologist E. A. Ross gave a lecture on "What the films are Doing to Young People." He argued that "more of the young people who were town people sixteen years ago or less are sex-wise, sex-excited, and sex-absorbed than any generation of which we have knowledge. Thanks to their premature exposure to stimulating films, their sex instincts were stirred into life years sooner than used to be the case with boys and girls from good homes" (Ross 1928: 179). Ross went on to make the movies "responsible for less-concealing fashions, pornographic literature, provocative dances and briefer bathing suits" (Sklar 1975: 138). Ross had no evidence to support his position: "This is not the place to cite evidence and I am not going to cite any" (1928: 179). Mead's anti-movie article "The Nature of Aesthetic Experience" had been published two years before Ross's address (1925–6).

Paradoxically, these criticisms from the vocal moral minority and the academic community emerged and took shape during the very period (1907–32) when film was becoming established as a new, international art form. Not only was D. W. Griffith inventing editing and camera strategies for modern narrative cinema during this time period, but German (Lang), Soviet (Eisenstein), French (Feuillade, le Bargy, and the Société Film d'art), and Italian (Caserini and Guazzioni) filmmakers were producing expressionism, the theory of montage, and early forms of realism and social consciousness films. At the same time, film stars of the stature of Chaplin, Keaton, Lloyd, Pickford, Garbo, and Fairbanks and directors like Griffith, Chaplin, Roach, and de Mille were making their presence felt in this new medium, as were a host of European filmmakers, including von Stroheim, Lubitsch, Murnea, Hitchcock, and Leni. As Cook (1981: 46) notes, "In some sectors the American film was gaining respectability as an art form: serious books were written about it (for example the poet Vachel Lindsay's *The Art of the Moving Picture* (1915) and the philosopher Hugo Munsterberg's *The Film: A Psychological Study* (1916)) and newspapers established regular columns for 'photoplay' reviews."

The Payne fund

Blumer took Mead's criticisms one step further. In 1928, William H. Short, executive director of the Motion Picture Research Council, a pro-movie censorship group, sought and received funds from the Payne Study and Experiment Fund,[4] a private foundation for the scholarly investigation of motion pictures and youth (Sklar 1975: 135).[5] Nineteen psychologists, sociologists, and educational researchers from seven universities joined the project. University of Chicago participants included

L. L. Thurstone, R. E. Park, Herbert Blumer, P. M. Hauser, Frederic Thrasher, and P. G. Cressey. W. W. Charters, director of the Bureau of Educational Research at Ohio State University, was chairman of the research group (Sklar 1975: 135). The studies were designed to answer a series of specific questions (see Charters 1933: viii–ix), including questions regarding the effects of movies on children's health, sleep, emotions, criminal conduct, knowledge of good and bad, and sex conduct (Blumer 1933: xi). The assumptions about the movies were all negative (Sklar 1975: 135). Charters (1933: xi) asked, for example, "Do children eventually become sophisticated and grow superior to pictures? Are the emotions of children harmfully excited?" The committee's work took four years (1929–32). At least thirteen monographs, four by Chicago faculty members, were produced.[6] They began to provide answers and evidence for Ross's assertion concerning movies and their negative effects on America's youth.

Hollywood's new production code

These works confirmed what might be regarded as an axiom of cultural, communication studies. Whenever a new information technology or art form is introduced into a cultural system, it is met with resistance and criticism (see Couch 1990). The negative reactions to Hollywood and the filmmakers were not unlike the moralistic controversies that surrounded Elizabethan theatre in the sixteenth century (Mast 1976: 123), the advent of the telegraph (see J. W. Carey 1989: 207) and photography in the nineteenth century (Cook 1981: 3–6), and the introduction, in the twentieth century, of radio (see Dewey 1934/86b)[7] and television (Mast 1976: 123). That philosophers, sociologists, and educators would agree with social moralists on the negative impact of the movies on American society is, therefore, not surprising. (The myth surrounding the Chicago school and its so-called liberalism is challenged by its willingness to conduct research that would support the conservative moral position of the day.[8])

The works sponsored by the Payne Fund contributed to the emergence of a Hollywood production code in 1934 which prohibited the presentation of violence, alcoholic drinking, sexual intimacy, homosexuality, interracial sex, abortion, incest, profanity, and drug use on screen (Sklar 1975: 174). The code also demanded that criminal characters be severely punished (if not killed) for their crimes. Herbert Blumer's (1933) *Movies and Conduct* and his and Hauser's *Movies, Delinquency, and Crime* (1933) were two of the works that contributed to this code.

Blumer's movie studies

In these two works Blumer (and Hauser) utilized movie autobiographies. Their respondents recall in their own words particular movies, scenes from movies, leading actors and actresses, and their effects on their dress, their daydreams and fantasies, their fears, their experiences with passionate (sexual) love, their views of their parents and their homes, their goals and ambitions in life, and criminal ideas they learned from the movies (see Denzin 1990f for a more detailed discussion of this project).[9] The movies provided rich materials for dreams about sexual partners, although Blumer offered no explicit treatment of sexual fantasies, noting that "their inclusion has been found inadvisable" (1933: xi). He includes only "milder, but representative, incidents" (p 71) of this kind of effect. Such fantasy, he suggests (1933: 70–1), "is largely monopolized by kinds of experiences which are tabooed by the moral standards of community life."

Blumer argued that in many cases the movies may "conflict with other educational institutions . . . [and] challenge what other institutions take for granted. The schemes of conduct which they present may . . . also cut athwart the standards and values which these latter institutions seek to inculcate" (p. 197). In some cases the emotions aroused by passionate love movies "represent an attack on the mores of our contemporary life" (p. 116).

Blumer partially undermines his findings in the following statement: "The writer is not unaware of the criticisms which are often made of autobiographical statements" (p. 192). He counters this charge with the claim that on "major items they (the accounts) substantiate one another . . . [and this is] a substantial indication of their reliability and accuracy" (p. 192). He "feels that the statement of findings in this report errs, if at all, on the side of caution and conservatism. To an appreciable extent the people who furnished their experiences represent a sophisticated and cultured group . . . the degree of influence of motion pictures is less in the cultured classes than it is in the case of others. With this one qualification the writer believes that his findings apply to the bulk of movie-goers" (p. 193). Thus Blumer provided evidence for Ross's assertions: Yes, the movies did influence conduct, and that influence was bad.

The judgments recorded in *Movies, Delinquency, and Crime* (1933) were even more harsh. Indirectly, through the manipulation of the unconscious, and directly, through the teaching of criminal techniques, movies are "a factor of importance in the [formation] of delinquent and criminal careers" (p. 198).[10] Those shown in correctional and penal institutions have little recreational, disciplinary, or reformatory value. They induce resentment and feelings of revenge on "society for the injustice they [the inmates] feel has been meted out to them" (p. 201). Such effects may lead "to disciplinary problems" (p. 201). Love and sex pictures "may create some problems of discipline in so far as they may lead to autoerotic and homosexual behavior" (p. 201). When movies lead to misconduct, crime, and delinquency, they "raise problems of social control" (p. 202).

Reading Blumer

How is Blumer's film study to be read today? It was clearly an interpretive project committed to digging out the facts about movies and their effects. It took a value position, pro-middle class and anti-film. It assumed that films mapped a reality that was having a negative impact on youth. Blumer read the autobiographies he collected as literal representations of these effects, even editing out those which were too lurid and dramatic. His readings presumed a theory of the child and adolescent mind and a theory of how media images affect that mind.

Blumer's theory of media effects

Politically conservative, his readings, if not directly arguing for censorship, were certainly used for that purpose (see Forman 1933). They articulated a theory of media effects which presumed that films worked their influence through the unconscious (Blumer and Hauser 1933: 72) by arousing "impulses and ideas of crime" (p. 37), "desires for easy money and luxury, and by suggesting questionable methods for their achievement" (p. 198). Blumer (1933) appeared to endorse Mead's aesthetic theory, which argued that films fuelled daydreams and reverie and promoted escapist and compensatory values. Blumer's theory of arousal assumed that the films "induced a spirit of bravado, toughness and adventurousness . . . intense sexual desires and by invoking daydreaming or criminal roles . . . created attitudes and furnished techniques conducive, quite unwittingly, to delinquent or criminal behavior" (Blumer and Hauser 1933: 198).

These effects cut across gender. Movies did for women what they did for men, only perhaps more so, or at least more so sexually.

> Motion pictures ... play a ... role in female delinquency and crime by arousing sexual passion, by instilling the desire to live a gay, wild, fast life, by evoking longings for luxury and smart appearance, and by suggesting to some girls questionable methods of easily attaining them; by the display of modes of beautification and love techniques; by the depiction of various forms of crime readily initiated by girls and young women; and by competing with home and school for an important place in the life of girls. (p. 199)

Presumably Blumer is speaking of prostitution here.

Blumer stopped short of endorsing the blank slate theory of mind, used by Forman (1933: 127) in his summary of the Payne Fund studies ("The virgin unmarked slates had been all indelibly written upon with a pencil of peculiar force").[11] Still, he saw movies as inciting conduct. "While under its influence the individual may be quite likely to experience temptation along the lines awakened by the impulse, and because of relaxed self-control to succumb to such temptations" (Blumer 1933: 128). A film's influence, he argued, is heightened by the circumstances surrounding its presentation.

> It is important to consider that the movies do not come merely as a film that is thrown on a screen; their witnessing is an experience which is undergone in a very complex setting. There is the darkened theater – itself of no slight significance, especially in the case of sex and love pictures; there is the music which is ... suggestive ... and is also designed to raise the pitch of excitement ... there are the furnishings – sometimes gaudy and gorgeous, which help to tone the experience. (p. 195)

In this setting the individual comes under the movie's spell. A film's chief effects, he argued, are emotional; "the forte of motion pictures is in their emotional effect" (p. 198). This emotional effect is realized through impersonation (for children, "playing 'cowboys' and 'Indians'," e.g. p. 13), imitation, and copying (for adolescents, "the copying of make-up, mannerisms and technique ... the actual utilization in ordinary conduct of life of what is imitated," e.g.; p. 30), and daydreaming and fantasy (p. 59).

These three effects are structured by the process of emotional possession. Movies produce what he called emotional possession: "having his emotions aroused, the individual loses self-control" (p. 74). Emotional possession occurs when the individual identifies "himself closely with the picture and so to lose himself in it" (p. 129). It takes several forms, including the production of fear, terror, sorrow, pathos, love, passion, thrill, and excitement; while it also influences daydreaming, fantasies, imitation, and impersonation. Emotional detachment (Scheff's (1979) underdistanced emotion), by contrast, is a method of controlling one's reactions (p. 129). In detachment the person maintains a critical, reflective attitude toward a film and its action. The viewer is then led to discount the film. There are three ways of producing emotional distance: (1) through instruction, (2) through a response to the attitudes of one's group, and (3) through disillusionment (p. 131).

Censorship and detachment

Blumer goes on to note that "this discussion of emotional detachment may throw some light on the problem of controlling conduct in the face of the influence wielded by motion pictures". At present, "chief reliance is being placed on censorship as a form of control" (p. 140). He suggests that this is a negative kind of control, "confined to deletion and rejection of pictures, and functioning under circumstances which make very questionable its effectiveness" (p. 140). In good Durkheimian fashion, he then encourages education and instruction as better methods of control: "The more effective and so desirable form of control comes . . . through instruction and through frank discussion." This requires a "greater willingness on the part of parent and teacher to talk about pictures with children and adolescents" (p. 140). Such talk allows the local moral community to counter the negative effects of films on the schemes of life children and adolescents develop, including their attitudes toward love, sex, family, church, wealth, leisure, and crime as a way of life.

Dewey on Blumer and the Payne Fund Studies

In 1934 Dewey (1934/86a: 188) commented indirectly on the Payne Fund studies and the Blumer research. He stated: "Recent investigations, conducted with scientific care, have shown that girls and boys have been stimulated in unwholesome ways by the movies." Going one step beyond Blumer, Dewey argued that these unwholesome effects were mediated by the "general tone and level of the child's surroundings" (p. 188). He then contrasted the environment of the well-to-do with the world of the child in a congested tenement district (pp. 188–9). The negative effects of movies could be counteracted by better education of parents, better recreation for the young, and improved material conditions (pp. 190–1). But of greatest importance, Dewey argued, should be the "organizations of business and professional men [who] should exercise . . . a powerful influence upon the kinds of movies that are shown in the community" (p. 193). This is censorship of another form; the captains of industry determine what goes on the screen.

Our movie made children

Forman's *Our Movie Made Children* (1933) provides a full-scale interpretation of the Payne Fund studies. In it he draws heavily on the two Blumer monographs. The dust jacket describes it thus: "Here is a book showing the movies for what they are – a monster Pied Piper, with marvelous trappings, playing tunes irresistibly alluring to the youth of the present day." Forman's book is presented as showing the movies to be "a sort of superimposed system of education for the young, a system with which established social institutions, such as the School and the Church, cannot compete in attraction or appeal." Forman (pp. 5–6) draws upon statements by Nicholas Murray Butler, the president of Columbia University ("Daily broadcasting of the passions and caprices . . . on the screen, [is] destructive of ideals that have proved to be wholesome"), and Ernest Burgess ("The boy comes into contact with influences in the motion pictures . . . that are in conflict with the standard of the home, the school and the church") to support his negative views of the movies. He states: "The facts are grave . . . it [the movies] is a social problem which touches everyone of us" (p. 283).[12]

Back to Blumer

As Sklar (1975: 139) notes, Blumer read these films from the perspective of the values of the middle class. The entire Payne project, Sklar contends, assumed that the "movies were tearing down American culture rather than representing and reinforcing it." He goes on: "If we took Blumer at his word, we would never know that men and women experienced sexual passion before there were movies, or that social values in America had always been in a state of conflict, confusion and change" (p. 139). It is difficult to quarrel with Sklar.

Blumer's cinematographic realism led him to treat the world of cinema "as if narrative and imagery inhere in it" (Clough 1988: 95). Behind his reading of his respondents' stories lurks his master-reading of the films, wherein he observes how they work their emotional effects on the inner life of the viewer. Unwilling to grant the stories a status of their own, he replaces their meanings with his own.

But on what ground does Blumer base his reading? He clearly stood in two places at the same time. He was the scientist watching the films, and he was in possession of a value position that permitted him to make judgments about which values the films undermined and which ones they supported. His gaze became part of the panoptic prison structure. To his eye, these films, many of which are praised today, contributed to the disorganization that post-First World War American society was experiencing. He brought these privileged positions to bear upon his readings of the texts his respondents produced. He violated the very methodological principles that he would later advocate, even as he produced perhaps the first instance of a cultural studies project undertaken by a symbolic interactionist.

His film aesthetic, or his theory of art and experience, to use Dewey's phrase, complemented his ethics and his politics. Art should have a desired effect on the public. When it fails to produce this desired effect, something must be done. The social scientist must determine precisely how these failures occur, offer a theory of how they occur, and propose solutions to the problem. This is what his theory of the movies did. It documented their negative effects, spelled out a theory of how they emotionally aroused young viewers, and proposed family and school education as tools for correcting the situation.

Blumer's theory was social psychological. It presumed that the processes of identification, imitation, personification, and emotional possession produced a susceptibility to a film's effects. These effects were then realized directly in the form of imitation and personification and in their most extreme forms led to criminal conduct. The effects were then worked through the individual's existing scheme of life. In many cases they were stronger than the influence of family, school, or church. The movies defined roles, impulses, emotions, and ideas for conduct (Blumer 1933: 197). The movies carried an "authority and sanction" that these other educational forms lacked. Blumer saw the motion picture industry as having "no cultural aim, no cultural politics, no cultural program . . . movies are the product of secular business groups with commercial interests . . . Were the motion picture industry to seek to become a cultural institution inside a society of free masses it would quickly collapse" (1935: 126–7).[13] Blumer's movie-goer is unsophisticated. "He probably could not *understand* or even *read* a sophisticated book, but can *see* the thing in the movies and be stirred and possibly misled" (p. 197; emphasis original). Oddly, unlike Dewey, Blumer failed to specify how these effects were mediated by family and neighborhood.

In many respects his film study was forward-looking, for it took on a major culture- and meaning-making institution and attempted to understand how it worked its effects on individuals. But he was trapped within a set of crippling assumptions concerning the movies and popular culture, the "world out there," social texts about that world, and the interpretive process and its relationship to an empirical science (see Lyman and Vidich 1988: 36–42 for an alternative reading of Blumer's movie studies).

For a variety of reasons, then, he was unable, or unwilling, to see in the movies what Benjamin (1936/68: 236) was later to see:

By close-ups of the things around us, by focusing on hidden details of familiar objects, by exploring commonplace milieus under the ingenious guidance of the camera, the film . . . extends our comprehension of the necessities which rule our lives . . . [and] it manages to assure us of an immense and unexpected field of action. Our taverns and our metropolitan streets, our offices and furnished rooms, our railroad stations and our factories appeared to have us locked up hopelessly. Then came film and burst this prison-world asunder by the dynamite of the tenth of a second, so that now, in the midst of its far-flung ruins and debris, we calmly and adventurously go traveling.

In short, for Benjamin, the movies encouraged a new form of aesthetic experience which was political and directed away from the high culture experiences advocated by others. Such practices politicized art and experience in ways that Dewey and Blumer found unacceptable.

Blumer, Mills and the Frankfurt school

Compare Blumer to Mills and the Frankfurt school. Mills in *The Power Elite* (1956), and *The Sociological Imagination* (1959), the *White Collar* (1951), analyzed the banality of the mass media and aligned his project with the work of Adorno and Horkheimer (Mills 1963: 572). The

Frankfurt school's criticisms of the culture industries (popular culture) saw the mass media replacing the family as the primary socializing agent in society. In this they were like the Chicago sociologists and philosophers. The media were producing a one-dimensional man with false needs and desires necessary to the smooth reproduction of advanced capitalism (Kellner 1989: 136).

The media's effects

The psychoanalytic perspective of Fromm and others in the Frankfurt school is starkly different from Blumer's social psychological theory. These scholars elaborated a psychoanalytic model of identification, which also stressed the culture industries' ability to inhibit reflective self- (and class) awareness. The media engineered social consent by establishing a social psychological basis for social integration (Kellner 1989: 131). The culture industries were seen as coaxing "individuals into the privacy of their homes or the movie theaters, where they produce consumer-spectators of media events and escapist entertainment while subtly indoctrinating them with dominant ideologies" (Kellner 1989: 131; see also Habermas 1987: 388–9).

A materialistic social psychology "which would describe how individual thought and behavior are shaped by material conditions and socialization processes" (Kellner 1989: 36) was developed by Fromm. This involved a synthesis of Marx and Freud, in which Freud's basic instincts (life and death) represent adaptations to the material structures of social reality. For Fromm, natural instincts are part of the base of society. The psychoanalytic emphasis on the irrational in all areas of social life is then combined with Marx's analysis of historical materialism. "Fromm believes that an analytical social psychology can study the ways in which socioeconomic structure influences and shapes the instinctual apparatus of both individuals and groups" (Kellner 1989: 37). This led to the psychoanalytic emphasis on the family as the primary socializing agency in society. The family became the unit which universalizes the norms of bourgeois society. Capitalist society was seen as molding and adapting instincts to its basic structures (p. 38). Fromm and other members of the Frankfurt school then applied the traditional Freudian notions of repression, reaction formation, and sublimation and oral, anal, and genital personality types to the study of "how specific social structures produce and reward certain types of character traits while eliminating others" (p. 38).

In their intensive studies of anti-Semitism and prejudice, they identified what they regarded as the basic variables defining the right wing, authoritarian personality (conventionalism, submission to authority and stereotypes, cynicism, and preoccupation with power and sex; see Kellner 1989: 116). Lowenthal's studies of popular magazines in the twentieth century revealed how popular biographies reinforced the values of an individualistic, liberal society.

Adorno and Horkheimer,[14] like Mead and Blumer (but unlike Benjamin), also adopted a highbrow, lowbrow model of culture. Unlike Blumer, who wanted to change the movies in positive ways, the Frankfurt school regarded the culture industries (especially the movie industry) with contempt, although this was not the case with Benjamin (see Kellner 1989: 124–5, 142, and Benjamin 1936/68: 236–7, 242–3). Like Blumer, they dismissed in advance any specific film or television program or piece of popular music or other artifact of popular culture (see Kellner 1989: 142). But, unlike Blumer, they viewed these artifacts as "debased forms of culture and vehicles of ideology which are not worthy of detailed study or critique" (p. 142). Where Blumer found tendencies toward criminal or anti-social conduct in movies, Adorno saw debasement, commodification, reification, standardization, and "the total triumph of capital" (p. 143).

Mills, like Adorno, saw the media as central to the forms of political consciousness that exist in a society (1956: 333), but felt that in post-Second World War America, "commercial jazz, soap opera, pulp fiction, comic strips [and] the movies" (p. 333) appealed only to the urban masses, mass emotions, [and a formulaic treatment of pulp heroes (cowboys and detectives) and idols of leisure and consumption (p. 338)]. He saw the media as producing conformity to middle-class values, including the promotion of individual success. He believed that the entertainment media were "potent instruments of social control" (Kellner 1989: 135), because "popular culture is not tagged as 'propaganda' but as entertainment; people are often exposed to it when they are most relaxed of mind and tired of body; and its characters offer easy targets of identification, easy answers to stereotyped personal problems" (Mills 1956: 336). This echoes Blumer, who also saw the effects of movies being the greatest when individuals were most relaxed.

Reading the popular

Blumer, Mills, and the Frankfurt school read the popular as if it were cut from the same, common cloth. The popular is unworthy of study. They share a commitment to the position that the popular debases, and they each affirm the value of high art (also authentic art and the avant-garde). Beginning with these shared interpretive positions, they then part company.

For Mills, Adorno, and Horkheimer (and Benjamin, to a lesser degree), the media manipulate public political consciousness in the direction of supporting the status quo. The media discourage informed public opinion and create conditions which turn public discourse away from revolutionary, or critical, social change. They turn the public into victims of a homogenized mass culture. But the media constitute the cement of late capitalism, and the forms of experience they shape are forms which contribute to the perpetuation of the capitalist system.

Blumer, of course, took an opposite reading. For him the movies were undermining the moral character of American community life and contributing to the production of homosexuals and sexual and criminal delinquents. They were eroding parental authority. They were challenging the school systems and the churches and feeding into the gang system of the inner city that was taking immigrant youth away from the proper American way of life.

The Chicago school never produced structural and analytic studies of the Frankfurt school type. Its members never anchored their studies of the media in a specific historical or economic moment. Their concerns for democracy and its perpetuation led, instead, to an early preoccupation with how the media were undermining the democratic project.

The media self and the effects tradition

The media self is a self created in the media's eyes (Altheide 1988), a self molded out of the ideas, fantasies and daydreams commodified and reproduced by the mass media. The Chicago and Frankfurt schools each saw the same media self being produced by American popular culture. An effects, uses, and gratification model (see J. W. Carey 1989: 52–3) of the media self and the media experience is presented in their materials. Such a model assumes a sender–message–receiver paradigm, in which the message sent is the message received. This model connects a particular pattern of behavior (imitation or consumption) with an antecedent media message (a film or a commercial), attaches a motivation for action (a desire to be beautiful) based on the media message (to buy this product), and interprets the resulting action (buying a product or dressing in a particular way) in terms of the original message, its use, and the gratifications it produces. In its simplistic forms this theory assumes that the media, especially movies, "are so designed . . . that sustained thought is out of the question . . . the effort required for . . . response is semi-automatic, no scope is left for the imagination" (Horkheimer and Adorno 1972: 126–7). Carey offers an example: "A person sits down to watch a television program because he wants to be entertained and by some mysterious process ends up dispelling his tensions, restoring his morale, or establishing solidarity with a larger community" (1989: 54).

This functional, behavioral model has "the effect of dissolving the content of the experience . . . without ever inspecting the content of the experience itself" (p. 55). It pays no attention to the process of symbolic interaction whereby individuals interact with a character or message and bring those interactions into their lives. It does not treat communication as a ritual process, as a process which creates the several "cultural worlds in which people simultaneously exist" (p. 67). It assumes unilateral media effects and shared, unreflected needs and gratifications. It takes individuals out of their cultural settings. It makes them monads who sit in front of a media message (the screen) which will produce a media self that satisfies larger ideological concerns. It ignores and contradicts Dewey's pragmatic theory of art and experience.

Blumer's theory failed to accord with his own (1969) self-interpretation model of the self. It followed instead, as just noted, a mimetic theory of selfhood, according to which the self and its images flow from the images reflected from the movie screen. This is not unlike the media effects research model he would severely criticize in the 1940s and 1950s. His model failed to accord with his later work on the industrialization process, in which he showed how the effects of industrialization are filtered through "the patterns of group life that already exist" (1990: 133). These existing patterns of meaning can reject a new information technology like the movies. On the other hand, the technology can exist alongside a traditional order without being incorporated into it. It can also be entirely assimilated into a group's culture and strengthen or support existing patterns of meaning. Or, more drastically, the technology may be entirely disruptive to a group and its way of life (see Blumer 1990: 88–95).

Blumer's analysis of the movies stressed the disruptive, disorganizing effects of this new information technology and art form. He did not examine how the movies were rejected in some quarters, minimally adapted in others, entirely assimilated in some, and used to strengthen existing patterns in others. His model ignored the very humanistic features of symbolic interactionism that he would later celebrate.

The Frankfurt school's psychoanalytic Marxism represented, on the other hand, a form of naive theoretical work in which one theory was grafted onto another. Whereas this analytic turn in Marxism would take another twist with Lacan in the 1980s, the Frankfurt school's theory of the subject failed to accord with the dynamic, interactional social psychology that the Chicago school and the symbolic interactionists later attempted to formulate.

Critical Theory's cultural subject, like Blumer's adolescent, is a cultural dope. Mindless in front of these cultural machines (Mills), he or she uncritically accepts the messages that are sent from the media. Unable to read serious books or hold serious ideas in their minds such people fall easily into the trap of believing what the media present to them.

The Birmingham variant

Stuart Hall's project, as suggested in chapter 4, approaches the study of communications from an entirely different angle. He is concerned to show how the communication structures of capitalism continue to exert hegemonic control over the ideas and ideologies that circulate in everyday life. His project aims to "change society and open the road towards a socialist transformation of society" (1986c: 29). His model for encoding and decoding mass media messages examines how meaning structures are encoded into texts, then interpreted by interacting individuals in society. The codes that organize televisual, print, and cinematic texts are read in terms of their consensual (dominant hegemonic), negotiated, and oppositional meanings. Each code creates specific subject positions and is a "means by which power and ideology are made to signify particular discourses" (S. Hall 1980c: 134). These discourses reproduce particular ideological meanings concerning the dominant values of the culture, especially those involving class, race, and gender.

Hall's project is always historically specific and framed within specific national states (national cultures) and the larger international scene. For example, each specific cultural formation, like racism, is historically specific, within a specific state structure. His cultural subject is always a multiple thing, framed around gender, ethnic, racial, economic, class, political, and ideological antagonism and interests (1986a: 25). Cultural practices, the representations, languages, and customs of any specific historical society, interact in the production of a national popular culture (p. 26). It is within this national popular culture that the major ideologies of a culture are played out in daily discourse and in the local and national media.

Hall's cultural subject, then, is in part symbolic interactionist, for his social actors define for themselves the conditions in which they live. But the meanings this subject brings to his or her situation are shaped by the larger ideological forces in the culture, for consciousness is "always infused with ideological elements, and any analysis of social frameworks of understanding must take account of the elements of 'misrecognition' which are involved" (1980a: 24).

Back to the beginning: the politics of media studies

To summarize, I have attempted to bring the study of communication back into the interactionist tradition. In reviewing the early interactionist work on the media, especially the movies, and in contrasting that work with the work of the Frankfurt school (and Mills), I intended to expose the flaws and the failures in both projects, especially in their theories of the media's effects on the cultural subject.

History cannot be ignored. Both these projects were conducted during historical moments framed by fascism, struggles within international labor movements, mass emigration from Europe, concentration camps, totalitarian regimes, conservative challenges to liberal democracy, and worldwide economic and moral crises. These moments were defined by the new information technologies and the rise to power of the popular culture industries (e.g. Hollywood). At the same time, the family and the schools as socializing agents were under attack, and the new media forms were seen as replacing these traditional socializing institutions. The Chicago and Frankfurt schools attempted to make sense of this historical moment and all its changes. Their divergent and conflicting interpretations simply answer to the need for a thoroughly grounded, interpretive, critical cultural studies program. This is what Hall and J. W. Carey offer.

Their cultural studies project frames the interactionist communications project.[15] It addresses the gaps in the media effects research tradition that joins Mead and Blumer with Mills and the Frankfurt school. It offers a theory of the cultural subject and the state which is historical and fitted to the information technologies specific to each media age. At the same time, it opens the door for a politics of media studies which is neither cynical nor conservative.

The nascent interactionist communications tradition, with its zigzag trajectory, has, at least since Cooley, involved interactionists in the politics of democracy; after all, a free society has a freedom of the press that totalitarian societies lack. Furthermore, free societies, like the United States, require for their freedom a form of discourse among their members that only the press, the information technologies of the time, and the social and behavioral sciences can provide.

Each communication interactionist theorist has seen dangers to democracy in these new technologies. Cooley, like Lippman, thought that newspapers produced gossip, not solid facts about social life, and that, as a result, they eroded the creation of a free and open public. Mead and Blumer (as noted above) thought that the movies threatened central social values. Park saw the circulation of news as being vital to a free society. Mills (1963) saw the contemporary individual as caught in a media trap, in which the freedom and ability to make rational political choices was constantly under attack. Innis thought that media with a time bias promoted authoritarian structures (Couch 1990: 111). Duncan (1962) and Couch (1990) have shown how authoritarian state structures use the electronic media to undermine the foundations of representative democracy. In short, the study of the media has always involved interactionists in the politics of their research. The cultural studies agenda I have sketched in this and the previous chapter reasserts the importance of this tradition.

Such a project must, after Dewey, develop its own critical, aesthetic theory of the popular culture experience and the cultural subject who experiences such social texts. It must grasp how subjects are produced and shaped by social and cultural texts, even as they appropriate such texts for their own personal experience. It must also examine how new media technologies enter into, alter, challenge, change, and support existing group formations. (Blumer's work on the effects of industrialization can be easily adapted to the examination of this problem.) The form–content distinction, with its related concerns regarding genre, narrative traditions, and regimes of realism, must also be maintained. A project with these commitments should better illuminate how the media, in their various forms, create the realities which human beings live in and experience. It asks, that is, what an interactionist cultural studies can contribute to a worldwide socialist democracy.

But interactionists, including Blumer, have been hesitant to openly embrace politics, postmodernism, and cultural studies (but see Lyman and Vidich 1988: 106–19). There is a paradox here which cuts to the inner core of symbolic interactionist epistemology. In spirit and tenor, interactionism is the theory that should be most open to cultural studies and postmodernism. All but one of its cardinal tenets, including respect for the empirical world, fitting theory to that world, entering that world and becoming part of it, listening to the voices that speak in it and writing their interpretations, are postmodernist and cultural studies in orientation. What puts interactionists outside the postmodern space is the assertion that there is an empirical world out there that must be respected. The ontological status of this world, in the postmodern period, is never seriously questioned by interactionists (but see Plummer 1990).

Hence their continued commitment to the schizophrenic project of producing an interpretive, objective science of human group life; what some even call a performance science (Becker *et al.* 1989). This divided self, which separates interactionists from the postmodern, cultural studies community, must be overcome if symbolic interactionism is to become an interpretive voice that continues to speak to the world of lived experience in the late twentieth century. How to do this is the topic of the next chapter.

Notes

1 Park (1940/67) saw the news as a form of literature and the reporter as the producer of an important type of new literature. He also saw the news as a new type of commodity within the American economy. Joas (1987: 100–1) considers Park to have been one of the most enlightened early interactionists, citing his definition of the news as information, his commitment to the black perspective and the race problem in America, his interests in the possibilities of social control and democracy in a pluralistic culture, and his belief that there is a possibility for rational, collective decision making (see also Lyman 1990c. 1991).

2 Other factors, of course, were also operating. During the same period that members of the Frankfurt school (see below) were forming their cultural studies, communications tradition, the Chicago interactionists were consolidating their theory and focusing their attention on race relations, collective behavior, family, deviance, and crime. A tradition of studying the communications industries other than the newspapers never emerged (except for Helen Hughes, M.Janowitz, Kurt and Gladys Lang, Francis Merrill, and Leo Zakuta. See the Merrill essay in Shibutani (ed.) 1970). This began to change in the postwar years; see Table 1.

3 Each art form employs different media (e.g. architecture and sculpture use stone and concrete) and reflects different values. For example, "the monuments of sculpture are the embodiment of the past" (Ulbrecht 1953: 20); painting expresses "nature and the human scene as a spectacle" (Dewey 1939: 235); music expresses change, suddenness, and emotionality; and literature expresses the values of collective life. Every work of art produces a "complete experience, rendering it more intensely . . . felt" (p. 52).

4 Portions of this section draw from Denzin 1990f.

5 Short's project was a reaction to the above issues.

6 *Motion Pictures and the Social Attitudes of Children*, by R. C. Peterson and L. L. Thurstone: *Boys, Movies, and City Streets*, by P. Cressey and F. Thrasher, and the two Blumer books.

7 Calling the radio the "most powerful instrument of social education the world has ever seen," Dewey (1934/86b: 309) also noted that the radio lends

itself to propaganda on behalf of special interests and can be used "to distort facts and mislead the public mind."

8 The involvement of Chicago sociologists (and philosophers) in civic and policy issues throughout the 1920s and 1930s is well documented. This included work with the Civic Federation of Chicago, the Chicago Commission on Race Relations, Hull House, the Charity Organization Society, and the Institute for Juvenile Research (see J. T. Carey 1975, ch. 3; Dykhuizen 1973: 102–3). The Chicago philosophy group, according to Dykhuizen (p. 103) "did not believe in drastic cures for society's ills. They were not extremists of the Marxist . . . type. They believed in the existing capitalist society, but taught that it should be controlled or modified to eliminate or lessen the evils and abuses which attend an unrestricted laissez-faire economy. None of them were as extreme as Veblen, Small or W. I. Thomas" (p. 104). The Chicago faculty appeared to be quite willing to produce works that agreed with the conservative politics and morality of the Chicago business community.

9 Unfortunately the names of specific films and actors are not given in the second book; this was "in compliance with editorial suggestions" (Blumer and Hauser 1933: x). This makes it impossible to provide alternative, oppositional readings of the films in question and their "presumed" effects. The first book records the film titles given in the autobiographical accounts – e.g. *The Phantom of the Opera, Dr Jekyll and Mr Hyde, The Gorilla, While the City Sleeps, Shadows of the Night, London after Midnight, The Gaucho,* and *The Lost World.*

10 Blumer and Hauser (1933) estimate this effect to be of importance in about 10 percent of male and 25 percent of female offenders, although he argues that these are conservative figures and the rate is probably higher (p. 198). Of those in prison, 49 percent of the sample indicated that the movies had shaped their criminal conduct (p. 36).

11 Forman is here describing the effects of *The Birth of a Nation* on children's minds: "Prejudice against the Negro had been clearly increased in these children's minds by the movie, *The Birth of a Nation*" (1933: 127).

12 Lyman and Vidich (1988: 129) argue that in Forman's book Blumer's "findings were distorted to support the censorious interests of the Payne Fund." Kimball Young (1935: 5–225) complained (Lyman and Scott 1988: 129) that Forman's book had done social psychology, education, and sociology a disservice. He predicted that Forman's version of Blumer's studies would awaken "a wave of sentiment against the movies."

13 Clearly a cultural institution, for Blumer, is one which supports the moral values of society. To argue that Hollywood had no cultural politics or cultural program makes no sense, given the history of the medium during and after prohibition, when anti-alcoholism and anti-crime films were repeatedly produced (see Denzin 1991b ch. 1). Furthermore (Cook 1981: 393–5), during the Second World War, President Roosevelt's Bureau of Motion Picture Affairs, in conjunction with Hollywood's War Activities Committee, worked to produce films which complemented the propaganda and morale-boosting programs of the government. The government (Cook 1981: 394) suggested six themes which Hollywood films should emphasize, including the themes that the war was being fought to support the American way of life, that the enemy was evil, that the United Nations was our ally, and that it was

the duty of American citizens to supply materials for victory. At the same time Hollywood was defined by the Selective Service System as an essential American industry. Supra-patriotic films were made (e.g. *Salute to Courage, The Devil with Hitler, To the Shores of Tripoli*).

14 They influenced, directly and indirectly, Mills, Riesman, Gouldner, Aronowitz, and of course Habermas (Kellner 1989: 137–8). Habermas's (1987) rather cumbersome theory of communicative action, with its speech act, its functional Parsonian and Freudian overtones, and its attempts to join Durkheim, Mead, and Piaget with Weber, fails to deliver what it promises – namely, a critical theory of communication. Still, his outline of the tasks for critical theory (pp. 378–9) are of value and will be discussed in chapter 6.

15 And thus transcends Habermas's theory of communicative action.

6 INTERACTIONIST CULTURAL CRITICISM

> The tradition of pragmatism – the most influential stream in American thought – is in need of an explicit political mode of cultural criticism.
> (West 1989: 212)

Implicitly and explicitly, interactionists have always been involved in cultural criticism (see Fisher and Strauss 1978: 461–82 for a discussion of the theories of social reform held by Thomas, Park, Hughes, and Blumer). This tendency to criticize existing social and cultural formations, both within and outside sociology, begins with James's arguments against the American war machine in the first decade of the twentieth century and continues in multiple lines from Cooley and Park on the newspapers through Mead and Blumer's criticisms of the movies in the 1920s and 1930s to Lindesmith's challenges to the drug laws in the 1940s; C. Wright Mills's attacks on the media in the 1950s; Becker and Goffman's analyses of moral entrepreneurs and the mental hospitals in the 1960s; Douglas's studies of morality and respectability in the 1970s; Lyman, Vidich; Manning, Altheide, Johnson, Couch, Hochschild, and Clough's investigations of race relations, the mass media, women, and democratic forms of government in the 1980s; and Blumer's critical analyses of American race relations and the labor movement from the 1940s to the 1980s (see Lyman and Vidich 1988).

In this chapter I intend to make cultural criticism an explicit part of the interactionist project. I will, accordingly, outline the tasks of an interactionist cultural criticism, drawing on the recent work of Cornel West (1989, 1988), Stuart Hall (1988a, b), Habermas (1987), Merleau-Ponty, and Sartre. I will offer a re-reading of the pragmatist tradition, especially the recent work of Richard Rorty (1979, 1982, 1989) and Cornel West (1989, 1988), and then turn to a pragmatic, aesthetic theory of cultural experience, including the tasks of a critical cultural studies. I will have occasion to return to Chuck Norris, whom we encountered in chapter 4.

Rorty's project

On the surface, Rorty is the symbolic interactionist's friend. More than any other contemporary American philosopher, he has promoted James and Dewey and the pragmatic tradition (West 1989: 199). He has offered pragmatism as a replacement for traditional American linguistic, analytic philosophy. At the same time, he has argued that pragmatism does what the recent existential, Marxist, poststructural turns in European philosophy (Nietzsche, Sartre, Heidegger, Foucault, Derrida, and Habermas) have been unable to do; that is, provide a philosophy which will "make our institutions and practices more just and less cruel . . . [while letting] us hold self-creation and justice, private perfection and human solidarity in a single vision" (Rorty 1989: xiv). He describes the pragmatic tradition thus: "On my view James and Dewey were not only waiting at the end of the dialectical road which analytic philosophy travelled, but are waiting at the end of the road which, for example, Foucault and Deleuze are currently travelling" (1982: xviii).[1] Rorty has served a double function for contemporary interactionist theorists. He justifies their pragmatic project, and he relieves them of the obligation of reading the European philosophers he dispenses with.

The key to Rorty's system lies in the resurrection of the separation between public and private values. He states: "The attempt to fuse the public and the private lies behind Plato's attempt to answer the question, 'Why is it in one's interest to be just?' and Christianity's claim that perfect self-realization can be attained through service to others" (1989: xiii). This desire to merge the public with the private is ill-fated, he contends, because it assumes that the "springs of private fulfillment and of human solidarity are the same" (p. xiii). But suppose, he argues, that there is no universal human nature or inner human essence, that "at the 'deepest' level of the self there is no sense of human solidarity" (p. xiii), then what is called "human" is only a product of the socialization process. The tension between public and private still prevails.

For Rorty, historicists like Foucault and Heidegger who long for self-creation and private autonomy see socialization as something antithetical to human experience. Historicists like Dewey and Habermas who "desire for a more just and free human community . . . are inclined to see the desire for private perfection as infected with 'irrationalism' and 'aestheticism'" (p. xiv).

Rorty wants to do justice to both groups of thinkers, arguing that we need not choose between them, but can give them "different weight for different purposes". Authors like "Kierkegaard, Nietszche, Baudelaire, Proust, Heidegger and Nabokov are useful as exemplars, as illustrations of what private perfection – as self-created, autonomous, human life – can be like. Authors such as Marx, Mill, Dewey, Habermas and Rawls [and Foucault] are fellow citizens, rather than exemplars. They are engaged in a shared social effort . . . to make our institutions and practices more just and less cruel" (p. xiv).

Rorty creates a questionable tension between these two schools of thought: "There is no way in which philosophy, or any other theoretical discipline will ever let us . . . hold self-creation and justice, private perfection and human solidarity, in a single vision" (p. xiv). He seems to be arguing that the private trouble (self-perfection) and the public issue (human solidarity) can never be joined. He states: "The closest we will ever come to joining these two quests is to see the aim of a just and free society as letting its citizens be as privatistic, 'irrationalist,' and aesthetic-ist as they please so long as they do it on their own time – causing no harm to others and using no resources needed by those less advantaged" (p. xiv).

His argument takes a linguistic turn, for the vocabulary for self-creation is necessarily "private, unshared, unsuited to argument," whereas the vocabulary of justice is "public and shared" (p. xiv). Hence the language and public values of the liberal society need not be compatible with the values and language of private life. Public life is the preserve of liberal values, including freedom, the eradication of inequality and suffering, and the attainment of human solidarity. These values are given by chance and contingency; they are the products of a particular set of historical situations. A liberal society is "one whose ideas can be fulfilled by persuasion rather than force, by reform rather than revolution" (1989: 60). Private experience and life, by contrast, are given over to self-transformation, self-reflection, and private morality, yet sustain the impulse "to adopt a self-identity which suits one for citizenship in such an ideally liberal state"

Rorty criticizes European philosophers for their nihilism and cynicism, while praising their attacks on realist epistemology. He finds in Foucault, Habermas, the Frankfurt school, and Derrida, however, unnecessary attacks on liberal democracy. His criticisms involve the private–public distinction. Ironist theorists like Hegel, Nietzsche, Foucault, and Derrida are useless when it comes to politics, but informative in "our attempt to form a private self-image" (p. 83). He faults Foucault for failing to see "the gains in freedom and expression" that have come in modern liberal societies and for failing to understand that increased modern constraints have been accompanied by decreases in pain (p. 63). He then attempts to assimilate Foucault into his utopian, liberal, reformist political view of contemporary culture (p. 64). In the process he dispenses with Foucault's analyses of the new kinds of subjectivities which the postliberal cultures have produced, including new regimes of power and sexuality. This move is justified, he contends, because Foucault, like Habermas, "still thinks in terms of something deep within human beings, which is deformed by acculturation" (p. 64); and he accepts (with Habermas) "Mead's view that the self is a creation of society" (p. 63).

If Foucault longs for social institutions that embody our autonomy, Habermas goes even further, only in a different direction. If Foucault is an ironist without being a liberal, then Habermas is a liberal without being an ironist (p. 65). For Rorty, Habermas thinks "it is essential to democratic society that its self-image embody the universalism, and some form of rationalism, of the Enlightenment" (p. 67). This position merely repeats the private–public distinction which Rorty regards as no longer useful. Habermas's ideal society rests on domination-free, rational communication, based on argumentative practices conducted within expert cultures. Such knowledge will not be overturned by romantic disclosures of new worlds (p. 66), the kind of poetry and narrative literature that Rorty favors. Habermas dispenses with Rorty's narrative turn, calling it an "unfortunate preoccupation of the 'world-disclosing function of language' as opposed to its 'problem-solving function'" (Rorty 1989: 66).

Rorty then criticizes Habermas's picture of the self and its three divisions ("the cognitive quest for true belief, the moral quest for right action, and the aesthetic quest for beauty"; p. 142), which have been reproduced in the three expert cultures of modern life (science, law and literary criticism). He suggests that Habermas's view of literature as a forum for the expression of feelings underestimates "the role which novels . . . have come to play in the reform of social institutions, and in the moral education of the young, and in the forming of the self-image of the intellectual" (p. 142). Quoting Dewey, Rorty (p. 69) insists that Habermas is unable to see how "the moral prophets of humanity have always been the poets."

In passages such as these, Rorty rejects virtually all the European critical theory and philosophy that has emerged since the Second World War. He states: "I think that contemporary liberal society already contains the institutions for its own improvement . . . Indeed my hunch is that Western social and political thought may have had the last *conceptual* revolution it needs" (1989: 63; emphasis original). In Dewey and James he finds a noncritical theory of contingency, chance, irony, and solidarity, which promotes the workings of this liberal, democratic society he values.

His cultural hero is the liberal ironist. "Liberals are the people who think that cruelty is the worst thing we do" (p. xv and ch. 3 and 6). An "ironist" is a person "who faces up to the contingency of his or her most central beliefs and desires – someone sufficiently historicist and nominalist to have abandoned the idea that those central beliefs and desires refer back to something beyond the reach of time and chance" (p. xv). Liberal ironists hope that human suffering will come to an end. But they know that there are no ultimate, final values that can be appealed to; "there is no answer to the question 'Why not be cruel?'" (p. xv). Anyone who thinks that there are "algorithms for resolving moral dilemmas . . . is still in his heart a theologian or metaphysician" (p. xv).

This position, he contends, is a minority position! The liberal ironic intellectual is outnumbered by people "who believe there *must* be" an ultimate moral position, including nonintellectuals who are "committed either to some form of religious faith or to some Enlightenment rationalism" (p. xv). However, the ironist is not hostile to democracy or human solidarity. Such persons seek a liberal utopia which is universal (p. xv), a postmetaphysical culture in which human solidarity would be a goal to be achieved, not by "inquiry but by imagination" (p. xvi). Solidarity is created by increasing sensitivity "to the particular details of the pain and humiliation of other, unfamiliar sorts of people" (p. xvi). Such thinking will make it more difficult to marginalize people who are different.

Neither positivistic science nor analytic philosophy can produce this kind of understanding and compassion. They are trapped within a viciously circular and apologetic set of arguments concerning their own perspective (West 1989: 200), which only repeats the same old language games and social practices (Rorty 1979: 10). The task of producing this compassionate understanding of the other falls, then, to the humanities (art and literature), the mass media, popular culture, and the humanistic versions of the social sciences (ethnography). This is a "task not for theory but for genres such as ethnography, the journalist's report, the comic book, the docudrama, and, especially the novel . . . the novel, the movie, and the TV program have, gradually but steadily, replaced the sermon and the treatise as the principal vehicles of moral change and progress" (1989: xvi). The authors whom Rorty likes include Dickens, Olive Schreiner, Richard Wright, George Orwell, Choderlos de Laclos,

Henry James, and Nabokov. Dickens and Wright provide insight into the kinds "of suffering being endured by people to whom we had previously not attended" (p. xvi). Writers like James, Nabokov, and Orwell "give us details about the sorts of cruelty we are ourselves capable of" (p. xvi and ch. 7 and 8).[2]

Rorty on aesthetics

Rorty's aesthetic theory (1989, ch. 2 and pp. 141–2) refuses the common distinction between works (books) with moral messages (books of conscience) and "books whose aims are aesthetic" and express artistic taste and values (p. 142). Both conscience and taste are matters of beliefs and desires, and in the traditional picture they lead to questions which judge a work's truth, morality, or beauty. Pragmatist that he is, Rorty asks instead: "What purposes does this book serve?" (p. 142). Purposes and books can be divided into two categories. There are those books which speak to the desire to produce some new, final vocabulary. A tiny fraction of such works will "make the greatest differences in the long run" (p. 143). Of these books, there will be those aimed at "working out a new *private* final vocabulary and those aimed at working out a new *public* final vocabulary" (p. 143; emphasis original).

The liberal ironist needs both kinds of works. This cultural hero reconstructs the moral-aesthetic divide by distinguishing between books that stimulate and those that relax. The morally autonomous person needs to relax occasionally and will read books that he or she finds relaxing. There is nothing wrong with this; these books are not immoral or useless (p. 144). The person who is not an ironist judges such works negatively, because they produce only pleasure. "They assume that a book which does supply pleasure cannot be a serious work . . . and cannot carry a 'moral message'" (p. 142).

In Rorty's liberal utopia there is a general turn away from science and philosophy to narrative and the narrative forms of expression. This stance recognizes that no single theory or philosophy can "hold all the sides of our life together in a single vision" (p. xiv). It takes note of the contingency of language; that there is no way to step outside a single perspective and form a metavocabulary or metalanguage that would provide a noncontingent epistemology which would account for "*all possible* vocabularies, all possibilities of judging and feeling" (p. xvi; emphasis original).

Reading Rorty

How can a symbolic interactionist use Rorty? He is not without his critics. Marxists have suggested that he presents a kind of "genial, clubbish, laid-back end-of-ideologies ideology that consecrates the status quo" (Eagleton 1990: 383). The cultural left has suggested that he is "blandly oblivious to the discourses of power [and] his ideal of private aesthetic experience can easily be translated into narcissistic, yuppie consumerism" (Klepp 1990: 124). The feminist position that the personal is political refutes Rorty's separation of public and private life. Fraser (1989: 103–4) points to the depoliticized, or apolitical, nature of Rorty's ironist theory and the atheoretical reformist practices he advocates. Rorty's politics simply become a form of community solidarity in which a modernized version of Dewey's social engineering replaces political struggle (p. 104). The cultural right (Bloom and Hirsch) would argue that his position leaves no objective ground for arriving at truth (Klepp 1990: 124). Science, scholarship, and politics are then abandoned to propaganda, irrational emotional appeals, and finally force. Analytic philosophers and philosophers of science predictably claim that his view of science as literature is false (Klepp 1990: 124).

It is, of course, impossible to sustain a division between the public and the private, between private troubles and the public, institutional response to such troubles. The two domains of experience are inextricably interwoven; each defines the other, as in Cooley's famous sentence "The individual and society are opposite sides of the same coin." Any attempt to tear these two structures apart produces two political projects, one for private life, the other for public life. Rorty's desire to resurrect this public–private, ethics–conscience division reflects an unwillingness to accept a radical, feminist politics predicated on the institutionalization of cultural and social differences. After all, it is when the individual experience violates the values of the public order that immediate, personal crises are experienced – for example, rape or family violence. A dialectical relationship obtains between the public and the private, sustained and mediated in part by the legal system and the mass media; the law, the media, the private, and the public mutually define one another.

This is one of the important lessons to be learned from Habermas, whose theme of the colonization of the lifeworld seems to go unnoticed by Rorty's liberal ironist. More deeply, Rorty fails to probe the depths of the problems that now characterize postliberal, postmodern societies, those outlined in earlier chapters (and below) concerning race, gender, the economy, the media, and the family (see Krug and Graham 1989).

Granted, there is no core self or essential human nature; nonetheless, there are cultural and political values that define the core of human nature as understood in particular historical moments, including the present. These are the values which Rorty and his mentor, Dewey, cherish. They will not be produced by wishful thinking or by the reading of good literature.

It is evident that a great deal of social engineering is necessary if the social democracies are to bring their politics into line with the private experiences of their citizens. Rorty's position that "contemporary liberal society already contains the institutions for its own improvement" cannot be allowed. Such a stance reinforces the status quo. Nor can his position that Western and political thought has had "the last conceptual revolution it needs" be allowed. By disallowing the criticisms of the Frankfurt school, Foucault, and others, Rorty seals the door on radical social change and radical social critique. In his romantic version of American society, all is well; a little cruelty here, a little insensitivity there, perhaps; but all in all, everything is just fine.

His political aesthetic thus dissolves into a passive pragmatism, which says that what works best is what worked best in the past.[3] The novels and books that make the "greatest difference in the long run" thus conform to the conventional, Western civilization, great literature canon. His aesthetic marginalizes the popular and values the private over the public, never detailing what a new, final public vocabulary might look like. In fact, if we take Rorty seriously, there can never be a final vocabulary of anything.

But there is a vocabulary right now which attempts to be final, and it is the language of the media, the language of the popular. This is a language with a shifting code that subsumes everything; a language of the new which reworks the old. This language takes many forms. It can speak of resistance and protest. It can also be a deterministic, patriarchal, sexist, violent, homophobic, racist, final language of social difference. It is a language which is changed and challenged daily, as it is reified in the popular. The aesthetics of this language and the popular art forms it defines (see below) can no longer be slighted in the name of authentic art or the high art of the past.

Rorty's project opens the door, then, for an interactionist cultural criticism. What he ignores must become the subject matter of the interactionist project. Parts of this project have been anticipated by Cornel West.

West's prophetic pragmatism

West's (1989) re-reading of the pragmatic tradition, from Emerson and Peirce through James to Dewey, Hook, Mills, Du Bois, Niebuhr, Trilling, Quine, Rorty, and Unger, concludes with a call for a prophetic pragmatism. In his reading, pragmatism refers to a heterogeneous tradition which results, in part, from the distinctive features of American civilization.[4] The diverse forms of pragmatism converge on a future-oriented instrumentalism which emphasizes thought "as a weapon to enable more effective action" (p. 5). Its "basic impulse is a plebeian radicalism that fuels an antipatrician rebelliousness for the moral aim of enriching individuals and expanding democracy" (p. 5). American pragmatism from James to Du Bois, Mills to Rorty, has been a "continuous cultural commentary or set of interpretations that attempt to explain America to itself at a particular historical moment" (p. 5).

West's prophetic pragmatism would attempt to capture Emerson's sense of the utopian, Dewey's conception of creative democracy, Du Bois' structural analysis of the limits of capitalist democracy, Hook and Trilling's sense of the tragic, James and Niebuhr's grasp of the religious, and Mills's "tortuous grappling with the vocation of the intellectual" (p. 212). West rejects Rorty's relativist, ahistorical, nontheoretical neo-pragmatism (pp. 208–9). Rooted in the above-mentioned American traditions, prophetic pragmatism, with "its hopes for the wretched of the earth, constitutes the best chance of promoting an Emersonian culture of creative democracy by means of critical intelligence and social action" (p. 212).

This project attempts to produce the following conditions.[5] First, it seeks to promote a society and a culture "where politically adjudicated forms of knowledge are produced in which human participation is encouraged" (p. 213). Social experimentation is to be encouraged only when those who must suffer the consequences have "effective control over the institutions that yield the consequences" (p. 213). This is creative democracy in the making. Second, politics, after Dewey and Mills, are regarded as being located in the everyday experiences of ordinary people. This leads to a form of empowered democracy (Unger 1987) in which constitutional law, under a critical legal studies agenda (Unger 1983), seeks to weaken the traditional hierarchical divisions of gender, race, and property. Third, in this utopian scheme (Dewey's creative democracy) there would be a large-scale reconstruction of the state and the "rest of the large-scale institutional structures of society" (Unger 1983: 25). This reconstruction would challenge the citadels of private power (factories, hospitals, state bureaucracies, and offices) which are presently insulated from effective democratic accountability (p. 28).

This means, fourth, that spaces must be created within the current institutional structures that control everyday life so that the voices, sentiments, and politics of ordinary people can be heard, felt, and implemented.[6] Fifth, the system of property, political, civic, and welfare rights that now organize democratic societies must be reconceptualized. The presently constituted system of rights reproduces the power structures that work against an empowered democracy. Unger proposes four types of rights – immunity, destabilization, market, and solidarity – which would establish "a distinctive style of human connection that contributes to a scheme of collective self-government and resists the influence of social division and hierarchy" Unger (1983: 39).[7] Each of these rights and the proposals on which they rest aim to "remake social life in the image of liberal politics [while changing] the liberal conception and practice of politics" Unger (1983: 42).

Sixth, from Gramsci, West (1989: 231–320) calls for a historically concrete politics of resistance that is "grounded in . . . reflections upon local struggles, yet theoretically sensitive to structural dynamics and international phenomena" (p. 231). This requires a sensitivity to the relationship between socially constructed identities, theories of human agency, and "ever-changing forms of class- [and gender-] ridden economic modes of production" (p. 231). Seventh, the aim of philosophy is to become part of "a social movement by nourishing and being nourished by the philosophical views of oppressed people" (p. 231). The elitist, arrogant, self-privileging stance of the intellectual who leads the people is thus undercut (see A. Ross 1989, ch. 7) and is replaced by an involved, engaged political stance that works at the local levels of resistance. This approach becomes embedded in those already formed (or to be formed) situations in which protest, and resistance to subordination can be organized. For West, this points to prophetic religious practices in churches, synagogues, temples, and mosques (p. 234). The social movement led by Martin Luther King, Jr, represents "the best of what the political dimension of prophetic pragmatism is all about" (p. 234).

West's pragmatism transcends Rorty's liberal irony, for which propaganda and truth are the same and there can be no answer to the question "Why not be cruel?" For West there is an answer, and it is given at the existential level of self-understanding and self-identity that flow from the crises and traumas of life (p. 233). West's vision is anchored in the burning cultural and political issues of the everyday lives of ordinary people – issues such as religious and nationalistic (usually xenophobic) revivals, the declining power of trade unions, escalating racial and sexual violence, pervasive drug addiction and alcoholism, breakdowns in the nuclear family, the cultural and political impact of the mass media (TV, radio, videos), and exponential increase of suicides and homicides. (p. 222)

West's pragmatism, unlike Rorty's, leads to a vision of a "walking *nihilism* [among the black underclass] . . . and a reality *that one cannot not know*. The ragged edges of the Real, of *Necessity*, not being able to eat, not having shelter, not having health care, all this is something that one cannot know" (1988: 277; emphasis original).

His politically engaged pragmatism, like Mills's, returns to the media, the popular, and popular culture (Bebop, avant-garde black music, James Brown, Michael Jackson, rap, Run/DMC, the oral artistry of black ministers, black sports). He finds in these formations an Africanization of black culture which is resistant to the pressures of commodification. These texts also subversively fuse religion with the popular. The black athlete styles an immediate reality, turning it into a spectacle with roots in African pageantry which projects a particular, enlivened, masculine image of self (1988: 283).

West takes interactionism to the next level of development, which is a pragmatic theory of cultural criticism. But first, a brief discussion of art, politics, and experience.

An interactionist aesthetics of experience

Everyday life has become aestheticized and politicized.[8] As Huyssen (1984/90: 261) observes (and as argued in chapter 4), this is an age of commodity aesthetics; "Capital itself has taken the aesthetic straight into the commodity in the form of styling, advertising and packaging." A political aesthetics structures and mediates the individual's relationship (and the group's) to the popular and the everyday lifeworld. This aesthetic transcends traditional views of the artistic experience (e.g. those of Dewey and Rorty; see Becker 1982: 145–50). It calls for a cultural criticism based on a pragmatic political aesthetics of experience. Such a position assumes, with Barthes (1957/72) that the media are the main carriers of the popular, and that ideology follows the route of the popular (see also Ray 1985: 20). It follows Benjamin (1936/68), who argued that the age of mechanical reproduction had created a new set of aesthetic practices whereby the function of art was reversed; instead of being based on ritual, it was now based on the practice of politics. (He predicted that the "logical result of Fascism is the introduction of aesthetics into political life" (p. 243), although he held out hope for a revolutionary art that would raise the political consciousness of millions of spectators (Kellner 1989: 124.) We now understand that "culture today is a matter of media" (Jameson 1991: 68), just as we know that contemporary cultural practices carried by television, video, popular film, music, and literature structure the formations of power and meaning that define the struggles of "everyday life and common sense" (Grossberg 1988b: 177).

Toward an interactional aesthetics

An interactional, political aesthetics must begin with Benjamin and work back to Dewey, modifying both in the process. The relationship between art and experience has never been just aesthetic (see Eagleton 1990: 8). Art has always been cultural, political, and ideological. Highbrow, middlebrow, and lowbrow (popular) artistic forms have simply carried different ideological views of taste, the sublime, sensibility, the beautiful, and the good. Each art form has contributed to the reproduction of particular cultural experiences and cultural subjectivities. These forms have embodied, in varying ways (even when they have denied them), the epistemologies of realism, discourses on the body (Eagleton 1990: 13), the political values of the state, and the classical distinction between science, art, and morality. The production, distribution, evaluation, and consumption of art objects has always been a gendered, ethnic, class-based, economic activity. This has led to the traditional distinction between high and popular art forms, the arts of the elites and the arts of the masses.

The aesthetic experience

Recall Dewey's discussion of the aesthetic experience. Unlike ordinary experience, with its routine flow, the encounter with an art object produces a vivid, complex interactional experience which is emotional, cognitive, and capable of integrating the individual with the environment in new ways. This experience is rhythmic, expressive, and fulfilling; it has a sense of unity and completeness. It involves a form of surrender (Dewey 1939: 976). The self yields to the emotional experience of the art object; it incorporates this object and its meanings into ongoing experience.

The aesthetic experience is a form of emotionality. "*It, like emotion, is a lived, believed-in, situated, temporally embodied experience that radiates through a person's stream of consciousness, is felt and runs through the body, and in the process of being lived, plunges the person into a world that is wholly constituted by the emotional-aesthetic experience*" (Denzin 1984b: 66; emphasis original). This experience is produced when the person confronts a cultural object defined in emotional-aesthetic terms: for example, a popular song, a painting, a building, a film, a tool, a TV show.

This interaction with the cultural object is experienced politically. It is defined in terms of the culturally approved meanings surrounding the key values of work, the individual, family, and sexuality (see Barthes 1975). Every aesthetic experience is potentially a political experience wherein the politics of the act are displaced into the emotionality and the emotional meanings brought to the experience. It is obvious, for example, that the singing of the national anthem before all sporting events in America evokes feelings of patriotism and nationalism. Less obvious are the politics involved in watching a Saturday morning cartoon like "Garfield & Friends" or "Teenage Mutant Ninja Turtles" or Public Television shows like "This Old House," "Pro Wrestling," "Louisiana Cookin'," or a rerun of "Magnum, P.I." or "A Night at the Opera" at the local university center for the performing arts, or an evening of blues music and jazz at a local night club.

But in each of these seemingly culturally diverse experiences lies a politics of experience, an affective economy (Grossberg 1988b: 178), an ideology of interaction, and the production of a set of desires which define and help people make sense of themselves and their projects. *These experiences become political when the actions and emotions they express connect to the political economies of everyday life in ways which reinforce class, race, and gender stereotypes.* In the aesthetic experience turned political, the individual experiences heightened feelings of moral worth, often coded in masculine-feminine, in-group, out-group terms. Such moments produce feelings of in-group solidarity and out-group hostility. Conduct is directed to the salient political stereotypes of the culture, and an exaggerated sense of self-worth is experienced.[9]

The political aesthetics of the cultural experience is thus produced by specific cultural practices which interact and collide with one another. Within any community there will be diverse cultural practices and different popular sensibilities. These practices will be rooted in specific gender, age, ethnic, racial, religious, political, and intellectual communities. They will be connected to various genre traditions, which move from high art to the popular, and within these domains there will be subcommunities of specific social worlds (see Strauss 1984) attached to various art or performance styles and traditions (e.g. classical, pop, rock and roll, punk, rap, heavy metal, folk, country, feminist, black music; cult, mainstream, and art film, etc.). These forms and practices and the communities attached to them are constantly changing, opposing, "undercutting and reinflecting each other" (Grossberg 1988b: 179).

Confronting the aesthetic object

When a work of art enters an individual's or a group's field of experience, it is confronted by a preexisting set of cultural, personal, and political meanings. These meanings are woven into the individual or the group's taken-for-granted understandings of the world. They constitute the individual or the group's definition of the place and the meanings that aesthetic objects have in their world. These definitions transform the aesthetic object into a form of experience that passes through three stages. In the first stage the object is assessed and given an interpretation. In the second stage a determination is made concerning which aspects of the individual or group's situation the object pertains to. In the third stage, a set of actions toward the object-as-an-experience are undertaken.[10] These situated interactions (Morrione 1985) give the aesthetic object a career, for its meanings are spread out over time, passing through the above three stages of perception, definition, and interaction.

The object-as-experience thus becomes an ongoing process which is defined by interacting individuals. These meanings, as noted in chapter 5, may be incorporated into the group's ongoing flow of experience and become part of its collective vocabulary and memory. On the other hand, they may be judged to have no relevance to what the members do and hence be rejected. Or they may create a disjunctive response, in which case they come to exist alongside other meanings the group holds, but are not fully incorporated into its collective or individual self-definitions. This interpretation contrasts with the supportive response in which an experience is defined as supporting and reinforcing a preestablished way of life. Finally, the experience may be disruptive and call into question cherished group values (on such responses, fitted to the study of the industrializing process, see Blumer 1990: 88–97).

An interactionally grounded set of experiences surrounds the meanings that are brought to any new information technology and the aesthetic objects and experiences which that technology creates. These interactional experiences frame and define the meanings that are brought to the aesthetic object. These definitions neutralize and reshape the meanings already coded into the aesthetic object by its producers. They reshape these objects in accordance with the group's ongoing definitions of its situation. Thus the meanings of an aesthetic object are always political, for its point of entry into a group is always a locus of struggle and definition.[11]

The politics of the popular, as interactionally interpreted, thus defines the aesthetic experience. That experience, in turn, further defines the political dimensions of art and the popular. In this way the personal becomes political, and the political personal. Art and the popular are no longer based on ritual; they are infused, through and through, by the practices of politics. Benjamin's predictions concerning the aestheticization of reality have come true; the political defines the aesthetic. Late capitalism "swallows virtually every resistance and opposition, requiring dissent to find unconventional, even nondiscursive forms" (Agger 1990: 204) of expression. Interactional aesthetic theory must now become political, in the ways suggested by West.

A pragmatic, interactionist cultural criticism

Dewey argued that the "moral prophets of humanity have always been the poets." Habermas (1985, 1987) argues for a political aesthetics of the artistic experience grounded in the modernist project of the Enlightenment and in the art forms which represent the "edifice of European art." Rorty (1989) calls for a liberal utopia in which artists and novelists take the lead in producing cultural works which contribute to the reduction of cruelty in everyday life and an increase in sensitivity to the problems of others.

Dewey, Habermas, and Rorty each propose a theory of aesthetics with political consequences. Each values the freedoms of discourse that define postliberal democracies. Yet each theory presumes a highbrow, lowbrow view of art and politics; high art, or authentic art, best embodies the cultural values of the democratic society. There are basic flaws in these models which need to be addressed.

Popular culture, not high art, carries the dominant cultural meanings in any historical moment. Works of popular culture must be valued and studied for the systems of cultural difference they embody. Prior aesthetic theory (Dewey, Habermas, and Rorty) has devalued the popular. There are also conservative implications in these theories (despite their approving nods in the directions of minority artists). The high cultural art experience they value embodies the very cultural, gender, and racial stereotypes that a postmodern, multicultural, ethnically diverse society must overcome. Cultural theory is sorely in need of a political aesthetics which values the popular as the main carrier of cultural values.

Reading the popular

Pragmatic cultural criticism today would build on, but diverge from, the work of Dewey, Blumer, Mills, the Frankfurt school, Habermas, and Rorty. It would begin by modifying Dewey's assertion about the poets and argue that the "moral prophets of 20th century America have been the film- and video-makers" (see also Jameson 1991: 68). With Sklar (1975: 3) it would argue that "for the first half of the twentieth century – from 1896–1946, to be exact – movies were the most popular and influential medium of culture in the United States." With the advent of commercial, network television (1946–8; see Monaco 1981: 503), the cultural impact of film would shift to this new video form.

Producing the cinematic, dramaturgical society

Film and television transformed American society into a video, visual culture. Representations of the real soon became stand-ins for actual, lived experience. America, Baudrillard (1987/8) argues, knows itself through cinema and the reflections of itself that the television and film camera project back on theater and home TV screens. Three implications follow from the cinematization of American society.

First, reality has become a staged, social production. Second, the real is judged against its staged, cinematic or video counterpart. Third, the metaphor of a dramaturgical society (Lyman 1990b: 221) or "life as theater" (Brissett and Edgley (eds) 1990: 2; Goffman 1959: 254–5) has now become an interactional reality. It is no longer necessary to restrict "the language and mask of the stage" (Goffman 1959: 254) to theatrical performances. The theatrical aspects of the dramaturgical metaphor have not only "creeped into everyday life" (p. 254); they have taken it over. Art not only mirrors life; it structures and reproduces it.

Unravelling the dramaturgical

A transactional, existential aesthetics (Kariel 1989: 26–43) which un-ravels the dramaturgical themes of contemporary cultural life is called for. Such an aesthetics would value the playful dimensions of culture. It would criticize those cultural rituals, beliefs, canons, and social institu-tions which oppressively center human experience within an oppressive, dramaturgical instrumentality that "derealizes familiar objects, social roles, and institutions to such a degree that the so-called realistic representations can no longer evoke reality except as nostalgia or mockery" (Lyotard 1979/84: 74; also quoted by Kariel 1989: 96).

This aesthetic perspective values those artistic and cultural productions which shock, mock, challenge, and ridicule the everyday (e.g. Christo's productions and Chaplin's films). It values those productions which reflexively reframe and challenge the mass culture's uses of the cinematic, video, and narrative codes of realism (e.g. the photography of Barbara Kruger, Sherrie Levine, and Richard Prince and the films of the Marx Brothers). It finds pleasure in texts which interrogate the dramaturgical urges of contemporary life (e.g. Beckett's plays), and challenge the accuracy of the cinematic eye (e.g. Hitchcock's *Rear Window* and *Vertigo* and Antonioni's *Blow-Up*).

Existential texts (see below) which bring human beings to the edge of hard, moral, political choices are valued. Artworks which engage the politics of freedom and choice and illuminate the terrors that are produced by specific political regimes are sought (e.g. *Salvador* and *Z*). Involved, committed, political art avoids a melodramatic, social realism that celebrates one political system over another (e.g. the noble worker). Sartre (1974: 14) expresses this commitment thus: "If literature is not everything, it is worth nothing. This is what I mean by 'commitment'. It wilts if it is reduced to innocence, or to songs. If a written sentence does not reverberate at every level of man and society, then it makes no sense."

This existential aesthetic perspective would read the popular and popular culture as diverse terrains which contain multiple, contradictory, and complex positions. It would call for the systematic study of all forms of the popular and would not dismiss in advance any cultural artifact. It would view the cultural as a contested landscape, rather "than a field of one-dimensional manipulation and illusion" (Kellner 1989: 141). It would see popular films as places where cultural dreams and nightmares are played out (e.g. *Blue Velvet*). It would examine particular films as instances of utopian thought (e.g. *Field of Dreams*) which reaffirm deeply held cultural values. It would study the most popular of the popular (e.g. the top box office and rental films) for what these texts say about the current generation and its fears, hopes, and aspirations. It would study the cult films (*Rocky Horror Picture Show*) and the flops for the meanings that circulate on the fringes of the popular. In the same vein, it would examine experimental, feminist, gay, African-American, Spanish-American, Asian, native American, Third World, and international cinema for its treatment of the "other" and of minority and marginal group experience.

Such a cultural studies would be critical, as Blumer, Mills, and the Frankfurt school were. Its critical stance, however, would be one that values difference and chaos. It would be one that sees popular culture as a place where a cultural politics of community can be formed. It would examine how the New Right sought, established, and now attempts to maintain control over the popular (Grossberg 1988a: 11). In particular, it would examine how family, work, and sexuality are configured within popular cinema, literature, and television. It would see these textual locations as the places where struggles over family, sexuality, and the individual are now occurring.

After Hall

Modifying Stuart Hall (1988a), such a program would build on the interactionist tradition of studying the interrelationships between the powerful and the underclass and the underdog. It would examine how the New Right, throughout the 1970s and the 1980s, attempted to undo the radical civil and human rights impulses of the late 1960s. These decades were characterized by a new anti-statism, vigorous law-and-order rhetorics, "Just Say No" drug programs, romantic nostalgia for the past, an authoritarian populism, and the rise in popularity of teleministry. The emphasis on a new politics of health and morality focused debates "around abortion, child abuse, sex education, gay rights and AIDs" (Hall 1988a; 282), family violence, alcoholism, and drug abuse. The New Right seized control of American popular culture by centering discourse on the family, the body, sexuality, desire and a patriotic individuality that made the military a new employment possibility for the underclass.

The Right, through "a series of ideological, religious, philosophical, political and juridical polemics" (Hall 1988a: 146), maintained its control over American society. It generated and participated in a series of economic and political crises (the crash of Wall Street, the Panama drug scandal, the Savings and Loan crisis, Grenada, the Middle East). These crises shifted attention away from civil and human rights and made patriotism the most important identity an American could have. At the same time, the underclass, the homeless, and drug addicts were defined as morally unworthy persons who were out of work because they chose to be.

Like Thatcherism, Reaganism (and now Bushism) played on common sense and ordinary American values. It did this by creating multiple fields of discourse wherein these common values were celebrated. In the field of education, "it has made itself the guardian of the 'return to standards' and [the] authority in the classroom" (Hall 1988a: 144). Here, as Hall noted, it helped create the figure of the worried parent "facing the harsh realities of a competitive world . . . aiming to secure . . . an education that will help his or her children to 'get on and compete'" (p. 144). The New Right's attacks on the liberals and their proposals to teach the literatures of racial and ethnic minorities were thus justified, because these "radical" individuals were undermining the patriotic agenda of the American school system. Hard work and family once again became central cultural values. Women who worked outside the home were frowned upon because they were letting their children down. The house-wife was defined as the moral center of American society. Abortion was defined as a crime against nature. The American woman was no longer safe on the streets of America. If she was a college student, she was under constant threat of being raped or mugged by a minority group member or an irresponsible "wealthy" white male.

In the area of crime, a series of moral panics were produced. These panics centered around minority youth gang members addicted to or dealing in crack and using guns randomly in the large cities to kill upright, white citizens. Delinquent teenagers who disrupted schools were attacked in popular films (e.g. *Stand and Deliver* and *Lean On Me*). Black rapists of white women were perceived as being on the loose, especially in New York City.

The welfare system was also attacked. The "spendthrift" state was scrutinized. The idea of "recklessly" giving money away to the needy was mocked and seen as an act which depleted the wealth of the nation (Hall 1988a: 144). The welfare system undermined self-confidence and perpe-tuated poverty. The welfare mother who drove a Cadillac was singled out as an example of the abuses this system produced. The plight of the ordinary man who worked to support his family was contrasted with the situation of the morally unfit black male who sold drugs. Here, as Hall notes, the "Protestant Ethic makes a late return" (p. 145). A new cultural racism united all the above moral panics under a single term, the non-white male who was a threat to the core values of American society.

In each case, the above moral panics took the shape of cultural texts. These texts attempted to capture the crisis in question, represent it through the media, and show how the New Right was containing such threats to the traditional order. These texts took many forms: front-page stories in local and national newspapers and weekly magazines, TV docudramas, sit coms and soap operas, popular films, New Age music, editorials in the *National Review*, and so on. Each of these textual formations can be undone through critical analysis, as Hall has done for Great Britain under Thatcher. They can be analyzed in terms of the stereotypes they reproduce, the simplistic solutions they propose, and their unyielding commitment to a law-and-order rhetoric.

The stories Chuck Norris tells

Consider again that textual figure called Chuck Norris. Remember his ACOA story, his resentments toward his father and his attempts to explain his problems in his autobiography. His life story, enacted by his screen persona, itself a textual production, is very much anchored in the politics of the New Right and the moral panics that defined the Right's relation to American culture throughout the 1980s. The titles and content of his films clearly reveal this relationship between Norris's cultural politics and the politics of the Right: *Force of One* (1979), *Good Guys Wear Black* (1979), *Eye for an Eye* (1981), *Slaughter in San Francisco* (1981), *Silent Rage* (1982), *Missing in Action, I and II*, and *Braddock: Missing in Action III* (1984, 1984, 1988), *Lone Wolf McQuade* (1983), *Code of Silence* (1985), *Delta Force* (1986), *Invasion U.S.A.* (1985), and *Fire Walker* (1986).

In these films Norris, like Sylvester Stallone, Clint Eastwood, and Charles Bronson, played on such themes as a worldwide communist conspiracy associated with terrorism (*Invasion U.S.A.*), pro-Vietnam military fantasies concerning veterans who return to Vietnam to free American POWs (the *Missing in Action* series) or strong heroes who took stands against the drug wars, underclass violence toward the police, and violence toward middle-class American women (*Lone Wolf McQuade*, *Delta Force*, and *Code of Silence*). These films represented a "curious mixture of anti-authoritarian individualism and extremely conservative law and order moralism that characterizes the populist American male"

(Ryan and Kellner 1988: 227). Norris and Canon Films made a cottage industry out of right-wing hero movies in the 1980s (Ryan and Kellner 1988: 227). These hero films fuelled the conservatism of the 1980s, amplified the moral panics of the decade, and contributed to a survivalist mentality that underwrote the Social Darwinism of the decade.

But this violent hero has a soft underside. In the *People Weekly* story about him, Norris emerges as a compassionate, feeling human being. Norris the man is a man filled with fears and plagued by physical and psychological insecurities that stayed with him until he learned martial arts. He overcame his character defects by becoming violent. Having learned to protect himself with his fists (and his feet), he could then enter those mean American streets and Viet Cong jungles where evil lurked. By saving himself, he saved America. Norris thus inscribed a form of masculinity that justified violence toward others as a means of saving oneself. He showed American youth how to return to that past which Ronald Reagan found so appealing. Here men were men, women were women, and real men protected their women.

Interventionist readings, like those of Hall (and this reading of the Norris films), buttressed by in-depth interactionist studies of the social worlds of the underclass, point in the direction of a politically engaged interactionism. I turn now to the tasks of such a program, finding its origins in the existentialism of Sartre and Merleau-Ponty.

Existential criticism

Sartre (1976) and Merleau-Ponty (1973) sought an existential Marxism. Asking always how humans are shaped by history, they each continued Marx's project of doing a phenomenology of life under capitalism. Their perspectives criticized the terrorism and inhumanity produced by democracy and communism. For each, the ideological formations of a given society are produced by a particular type of economic praxis that interweaves economy and ideology into the totality of lived history. A society is embedded in its methods of production. Its science, art, religion, and philosophical schemes are all extensions of this economic mode of production. The spirit of a society is transmitted and perceived through the cultural objects that it presents to its members. The bourgeois ideologies that contaminate all capitalist society prop up a world that is lived by human beings who seek their realization through alienation, the fetishism of goods, and the logics of experience that capitalism affords them.

The philosophers' tasks were clear: to offer a philosophical anthropology and an existential ethics that would permit human beings to seize their own history. Such an existentialism would not seek recourse in abstract principles. It would be committed to the fundamental belief that all action is political. Art, sociology, anthropology, and philosophy are charged with a political agenda: to present the human being as an agent of history, who "produces and plays his drama while he lives the contradictions of his situation, until either his individuality is shattered or his conflicts are resolved" (Sartre 1974: 11). Art and science become existential and political. The essential absurdity of the world is recognized (Lyman and Scott 1989: 2), but it is understood that humans create and give meaning to this world through their epiphanic, existential acts (see Douglas and Johnson (eds) 1977: vii; Kotarba and Fontana (eds) 1984, ch. 1 and 11; also Brown 1989: 150–1).

The tasks of critical, interaction theory

According to Habermas, the work of the Frankfurt school until the early 1940s was "essentially dominated by six themes" (1987: 378). These research interests focused on (1) the forms of integration in postliberal societies, (2) family socialization and ego development, (3) the mass media and mass culture, (4) the social psychology behind the demise of social and political protest, (5) the theory of art, and (6) the critique of positivism and science (pp. 378–9).

These six tasks, or areas of research and theorizing, establish a framework for a critical, existential cultural studies agenda (see also Fraser 1989, ch. 7 and 8). They reflect issues taken up in earlier chapters, especially chapters 5 and 6. They have, in their various forms been anticipated (and criticized) by Hall and West (see also Fraser 1989, ch. 7). I borrow and rework them for interactionist purposes.

The postliberal societies

With the exception of Mills, few interactionists have taken up the problems facing either liberalism, late capitalism, or national socialism. A theory of the state and state bureaucracy is lacking in interactionist political sociology (but see Couch 1984a, 1990; Lyman and Vidich 1988; Lyman 1990b; P. M. Hall 1985). While the cultural logics of late capitalism have been analyzed in earlier chapters (2–5), many issues remain. These include the decline of reason and rationality in post-modern societies, the increased colonization of the everyday lifeworld by the mass media, a sprawling, gender-based social welfare system committed to the logics of an illiberal practicality (Mills 1959: 95), and the constant production of moral panics and moral crises which divert attention from the basic agenda of a liberal democracy (Kroker *et al.* 1990: 446). This new form of liberalism works alongside the older, practical liberalism which was concerned with the maintenance of the political status quo. Classic liberalism is no longer concerned with radical social reform; it administers the welfare state (Mills 1959: 92). The new illiberal practicality is well-suited to conservative regimes in which there is little concern with "the battered human beings living at the bottom of society" (p. 95).

It has served to perpetuate a basic institutional framework characterized by the following: an economic division of labor organized for private profit rather than human need; a gender-based division of labor "that separates privatized childrearing from recognized and remunerated work"; gender and race-segmented "paid labor markets that generate a marginalized underclass"; and a world political economy and system of nation-states that "engage in crisis management in the form of segmented social welfare concessions and subsidized war production" (Fraser 1989: 107).

The family

The postmodern family is not the old socializing agent of the immediate post-Second World War years, in which children were cared for by two parents within an "idealized" protective and emotionally secure environment. This is no longer the American norm. The postmodern family is a single-parent family headed by a teenage mother, who may be drawn to drug and alcohol abuse. She and her children live in a household that is prone to violence. In addition, increasing numbers of children are now cared for by someone other than a parent. The day-care center has become a key factor in contemporary child development. In the home the presence of the television set cannot be discounted. It is from television that children learn the cultural myths of today. The postmodern child is cared for by the television set and the day-care center.

How these new structural and interactional environments affect the emergence of the self, the patterning of lived experiences, and the development of moral values and commitments to key cultural myths requires intensive study (see Leavitt and Power 1989). The family, in its traditional forms, as well as traditional formulations thereof (see Cheal 1991) is no longer present. This means that conventional concerns with the Oedipus complex and the ego–id–superego model (Habermas 1987; 386, 389), and the family's functions in society (Parsons) may no longer be relevant. In their place must emerge a more fractured, postmodern image of individuality, family, intimacy, and love. At the same time, how the media (below) perpetuate certain cultural, Oedipal myths about the family and its formations needs to be studied.

Mass media and mass culture

The mass media, as argued earlier, have erased the traditional boundaries between the private and the public. They completely permeate and dominate the languages and experiences of everyday life.[12] A variety of questions are raised by this situation. How do the media work within the private settings of the postmodern culture? How do they inform everyday talk? How do they shape and mold fantasies? How are their effects mediated by interacting individuals? (Davis 1990). How do the various forms of the popular which are carried by the mass media challenge dominant and marginal cultural values, and how are these challenges defined and institutionalized (e.g. the movie code, the new rating system for rock music, etc.)? How are the ideological messages of the media met and interpreted by various audiences?[13] What myths and mythical systems do the media reproduce? What epistemological logics, including simulational realism, do they employ? What is truth within a given media message?

Protest

A variety of emancipatory, resistance, and withdrawal protest publics and movements (Habermas 1987: 393) now struggle to redefine such issues as quality of life, human rights, peace, the environment, nuclear power plants, atomic waste, genetic engineering, "the storage and central utilization of private data" (p. 394; see also Lyman and Vidich 1988: 107–8), religious fundamentalism, minority group status (the elderly, gays, the handicapped, women,[14] African Americans, etc.), mental health, the violent, the incestuous family, drug and alcohol addiction, welfare, housing, work, taxes, and neighborhoods.

These protests occur along the "seams," to use Habermas's word, between the everyday lifeworld and the larger culture, or the private and the public spheres. They indicate that all is not alive and well in the private sphere. They show how special lifeworld interests have now become levers for changing the public order. These protests merge private troubles with public issues.

Art

The institution of modern art, in Habermas's (1981/3) version of art history, has moved through three key historical phases. In the Renaissance, art was part of the sacred. In the eighteenth century, "the fine arts and music were institutionalized as activities independent from sacred, courtly life" (1981/3: 10). Around "the middle of the nineteenth century an aestheticist conception of art emerged, which encouraged the artist to produce his work according to the distinct consciousness of art for art's sake" (p. 10). Art was alienated from life and ceased to perform its prior function (along with science and religion) as a major integrating institution in society. Subsequent modernist movements (surrealism, expressionism, dadaism, etc.) continued this split. They furthered the erosion of the cultural aesthetic sphere as a carrier of expressive, moral, community values.

A rational society, Habermas argues, needs the cultural tradition which the arts previously provided. But all is not lost. Contemporary bourgeois art has taught laypersons how to enjoy art, how to become educated on artistic matters, and how to become intelligent consumers of art objects (1981/3: 12). In this way laypersons are able to take over expert knowledge and learn how to put art to use in their everyday lives. Habermas values only certain art forms, in particular those which either represent the "edifice of European art" (p. 13) or those of the post-avant-garde with tendencies toward "realism and engagement with . . . authentic continuations of classic modern art" (1987: 398).

Habermas thus proposes a political aesthetics of the artistic experience which is grounded in the modernist project. His proposal opens the door for cultural criticisms of those art forms that do not conform to his version of the canon. It continues the line of analysis started by the Frankfurt school in the 1940s and shows dangerous parallels with the Dewey–Blumer statements in the 1930s. The existentially committed, political art that Sartre valued thus replaces Habermas's conservative aesthetic agenda.

The critique of positivism and science

The Critical Theory critique of positivism and science is by now well known. In many respects it anticipated the interpretive, postmodern move in anthropological theory (Geertz 1973, 1988; also Sartre 1963). It also has many similarities with the interactionist and feminist views of science (see also Smith 1987). Facts and values cannot be separated. Science must be dialectical and critical; it cannot be indifferent to the world of men and women. Science is based on a faith in reason and rationality which is no longer warranted.

Race and gender

As discussed above, race and gender must be added to the Frankfurt school's list of themes. An interactionist cultural politics is formed around the issues of cultural racism and sexism, the politics of the postliberal societies, the family, the media, social protest, art and the aesthetic experience, and the ongoing critique of positivism. It inter-rogates each of these issues at the three levels outlined in chapter 5: namely, at the level of the production, distribution, consumption, and exchange of cultural objects connected with each site; the textual analyses of the systems of discourse that contain these objects; and the connection of lived experiences to these sites. In each instance the emphasis on the epiphanic moment is maintained as the investigator attempts to connect personal troubles with public issues and their institutional transformations.

Critical, existential interactionism: why the merger with critical theory?

There are several reasons for joining interaction research with the items on this agenda, not least the long overdue reunion between Critical Theory, existentialism, and symbolic interactionism (see Novack 1975, ch. 14 and 16, on the relations between Marxism and pragmatism). Such a merger also has the virtue of moving interaction studies more directly into the fields of communications and media studies, as well as into studies of the popular and cultural racism and sexism. Of equal importance, this marriage, which also includes existentialism, elevates the political and the study of power to its rightfully central place in the interactionist tradition. In so doing, it addresses the problems of history and political economy which interactionists have always been weak on.[15] At the same time, it allows interactionists to reclaim from Habermas (and the Critical tradition) not only a critical pragmatism, but G. H. Mead as well.[16] It also allows interactionists to take back the interactionist perspective that this tradition has attempted to appropriate for its structural-functional purposes. Finally, this merger makes explicit the critical edge and the cultural criticism tradition that has always been implicit in interactionism. Hence critical interactionism (the joining of Critical Theory and existentialism with symbolic interactionism) would merge the gender interests of feminist theory with the class interests of classical Marxism, while openly embracing prophetic pragmatism's commitment to an empowering democracy.[17]

Toward an engaged political pragmatism

A politically self-conscious interactionist cultural studies program would organize itself around these thematic structural issues. They define the forms and types of individualities that are now being produced in the United States in the waning years of the twentieth century. This program would draw upon American pragmatism, but not on the consensualist pragmatism of the Chicago school. This must not be a consensualist, cultural relativism which is nihilistic, conservative, or politically naive.[18] However, as Downing (1987: 67) observes, there is a danger in such a pragmatic project, "since there is no firm vantage point from which theory might conduct its own critique; what emerges is a species of cultural relativism which in practice amounts to a dangerous political conservatism." It can be argued, for example, that Rorty's philosophy of "liberal consensus" results in an uncritical acceptance of the status quo (Downing 1987: 67; Norris 1985: 15).

A privileged criticism?

How can a pragmatic position privilege any critique?[19] A provisional answer lies in Foucault's (1980: 117) subversive genealogy "which is a form of history which can account for the constitution of knowledges and discourses and domains of objects." This genealogy refuses to accept those systems of discourse (economic, political, scientific, religious, or narrative) which "ignore who we are collectively and individually" (Racevskis 1983: 20) while attempting to determine who we are within specific sites of discourse and power. Foucault's project does not reject reason, but rather aligns reason with an unmasking process that seeks to "liberate us both from the state and from the type of individualization which is linked to the state. We have to promote new forms of subjectivity through the refusal of this kind of individuality which has been imposed on us for several centuries" (Foucault 1982: 216).

A pragmatic cultural studies project seeks its external grounding, such as it is, in a commitment to a post-Marxism with hope, but no guarantees (S. Hall 1986c: 58).[20] Such a project, borrowing its theme from West's prophetic pragmatism, understands that "human beings are perhaps more spoken by the forces of language than they are independent users of linguistic tools" (Downing 1987: 80). A revised pragmatic analysis situates language and its use within Foucault's "concern for the operations of power and systems of discourse" (Downing 1987: 80). It adopts Althusser's (1971: 21) view that "words are the site of an ambiguity, the stake of a decisive but undecided battle." It attempts to unravel how words, texts, and their meanings play a pivotal part in those critical "performances of race, class, and gender relations as they shape the emergent political conditions that we refer to as the postmodern world" (Downing 1987: 80).

An oppositional cultural aesthetic

An oppositional cultural aesthetic, based on the pragmatic tradition, can now be proposed. It has already been anticipated. Every cultural text carries multiple meanings which operate at several levels (the surface, the visual, the auditory, the written word, etc.). Within any cultural text at least three hypothetical positions, or codes, can be identified; what Stuart Hall (1980b: 136), calls the dominant, or hegemonic, the negotiated, and the oppositional. The dominant code carries the weight of cultural legitimacy. It "appears coterminous with what is 'natural', or 'inevitable', 'taken for granted about the social order'" (p. 137). Here history merges with its telling. The negotiated code accepts the dominant code at an abstract level, but at a restricted, "situated level it makes its own ground rules" (p. 137). This code is often filled with contradictions. (In the abstract a man may be opposed to striking women; but he may have specific reasons for liking *Blue Velvet,* a film which shows violence toward women.) In the oppositional code the message is "retotalized within some alternative framework" (p. 138). Hall observes that "One of the most significant political moments . . . is the point when events which are normally signified and decoded in a negotiated way begin to be given an oppositional reading. Here 'the politics of signification' – the struggle in discourse – is joined" (p. 138).

An oppositional cultural aesthetic aims to always subvert the meanings of a text, to show how its dominant and negotiated meanings can be opposed. It presumes that such readings can expose the ideological and political meanings that circulate within the text, particularly those which hide or displace racial, class, ethnic and gender biases. Such readings, as outlined in earlier chapters, analyze how texts address the problems of presence, lived experience, the real and its representations, and the issues of subjects, authors, and their intentionalities. In the unhinging of a text there is an attempt to illuminate the dominant code and its workings. Such readings then show how the mythologies of the culture work their way into the popular and the artistic expressions that cultural members appear to value (Barthes 1957/72).

The oppositional reading frees up the text so as to allow the reader to find alternative meanings heretofore hidden. Alternative readings create the spaces for a public voice (Agger 1990: 213–19) which seeks to engage the politics of liberation that have always defined the liberal democracies. In such work interactionism returns to its beginnings, where its early practitioners routinely wrote about and addressed the problems of a democratic society.

Notes

1 These lines have been approvingly quoted by such interactionists as Joas (1987: 111) and Perinbanayagam (1985: xvi), who also places Mead at the end of this road ("I may add that in my view, the one who has been furthest along this road is the redoubtable figure G. H. Mead").

2 He resists the temptation (e.g. the Bloom–Hirsch project) to create an approved cultural reading list (for an example of such lists, see Searle 1990); but he does make a distinction (p. 143) between the stimulating (the classics; e.g. *King Lear*) and the relaxing (the popular; e.g. *Murder on the Orient Express, Thunderball*). Later (pp. 141–2) he distinguishes between books which help us to become more autonomous and those that help us to become less cruel. In the end, he has his own approved reading list.

3 Mills (1943/63: 167) anticipated these problems with pragmatism, noting that, "in lesser hands than Dewey's many things may happen."

4 These include its revolutionary beginning in combination with a slave-based economy; an elastic liberal rule of law combined with an entrenched,

business-dominated status quo; a hybrid culture combining a moralistic impulse with a desire for collective self-definition and community and an obsession with mobility and wealth; and an impatience with abstract philosophies and theories, alongside "ingenious technological innovation [and] political strategies of compromise" (West 1989: 5).

5 In this section I draw from Roberto Unger's (1983, 1987) critical legal studies project which proposes a radical re-doing of American constitutional law and economic theory.

6 This proposal calls for an increase in the spaces now occupied by labor unions, EAP programs, institutionalized self-help groups, and environmental, welfare, minority group, human rights, peace, gay and lesbian, and women's programs.

7 Immunity rights protect individuals against the state, other organizations, and other individuals Unger (1983: 39); destabilization rights allow citizens to disrupt established institutions; market rights entitle individuals and groups to part of the collective capital of the society; and solidarity rights entitle persons to a communal life that has not been constructed by the state.

8 Park saw this in 1940 in his discussion of the news. "The extent to which news circulates, within a political unit, or a political society, determines the extent to which the members of a society may be said to participate, not in its collective life . . . but in its political acts" (1940/67: 42). He elaborates thus: "Politics is present history . . . News . . . [which] . . . is neither history nor politics . . . is . . . the stuff which makes political action possible" (pp.42–3).

9 Country and western music provides an apt example. Lines and titles like "Up against the Wall, Redneck Motherfucker" are intended to create such feelings.

10 Consider a family deciding which movie to go see on a Saturday night. They collectively examine the movie listing in the local newspaper and pick a film which all members agree upon. They then set a time to go to the movie, checking the times it is playing. They then go to the theater, see the movie, and afterward discuss its meanings for them, individually and collectively.

11 Compare here the meanings recently brought to rock and roll music, especially heavy metal, where national organizations of parents have sought to ban certain songs (and the groups that write and sing them), claiming that they incite listeners to violence, while the producers of the music and their youthful listeners make no such claims. (On these and related issues, see Kotarba 1991 and Grossberg 1988a: 49–60).

12 The VCR, which turns every TV set into a movie screen, now permits the private consumption of movies as cultural commodities in ways which were previously not possible.

13 Habermas (1987: 391) dismisses each of these questions, arguing that the media do not present a single, ideological perspective, that their messages are often missed, that they do not reflect the standards of mass culture, and that the professional codes of journalism require that they do their work without distortion. His position is based on the weakest of evidence and flies in the face of a large counter-literature that points to how the news and the media reflect certain dominant class and ideological interests (see Jansen 1988).

14 Fraser (1989: 114) notes that Habermas does not deal with gender in the *Theory of Communicative Action*, except to make note of the women's movement.

15 Novack (1975: 278) observes that Marxism "is the militant ideology of the revolutionary working class . . . [and] Pragmatism is the conciliatory philosophical instrument of the middle classes." Perhaps so. But then Marxism, with its emphasis on class, has been noticeably silent on gender (see MacKinnon 1983), as was existentialism until Simone de Beauvoir.

16 Habermas's Mead (1987: 3–46, 92–111), after many twists and turns around Wittgenstein, Durkheim, and Parsons, is finally fitted to Freud and Piaget (p. 389) and an analytic, object relations, cognitive, and sociomoral developmental model. For a far better merger of Durkheim and Mead, see Wiley (1989), and for another, pivotal reading of Mead see Joas (1985). On Habermas's weaknesses, see also Joas 1987: 110–11.

17 For a discussion of Robert Park's attempts in this direction, see Joas 1987: 100–1.

18 J. W. Carey (1989: 46) openly addresses these problems, which he calls, after Geertz (1973: 194), "Mannheim's Paradox," asking how sociology is to deal with the distrust of reason, while recognizing that no writer is free of ideology or in a privileged position which permits escape from this dilemma. He contends that "Cultural studies does not, however, escape Mannheim's paradox; it embraces it" (p. 56). Noting, like Barthes (1957/72: 145–55), that right-wing scholarship has an ideology, but no method for its analysis, and that the Left "has a dozen different analyses of ideology; it just does not have an ideology – in the sense of a plan for political action" (p. 102), he argues for a cultural studies that evaluates and critiques its own moral and political commitments (p. 104), while refusing to reduce culture to ideology (p. 109), resisting an Althusserian determinism (p. 106) and the positivism of the behavioral sciences, and maintaining a commitment to an interpretive, interactionism (p. 96), which is sympathetic to the neo–Marxist (p. 99) project which centers "the mass media as a *site* on which to engage the general question of social theory . . . [for] it is through communication, through the intergraded relations of symbols and social structure, that societies . . . are created, maintained and transformed" (p. 110).

19 This, of course, is the problem Habermas (1985) confronts when he attacks Lyotard, Baudrillard, and Foucault. His solution, which is unacceptable, lies within a universal pragmatics grounded in a "modernist" theorizing project.

20 In making this statement, I reject the transcendental, totalizing, scientific claims of certain Marxisms and adopt, instead, the humanizing, interpretive Marxism of Merleau-Ponty (1964, 1969) and Sartre (1976); see also Agger 1989.

7 INTO POLITICS

If I may be permitted to look at the crystal ball, I would see in it for the next twenty-five years of symbolic interaction theory an accelerated development of research techniques on the one hand, and a coalescing of most of the separate subtheories under consideration in this paper on the other.

(Kuhn 1964a/72: 72)

Symbolic interactionism has gotten now very much under your skin.
(Variation on Robert Oppenheimer[1] as quoted by Saxton 1989: 9)

We are practical beings each with limitations and duties to perform. Each is bound to feel intensely the importance of duties and the significance of the situations that call these forth. But this feeling in each of us is a vital secret for sympathy with which we vainly look to others. The others are too much absorbed in their own vital secrets to take an interest in ours.
(William James, "A Certain Blindness in Human Beings," 1898, quoted by Park 1934/50: 66)[2]

It has been nearly 30 years since Manford Kuhn, in his presidential address to the Midwest Sociological Society, presented what has become a classic reading[3] of symbolic interactionist texts. The chapters in this book have been written in the spirit of Kuhn's critique.[4] *Throughout, I have wrestled with two problems: how to make interpretive sense of this shifting theoretical paradigm called symbolic interactionism and how to recast this framework into a critical cultural studies program for the human disciplines.* I have constantly looked into a crystal ball, as Kuhn did, while attempting to project a future for symbolic interactionist thought.

Symbolic interactionism is very much under my skin, as it was for Kuhn. In this chapter I hope to show why this is the case. I will do this by briefly summarizing my arguments to this point. I will then return to Kuhn's address and locate it, along with subsequent interactionist work, within the modernist tradition in science. I will evaluate that work from a postmodernist position (as outlined in earlier chapters). By way of conclusion I will propose a research agenda for interactionism in the next 25 years. This will bring me back to the quote from William James on a "Certain Blindness in Human Beings."

Reading the past

I have read interactionist work through the lens of a critical, poststructural perspective, arguing that symbolic interactionists are cultural romantics. They write in praise of little people, deviants, and outsiders, seeing in these social types heroes and heroines who have taken a stance against the oppressive powers of a cruel society. Never embracing a totalizing theory of society, like Marxism or functionalism, interactionists believe in the contingency of self and society and see reality as something that can be changed and transformed through well-intended, humanistic, Promethean human effort. This romantic, tragic, ironic, romantic view of the self and its societies stands in a direct line with the works of Emerson, Thoreau, Marx, James, Dewey, Hook, Trilling, Du Bois, Niebuhr, Mills, Gramsci, Foucault, Unger, Sartre, Merleau-Ponty, and Martin Luther King, Jr.

Interactionist works have always been organized around the various forms that this romantic view can take. In each historical phase – that of the canon (1890–1932), of empirical/theoretical developments (1933–50), the transition to new texts (1951–62), criticism and ferment (1963–70), ethnography (1971–80), and diversity and new theory (1981–90) – interactionist texts articulated a social and political ideology that was sympathetic to the plight of America's minorities and their social problems. These texts expressed a humanistic, scientific perspective that insisted on the separation of facts from values. Haunted always by the individual and his or her subjective experiences, interactionists wanted a social science that made a difference, but a difference grounded in very specific terms. While siding always with the underclass, interactionists try not to let their personal sympathies get in the way of moral and political progress.

Their personal sympathies were divided. They valued democracy and the moral reforms that capitalism was producing, but they abhorred revolutions and violence. Hence help for the underclass could come only through changes made from within American society, in particular changes in the family, the school, and the mass media as educators of the masses. In this they were conservative, cultural romantics.

From 1890 through the 1933–50 period, classic interactionist texts were organized and shaped by the following systems of discourse: (1) Darwinian evolutionary theory and the emergence of functional psychology as an alternative to structuralism, psychoanalysis, and behaviorism,[5] (2) the liberal theory of the democratic state, with its divisions between public and private life, including the concept of a mass society defined and informed by the mass media; (3) Marxism, socialism, the international labor movement, and pragmatism as an alternative to Marxism; (4) the mediating relationship between science, technology, and capitalism and the American university as the place where these forces came together, including the social sciences as major information-gatherers for the capitalist society; (5) mass movements of Europeans and African-Americans into the major American cities, producing new social problems for the democratic society; (6) a cultural morality with links to Victorianism, traditional religion, temperance, and prohibition; (7) the production of a social theory grounded in realist epistemologies, with a simultaneous commitment to a science of subjective experience; (8) a behavioral theory of language (see Rochberg-Halton 1986);[6] and (9) a gender and racial stratification system which perpetuated a white, patriarchal system of knowledge and truth in the universities.[7]

These systems of discourse produced a certain kind of structural blindness in interaction theory, a blindness, as Reynolds (1990: 157), Farberman (1979: 9), and Mills (1943/63: 532, 543, 551–2) note, to economic processes in favor of ecological, interactional, and communicational factors (see discussion below). (This blindness has inhibited the development of the cultural studies program I have called for in this book.) The early interactionists (along with most other American social scientists) believed in classic liberalism, with elements of Social Darwinism. This produced a bias that stressed communication, interaction, and human ecology over the economic, ideological, and historical forces of class, status, and power (J. W. Carey 1989: 98). It shaped an ideological bias that emphasized the situational, adjustive, normative approach to social problems (Mills 1943/63: 532, 551–2). It assumed a basically cooperative, assimilative, nonconflictual view of the social, although conflict was regarded as the *sine qua non* of a democratic society, for struggles between groups would produce "relatively progressive forms of association" (see Fisher and Strauss 1978: 491).

Farberman summarizes the way in which the above forces shaped interactionism: "Social Darwinism contained the key rhetorical elements. Jeffersonian agrarianism and Manchester Liberalism provided the idea that least government was best government. The 'religious' principle that the ability to make money was a signal of divine approbation coupled with the sanctity of private property provided a moral patina." Spencer's doctrine of the survival of the fittest "capped off an impregnable justification for the American business establishment" (Farberman 1979: 6).[8]

This is the intellectual and political heritage that defines the modern period of interactionist work – that is, the transition to new texts (1951–62).

Kuhn's reading of the past

When Manford Kuhn surveyed American interactionist literature in 1962, he marked 1937 as a watershed year, this date falling in the middle of the four-year period which saw the publication of three of Mead's major works. The publication of Mead's work, Kuhn argued, signalled the end of the "oral tradition" in interactionist thought and the beginning of the "age of inquiry." The oral tradition, he suggested, had been characterized by attempts to get the orthodoxy right, by repetitions of past "truths," and by more emphasis on criticism than inquiry and creativity. The age of inquiry (1937–62), on the other hand, saw the emergence of interactionist social psychology textbooks, the beginning of a period of hypothesis testing, and the appearance of a multiplicity of theories, including Kuhn's self theory, Parsons's role theory, Merton and Kitt's reference group theory, the person perception literature, dramaturgical sociology (Goffman and Burke), identity theory (Foote, Stone, and Strauss), the work and career studies of Hughes, Strauss, and Becker, the language and culture studies of Sapir, phenomenological theory, and Sullivan's (1953) interpersonal theory of psychiatry.

Kuhn predicted, as he looked into his crystal ball, that in the next 25 years symbolic interactionism would see a refinement of research techniques and a coalescing of the separate subtheories he had identified. Early in his address, Kuhn observed that interactionists do not have their own professional organization, their own journal, their own pontifical leader or tight-knit clique of leaders.[9] He suggested, however, that interactionism would hold its own against psychoanalysis, learning theories, and field theory. He concluded that only interactionism is logically consistent with the basic propositions of the social sciences: "the psychic unit of man; the extreme cultural variability of man; the continual socializability of man; and man's ability to feed back complex directives to his behavior without engaging in trial and error, or conditioning learning" (Kuhn 1964a/72: 72).

Reading Manford Kuhn and his children

The oral tradition, which Kuhn perpetuates in his 1962 address, sustains a narrow, mythic vision of interactionist thought, which continues to the present day. I wish to elaborate this charge.

Kuhn, Blumer, H. Hughes, and those who have followed in their footsteps have persisted in holding to a "modernist" version of science, empirical inquiry, and the growth of scientific knowledge. By this I mean the following. They hold (in varying degrees) to a verificationist view of science, to a "realist" conception of the social – there is an obdurate world out there – and to the view that interactionist thought, more than any other kind, maps the social, the self, and social process. From this point of view, interactionist knowledge cumulates, bit by bit, piece by piece, into a castle-like structure that houses interactionist "truth". But this castle is a prison. Its truths have long been guarded by prophets who have read the sacred texts. These same people have pointed their followers into the empirical world of the social with the proper methods of empirical inquiry. Whether it was the injunction to "look, listen and see," to administer TSTs, to video-tape, or to return to Peirce's pragmatism, the interactionist prophets have, in keeping alive the oral tradition, maintained an ideological control over inquiry. The same tendency is observed in those who criticize contemporary interactionists for turning to a cultural studies perspective (e.g. Farberman 1991). The prophets have formed, through their own power and control, a body of knowledge about the social that is justified by recourse to the grand narrative myth of science as a cumulative, empirical enterprise.

But since these prophets read the texts for their followers – that is, Mead, Simmel and E. Hughes – they undermined from within the very empirical agenda they wished to put in place. They canonized knowledge. They arrogated to themselves the privilege of deciding empirical issues. They excluded literatures that fell outside the canon. They essentially eliminated any ambiguities lurking within the symbolic interaction orientation. In so doing, they followed a modernist agenda. They sought – and seek – a science of the social. They struggle to develop a totalizing theory that embraces the self, society, interaction, and even entire civilizations. They formulate a gender-free, universal theory of the social, which stands outside the economic, material infrastructures of society.

Science is always mythic. It is always contained within an oral tradition which rests on language games that are conflictual, narrative-like, and based on storytelling (Lyotard 1979/84). These language games consist of rules for pushing words around on pieces of paper. The storytelling myths of symbolic interactionists are like the myths of any other scientific community within or outside sociology (e.g. physicists, chemists, biologists, the Iowa, Chicago, Stanford, Harvard, Minnesota, Wisconsin, or Columbia schools in sociology). Our words are simply different: self, object, language, drama, interaction, process, futures, identities, dyads, etc., and we have different rules for putting them together. Modernist science has always justified itself in terms of two grand narrative myths: science will free humankind, and knowledge of the world cumulates in a positive manner. Science, in this sense, has always been ideological. Being empirical has always been the veil that scientists have stood behind as they conduct their oral, mythic enterprises. This is the veil that Kuhn stood behind. But the veil hangs in a house of mirrors, and all we see are multiple images of first this version, then that version of the real.

The postmodern turn

This interpretation of Kuhn's text is based on a postmodernist reading of science. On this reading there can be no science of the real, no theory of the totality, no cumulation of verified knowledge. There is only situated, practical activity, organized and legitimated under the heading of one theory or another. We must abandon the modernist project that has organized the symbolic interactionist project since 1937.[10]

What does this mean? First, canonical readings of our classic and neo-classic texts – what Blumer meant, what Kuhn didn't say but meant, what Mead said but didn't mean, why Goffman didn't write the magnum opus – while harmless enterprises, divert our attention from reading, interpreting, and engaging the postmodern situation. Second, a project, which aims for a science of the social as a totality must be abandoned. Third, interpretive readings of the Chicago or the old or the new Iowa schools must be seen as narrative exercises that perpetuate the myths of symbolic interactionism. They keep our prophets alive. This means that we continually read our actions in the present in light of these recon-structed histories of the past. These stories allow us to live in the past. We map the present into the past. This gives interactionist texts a curious sense of temporality. We rely on Mead to tell us about life in the postmodern moment, or we use Simmel's theories of the dyad, formu-lated in the early 1900s, to tell us about postmodern relational life.

Contemporary interactionist myth reproduces the problems of the past in the present. The past, the work of dead theorists, remains the conceptual model for understanding the present. Interactionist texts thereby see the present moment in terms of the problems of the past. The past becomes the present, and the future is always a present moment read in light of past concerns. Thus do interactionists back into the postmo-dern moment. By shutting their eyes to the present, they allow the veils of the past to determine how they see what they see. As they do this, the social dies in front of them, and they, like other modernists who are also unaware of this passing of the social, persist in studying an empirical world of their own making. This is a safe world. It has its prophets, its texts, and its stories; and, most important, it has the self-serving myth of being empirical.

Fourth, this is how we came to have our own association, our society with elected leaders, our own journals, our own annual meetings, and our own sessions at other meetings. The age of inquiry keeps the oral tradition alive.

So if, in 1991, we look back into Kuhn's crystal ball, we find that we have not moved forward as he predicted. We have simply played different language games (but see Perinbanayagam 1991: 196). But we are still in the oral tradition; our journals merely report the folklore of our storytellers. We have added one or two new methods to our canon, but we are still using the empirical as we did in 1962. No new theories have appeared, because we have all the theory we need in our ancient texts. Indeed, we don't want new theories for they would cause us to read what we judge to be unreadable. Besides, new theories would challenge our sacred texts.

Out of the past: undoing a certain blindness

It hardly seems necessary to repeat the point that, by seeing society as symbolic interaction, interactionists from Blumer (1969, 1990) to Strauss (1978), Becker (1986a), and Lyman and Vidich (1988) have focused our attention on how social order is constructed and given meaning in concrete interactional situations. Eschewing efforts to conceptualize societies as interactional ritual chains, as dualities of structure, functional subsystems, or as social networks, interactionists have offered a picture of society as a conflict-riddled, negotiated order that turns on the intersection of endlessly proliferated social worlds. Recent Marxist- and feminist-oriented interactionists have pointed to the material substrata of the social order and have attempted to build an image of the brute human being who is daily caught up in frightening struggles to reproduce order and sanity. This phenomenologically, existentially driven view of humans and society positions self, emotionality, power, ideology, violence, and sexuality at the center of the interactionist's interpretive problems. These are the topics that an interactionist cultural studies aims to address.

Into politics

These concerns move interactionist sociology out of the past that Kuhn mapped.[11] They open the door for a more fully engaged political interactionism that transcends the conservative boundaries established in the 1890–1950 period of the perspective's history.

Disclaimers first. Symbolic interactionism allows us to escape the kind of blindness that James noted and Park quoted. It provides the foundations for a profoundly existential and practical philosophy. This philosophy is at the same time critical, feminist, and prophetic. It is premised on two fundamental beliefs. First, before you act on behalf of another, you need to have shared in his or her experiences and taken his or her point of view in the situation. Even then, you cannot be sure that you have grasped the other's perspective. Second, the ethical standards for acting are not given by some ultimate, final, external source (religion, politics, philosophy, or science). Individuals create their own values through action and by assuming full responsibility for the consequences of their conduct.[12] The existential self "accepts the tension of absolute freedom and total responsibility" (Barnes 1956: xliii). This self "gives up the role of spectator and voluntarily commits his [her] freedom to the cause" of human suffering (p. xliii). In this commitment, critical, existential interactionism is romantic to the core. It is always preoccupied with human agency, the inability to ever understand the other fully, the constraints on freedom that structural conditions produce, and the inhumane acts that human beings direct to one another.

But alongside this humanistic turn in the theory exists that tendency in the early period (noted above) not to see the transcendent political, economic, gender, racial, and cultural structures of everyday life, the structures that produced the interactional blindness which Park and others wished to erase. The early Chicago ecology–conflict model (see Park 1926/67), with its theory of the cycle of race and labor relations, assumed that "conflict and accommodation between groups defines and constitutes the democratic process" (Fisher and Strauss 1978: 477). In this model, the democratic society spontaneously produced creative conflict (Fisher and Strauss 1978: 477). Park is instructive on this point. He argued that "the race problem turns out, then, in one of its aspects at least, to be a problem of communication . . . the barriers to communication are not differences of language . . . but more particularly of self-consciousness, [and] race consciousness" (Park 1926/50: 253–4).[13] The implications are clear. If the races could only communicate better, the race problem would go away.[14]

This emphasis on communication as the structure which would produce a better society stressed primary groups and solidarity relations (Mills 1943/63: 543) anchored in the private sphere of family life (Farberman 1979: 17). This image of the social rested on a distinction between the public sphere, with its economic and political orders, and the private spheres of family life, friendship, and leisure activities (pp. 16–17). The anonymity of public life, which produced a degree of freedom, was reinforced by "moral regions" of experience in private life, where a certain consciousness of mind was shared (p. 15).

The interactionist theory of the state was noninterventionist. The public good would be expressed through the free and open communication of informed citizens in small, public interest groups. The media, the schools, and the social sciences would present the knowledge necessary for the public to make the correct decisions in any problematic situation. Reforms would always be worked from within the system. There would never be a radical critique of democracy or American capitalism.

Such a critique was not necessary, because "Civilization in the interests of the common welfare, demands the suppression sometimes, and the control always of [man's] wild, natural dispositions" (Park 1925/67, quoted by Farberman 1979: 14). That is, man's human nature required submission to the social order. Besides, attempts at revolt have never succeeded. "In the modern democratic states, the classes have as yet attained no effective organization. Socialism, founded as an effort to create an organization based on 'class consciousness' has never succeeded, except perhaps in Russia, in creating more than a political party" (Park 1925/67, quoted by Farberman 1979: 15; see also Mead, in Shalin 1987b: 275).[15]

The state, then, must speak on behalf of its citizens. Discussing strikes by labor, Blumer (1958: 43) argues: "No government should forfeit its fundamental function of action to prevent injury to the public interest . . . any government is freely justified to control the major strike that inflicts such injury." Regarding the right to strike as a basic public right, Blumer contended "that right might move against the general welfare which the government is pledged to protect" (Lyman and Vidich 1988: 115). Who defines the general welfare? The state?

The interactionist theory of the state thus cedes the right to control what is in the general good to the very unit which decides when that good has been challenged. This is classic, *laissez-faire* liberal capitalism. Completely absent in this formulation is any notion of Mills' power elite or the idea that the state is ruled by the governing interests of those individuals, groups, and institutions which have the greatest power in the society. In taking a noncritical stance toward the state and the doings of capitalism, the interactionists allowed Darwinian theory to work its way through the survival of the fittest doctrine. This move then compartmentalized the Marxist–Socialist agenda and allowed the capitalist marketplace to work its way with the minority and immigrant group members who were flooding into the industrialized cities of the North.[16]

The limits of the Chicago model

The major political weaknesses of the classic interactionist–ecology–conflict model are now clear. Explanations based on such models, Gans argues, "are most applicable if the subjects under study lack the ability to *make choices*, be they plants, animals or human beings" (Gans 1962: 639), emphasis original). Despite its imagery of the free human agent, the interactionist self is free only within the constraints set by the ecological collective order. A structural blindness prohibited interactionists from seeing this contradiction in their theory.

Blumer's (1981: 157–8) comments on Marxism are relevant in this context. He contends that Marxism (he does not cite a specific Marxist theorist) is logically committed to "the premise that social acts (as defined by Mead) have their origin in the given class structure and are to be accounted for by that structure." Marx said that social experience was shaped by historical, material, and economic conditions and relationships, not necessarily class structure. He (as well as Mills) said that human consciousness is molded by material conditions which are mediated by structures of communication. Blumer thus creates a false image of Marx. This is continued in his next assertion, that Marxism assumes "that the interpretive process is determined by the class structure . . . Mead's scheme . . . allows for a variability in defining situations that the Marxist scheme does not permit" (pp. 157–8).

In a single stroke Blumer makes his human agent free; free, that is, to define situations in ways that transcend the very material conditions of life that Marxism, Critical Theory, and existentialism say shape human consciousness. For Blumer (and Mead) consciousness determines existence. For Marx, Mills, Sartre, and the Critical school, human consciousness does not determine existence; nor does existence determine consciousness. Between consciousness and existence resides communication and culture. These two processes dialectically structure existence and consciousness.

Into the future

That was then, and this is now. Much of what the Chicago school did must now be undone. If symbolic interactionism is to continue to thrive and develop into the twenty-first century, it will have to confront many of the issues raised in the preceding chapters. Here are the kinds of changes that I propose.

The concept of the state, states' rights, and the ideology of informed publics must be re-done, if only in the ways suggested by Foucault and Unger, who are suspicious of grand, totalizing theories. Society *is* more than symbolic interaction. What goes on in a society at the level of opinion, news, social welfare, education, labor, the courts, the military, and the family involves more than informed publics exercising their will. Entrenched elites connected to the class, status, and power groups of the social order maintain some degree of hegemonic control over what occurs within any society. How these elites work and how their efforts shape what passes for public opinion must be examined. The interactionist preference for local narratives and small-scale, close-up studies which tell how people do things with and to one another needs to be challenged again. This type of work needs to be combined with larger, historical studies which connect to the three prongs of cultural studies outlined in earlier chapters.

The study of everyday life in America, as it is shaped by the cultural logics of late capitalism, must become a central priority, including how personal troubles become public issues. Here Park's belief that the "moral regions of experience in private life" provide a buffer against the ruthless anonymity of the public sphere can no longer be allowed. The boundaries between the public and the private, as argued in chapter 4, have been dissolved. The personal has become public, and the public now believes that it has the right to know all that is personal. This erasure has produced a situation which divorces ethics from politics, for the personal has become political. As a consequence, the liberal theory of the state which presumed a strict separation between public, civic life and private, secret life no longer holds. The consequences of this transformation for the theory of the democratic society have not been well worked out (see Unger 1987). But what is clear is that a moral and social theory of democracy can no longer presume a sacred sphere of social life.

The concept of the interactionist text requires revision. Successive generations of interactionists have displayed a commitment to the production of a realist, melodramatic, social problems text embodying an identification with the powerless in American society. This realist commitment has been displayed throughout the three ages of realism (textual-cinematic, emotional, and simulational) and has been carried to a high scholarly level in the works of Blumer, Becker, and Goffman. The forms of realism which such authors reproduce mirror, rather than challenge, however, the social structures that need to be changed. A new, multivocal, interventionist form of interactionist writing needs to be explored. This would include performance and multimedia, visual texts which tell various versions of "mystory" or "my history" as it has been shaped by my biography, by popular local culture, and by systems of scholarly discourse (see Ulmer 1989, ch. 1 and pt 3).

The poststructural (and feminist) turn has yet to be felt in the meanings which interactionists bring to their key terms, including "symbol," "social object," "social act," and "self." Mead's self must be rewritten in existential, gendered, and class ways (see Lyman 1990b: 250 and the discussion in chapter 2). While interactionists hunger after lived experience and seek its representation in their ethnographic texts (see Ellis 1991), texts always displace, through the words they use, the experiences they seek to record. The words that subjects speak are always already given elsewhere, in other texts. Hence a subject's words are themselves transformations of prior textual expressions.

The cultural studies of the Chicago pragmatists, their aesthetic theories, and their analyses of the media, need to be reworked in light of current understandings concerning popular culture, politics, and the aesthetic dimensions of everyday experience. This will require the development of an explicitly political model of cultural criticism. The themes that organized the Frankfurt school's project up to the 1940s need to be reworked to fit the tasks of an existential, interactionist cultural studies program.

On being something else

James's "certain blindness" haunted Park, who sought a sociology that would undo the cultural masks that people wore, the masks that produced a blindness to another's position. In his hands, this sociology was acutely attuned to the race relations problems in America and to the press and the media as the chief vehicles for positive, social, democratic change. Park set an agenda that was followed by others. He created a public identity for the American sociologist as an intellectual who could speak to ordinary citizens as well as to people in power (see Lyman 1990c). Like Mills's social scientist, Park directed his "work *at* kings as well as *to* publics" (Mills 1959: 181).

Throughout their collective, cultural history, until the criticism and ferment period of the 1960s, interactionists routinely followed Park's lead. They wrote about the pressing political issues of the day. One has only to examine the bibliographies of Thomas, Park, Burgess, E. Hughes, and Blumer to confirm this point. These American intellectuals, ideological and sometimes conservative, wrote about the problems facing a democratic social order. They took themselves and their discipline seriously.

In the 1960s something happened, and it is still happening today. Interactionism became a recognized school of thought. It entered Kuhn's age of inquiry, Mullins's period of specialization, and Meltzer, Petras, and Reynolds's phase of major varieties. When these things happened, interactionists stopped writing (not entirely of course) about the problems of the day and wrote, instead, about their problems as a theory group in American sociology. It is not that a failure of nerve struck down the post-1960 interactionists. Rather, it seems that it became more important to write for scholarly audiences than for the American public.

It is time to reengage in American society and the international political arena that frames this social order. Such a move will take up where Mills left off. It will rest on a belief that the critical, interactionist sociological imagination can make a difference in the lives that people lead. This means that interactionists must deliberately present controversial research and theory so as to encourage controversy. They must learn to write in ways that are free of complex jargon. They must always link the political with the personal. They must study how those in power (the economic, political, and cultural elites) constantly define the personal in terms which further their own political agendas.

In the end

Turning interactionism into a critical perspective means, by way of summary, the commitment to a sociology which establishes new interpretive roots. Such roots will branch out in two directions at the same time. Theoretically they will extend into the critical, feminist traditions that presently exist in the human disciplines. These roots will be anchored in the bedrock worlds of material existence that shape human consciousness. At the level of practice, this perspective will no longer adhere to the elitist theory of publics and the public interest that drove the Chicago school's model of political involvement. It will work, instead, at the level of local political resistance. It will seek to assist those groups in which personal troubles are transformed into demands for a greater stake in the public good.

Such efforts should help to construct a politically critical interactionism which would make a difference. It is not sufficient, as Marx argued so many times, to just understand the world; the key is to change it.[17] It is one thing to understand, as Park did, how masks get put in place. It is another thing to change the conditions that produced the masks in the first place. If the dramaturgical, postmodern society is to be unravelled and made more humane, then the masks that we all wear must be pulled off. This is what critical interactionism aims to do.

In conclusion

The recourse to William James's essay "A Certain Blindness in Human Beings" is motivated by an ironic postmodernist agenda. His essay turns on vision, looking, and the belief that one set of looks can overcome another way of looking, of being blind to the situation of the other. His essay implies a compassionate voyeur who sees in the name of the other. In pursuing a sociology which unmasks the dramaturgical society, interactionists have made a hero of the ethnographer-voyeur who comes back from the field with moving tales of the powerless. They have made gazing on others a legitimate interactionist preoccupation.

Classic Chicago sociology was framed by these arguments. It perpetuated two myths: first, that urban man (and woman) still had an enclave of privacy that urban society could not touch; second, that the skilled interactionist ethnographer could make sense of the worlds of experience.

But now these myths are under assault. Now we know that there are many ways to tell the same story and that maybe it isn't the same story any longer. The myth of a total, realist ethnographic Chicago sociology, like its counterpart, the myth of total cinema, is on the verge of collapsing. Traditional, realist, narrative cinema, like traditional ethnographic sociology, tells only one version of the story, a version which has a zero degree of textual politics. Such texts perpetuate the illusions that stories have happy endings; that heroes always prevail, that the private is sacred, and that in the end man and woman will be joined in peaceful bliss.

Progressive, reflective, political sociological texts force us to see things differently. They make ideology a spectacle and, in so doing, objectify the presence and activity of ideological meanings which too often go unnoticed in the traditional, realist text; texts which blur the distinctions between nature and history (Barthes 1957/72: 11). These texts presume a political aesthetic which both pushes and forces into view the underlying ideological presuppositions of the traditional narrative text. Such works rupture the veneer of their own premises. They deconstruct themselves from within. In so doing, they expose the limits of the standard, classic text.

As interactionists, we have invaded the private spaces of the postmodern. We have perpetuated the ideological illusion that we are keeping the sacred safe from and for the public. We, like the Chicago sociologists of old, have contributed to an opiate of the masses; the opiate which says that sociological knowledge will protect this democratic society from itself. We can no longer justify our voyeurism in the name of democracy. We must, instead, turn our searching eye inward upon our own consciences. We may then see how our reflective gazes have contributed to this surveillance society. We may see (and hear) how we have perpetuated the illusion that the scientific gaze is politically neutral and really beneficial to all. We turn to the production of progressive, reflective texts and begin the difficult task of unmasking the taken-for-granted ideologies which have for far too long justified our self-serving voyeuristic project.

Still, contemporary society believes that it needs some version of the voyeur. He or she exposes the truth which others refuse to see or cover up. But in so doing, the voyeur argues that there is a greater truth. This is the truth which resonates with the great myths of late capitalism, that there is, after all, a real world out there and it is structured by recurring truths concerning family and heroes who dare to take risks and give their lives and their sanity for the rest of us. The deconstruction of this myth of the voyeur, as this figure is implicated in traditional interactionist work, should serve to further expose the central cultural logics of late capitalism; namely, the fiction that there are ultimate, final truths about the dramaturgical, postmodern society.

As a perspective, interactionism is moving in several directions, both vertically and horizontally, at the same time (Fine 1990). This means that the interactionist tradition must confront, absorb, debate, and be in conflict with the new terrains of theory which continue to appear in the postmodern period (e.g. hermeneutics, phenomenology, structuralism, poststructuralism, postmodern theory, psychoanalysis, semiotics, post-Marxism, cultural studies, feminist theory, film theory, etc.). This is as it should be. We are alive, if not lively, and we shall become all the more so as we let go of the past and more fully embrace this uncertain postmodern world that engulfs us all.

Notes

1 The full quote is: "Robert Oppenheimer wrote a family friend, 'I take it . . . that physics has gotten now very much under your skin, physics and the obvious excellences of the life it brings.'"
2 Park's use of these lines from James was in the context of his review of a very sad book by C. S. Johnson, *Shadow of the Plantation* (1934).
3 The title of Kuhn's address was "Major Trends in Symbolic Interaction Theory in the Past Twenty-Five Years." Delivered in 1962, it was published in *The Sociological Quarterly* (in 1964) and reprinted in the 2nd edn of *Symbolic Interaction: A Reader in Social Psychology* ed. Jerome G. Manis and Bernard N. Meltzer in 1972. I take my quotations from this last source.

4 Portions of this chapter, in underdeveloped form, appeared in Denzin 1987e.
5 This psychology, in contrast to structuralism, which analyzed and described consciousness, considered the mental processes of sense perception, emotion, volition, and thought as functions of the biological organism in its adaptation to and control of its environment. As argued in chapter 1, James's psychology had traces of a structuralism (e.g. the stream of consciousness) which Mead attempted to override. Functional psychology and social behaviorism thus maintained commitments to the Darwinian, evolutionary model of human experience and human society.
6 Blumer would turn this theory in an interactional direction, and Goffman would later modify it, first in structural and sociolinguistic and then in poststructural ways.
7 This section glosses Wiley's (1986) brilliant analysis of the Chicago school and the forces that shaped its social theories, especially Thomas and Znaniecki's *The Polish Peasant*.
8 Wiley (1986: 23) argues that Thomas and Znaniecki broke with the Darwinian, biological perspective through the introduction of the "symbolic level" and the concepts of attitude and value and the definition of the situation into their general theory. This allowed them to escape a strict biological determinism, while introducing a moral dimension into the discussion of ethnicity in American life. Wiley states: "Thomas and Znaniecki gave the United States a major intellectual resource for maintaining what civil liberties and democracy it did maintain in the Twentieth Century" (p. 23). Wiley (in conversation) also suggests that there were really two Chicago schools: the earlier Thomas and Znaniecki *Polish Peasant* school which emphasized culture and interaction and the later Park–Burgess ecological school which deemphasized the cultural.
9 As noted in the Preface, today interactionists do have a professional organization and at least two journals.
10 This is Kuhn's date, not mine. On my reading, the age of inquiry was present from the beginning (e.g. during the 1890–1932 period).
11 Note that his reading of the past was completely apolitical.
12 This is where existentialism departs from pragmatism, which has always been weak on the individual's acceptance of the consequences of conduct. In Sartre's words (1943/56: 626): "Man made himself man in order to be God . . . one could just as well say that man loses himself in order that the self-cause may exist . . . Man pursues being blindly by hiding from himself the free project which is this pursuit."
13 Blumer (1958/88: 206) provides a structural corrective to Park's position: "The proper . . . area in which race prejudice should be studied is the collective process through which a sense of group position is formed . . . to seek to understand it . . . in the arena of individual feeling and individual experience seems to me to be clearly misdirected."
14 Structural blindness does not produce astructural biases, as many have argued (e.g. Reynolds 1990; Prendergast and Knottnerus 1990). It produces, instead, a selective bias which emphasizes some structures over others. The interactionists were not blind to racial cultures, discriminatory practices, racial prejudice, inter-group and power conflicts, collective processes of protest, group tensions, interest organizations, industrial structures, labor markets, the mass society, publics, public opinion and the public interest,

mass markets, and the mass communications industries (see the Blumer essays in Lyman and Vidich 1988; also Maines and Morrione (eds) 1990).

15 Mead (in Shalin 1987: 275) states that "socialism has never been the articulate voice of democracy or even of labor in America."

16 At the same time it cleared a space for a strange merger of functional psychology with psychoanalysis. If human beings had wild instincts, passions, appetites, and impulses that ran counter to the needs of civilization, as Freud argued, then a rational, cognitive social psychology could curb these tendencies. This would not be a Watsonian behaviorism which cut off people's heads. Pragmatism and the belief in the integrity of the individual would not allow this. James's and Dewey's functional psychology, Mead's social behaviorism, and Cooley's solipsistic idealism countered such a behaviorism with a soft, interpretive, humanistic social psychology. Cooley, James, Dewey, and Mead offered a theory which comfortably fitted the individual to the group, where the individual's needs and ideals were those learned from the generalized other. Now the media's place became clear. They were given two functions: first, to provide entertainment and news which did not arouse man's primitive, animal instincts; second, to provide factual news about society and its needs and problems.

17 Blumer disagrees. "There is an advantage in seeing the difference between trying to understand something and trying to change it. You can only be effective in trying to change it if you understand it. The understanding is the important thing to me" (Morrione and Farberman 1981b: 281).

REFERENCES

Adler, Patricia A. and Peter Adler 1987: *Membership Roles in Field Research*. Newbury Park, Calif.: Sage.

——, Peter Adler, and Andrea Fontana 1987: Everyday Life Sociology. *Annual Review of Sociology*, 13, 217–35.

Agger, Ben 1989: *Fast Capitalism*. Urbana: University of Illinois Press.

—— 1990: *The Decline of Discourse*. New York: Falmer Press.

Alcoholics Anonymous 1976: *Alcoholics Anonymous*. New York: Alcoholics Anonymous World Services.

Alexander, Jeffrey 1987: The Centrality of the Classics. In A. Giddens and J. Turner (eds), *Social Theory Today*, Stanford: Stanford University Press, 11–57.

—— and Bernhard Giesen 1987: From Reduction to Linkage: The Long View of the Micro-Macro Link. In J. C. Alexander *et al.* (eds), *The Micro-Macro Link*, Berkeley: University of California Press, 1–42.

Altheide, David L. 1985: *Media Power*. Beverley Hills, Calif.: Sage.

—— 1988: Computer Formats and Bureaucratic Structures. In Maines and Couch (eds) 1988: 215–30.

—— and John M. Johnson 1980: *Bureaucratic Propaganda*. Boston: Allyn and Bacon.

—— and Robert P. Snow 1979: *Media Logic*. Beverly Hills, Calif.: Sage.

—— 1991: *Media Worlds in the Era of Postjournalism*. New York: Aldine de Gruyter.

Althusser, Louis 1971: *Lenin and Philosophy and Other Essays*. New York: Monthly Review.

Ames, Van Meter 1956: Mead and Sartre on Man. *Journal of Philosophy*, 53, 205–19.

Antonio, Robert J. 1989: The Normative Foundations of Emancipatory Theory: Evolutionary versus Pragmatic Perspectives. *American Journal of Sociology* 94, 721–48.

Ashmore, Malcolm C. 1989: *The Reflexive Thesis: Wrighting Sociology of Scientific Knowledge*. Chicago: University of Chicago Press.

Athens, Lonnie 1984: Blumer's Method of Naturalistic Inquiry: A Critical Examination. *Studies in Symbolic Interaction*, 5, 241–57.

—— 1989: *The Creation of Violent Criminals*. New York: Routledge.

Atkinson, J. M. and John C. Heritage (eds) 1984: *Structures of Social Action: Studies in Conversation Analysis*. Cambridge: Cambridge University Press.

Atkinson, Paul 1988: Ethnomethodology: A Critical Review. *Annual Review of Sociology*, 14, 441–65.

Baldwin, James Mark 1899: *Social and Ethical Interpretations in Mental Development: A Study in Social Psychology*. New York: Macmillan.

Balsamo, Ann 1988: Reading Cyborgs Writing Feminism. *Communication*, 10, 331–44.

—— 1989: Imagining Cyborgs: Postmodernism and Symbolic Interactionism. *Studies in Symbolic Interaction*, 10, 369–79.

—— 1990: Rethinking Ethnography: A Work for the Feminist Imagination. *Studies in Symbolic Interaction*, 11, 45–57.

—— 1991: Technologies of the Gendered Body: A Feminist Cultural Study. Unpublished doctoral dissertation, Institute of Communications Research, University of Illinois at Urbana-Champaign.

Barnes, Hazel 1956: Translator's Introduction to Sartre 1956: viii–xliii.

Barthes, Roland 1957/72: *Mythologies*. New York: Hill and Wang.

—— 1975: *Pleasure of the Text*. New York: Hill and Wang.

—— 1977/82: From Writing Degree Zero. In Susan Sontag (ed.), *A Barthes Reader*, New York: Hill and Wang, 31–61.

—— 1985: *The Grain of the Voice: Interviews 1962–1980*. New York: Hill and Wang.

Bateson, G. 1972: *Steps to an Ecology of the Mind*. San Francisco: Chandler.

—— and Jürgen Ruesch 1951: *Communication: The Social Matrix of Psychiatry*. New York: Norton.

Baudrillard, Jean 1968: *Le Système des Objets*. Paris: Gallimard.

—— 1970: *La Société de Consommation: Ses Mythes, Ses Structures*. Paris: Gallimard.

—— 1972: *Pour une Critique de l'Economie Politique du Signe*. Paris: Gallimard.

—— 1975: *The Mirror of Production*. St Louis: Telos Press.

—— 1976: *L'Échange Symbolique et la Mort*. Paris: Gallimard.

—— 1981: *For a Critique of the Political Economy of the Sign*. St Louis: Telos Press.

—— 1983a: The Ecstasy of Communication. In John Foster (ed.) *The*

Anti-Aesthetic: Essays on Postmodern Culture, Port Townsend, Wash: Bay Press, 126–34.

—— 1983b: *Simulations*. New York: Semiotext (e), Foreign Agent Press.

—— 1987/8: *America*. New York: Verso.

—— 1988: *The Ecstasy of Communication*. New York: Semiotext(e).

—— 1990: *Cool Memories*. London: Verso.

Baugh, Kenneth Jr. 1990: *The Methodology of Herbert Blumer*. New York: Cambridge University Press.

Bazin, André 1967: *What is Cinema?* Berkeley: University of California Press.

Becker, Howard S. 1963: *The Outsiders*. New York: Free Press.

—— 1966: Introduction to Shaw 1966: v–xviii.

—— 1967: Whose Side Are We On? *Social Problems*, 14, 239–48.

—— 1970: *Sociological Work*. Chicago: Aldine.

—— 1981: *Exploring Society Photographically*. Evanston, Ill.: Northwestern University Press.

—— 1982: *Art Worlds*. Berkeley: University of California Press.

—— 1986a: *Doing Things Together*. Evanston, Ill.: Northwestern University Press.

—— 1986b: *Writing for Social Scientists*. Chicago: University of Chicago Press.

—— and M. M. McCall 1990: Introduction to H. Becker and M. McCall (eds), *Symbolic Interaction and Cultural Studies*. Chicago: University of Chicago Press, 1–15.

——, Everett C. Hughes, Anselm L. Strauss, and Blanche Geer 1961: *Boys in White*. Chicago: University of Chicago Press.

——, Blanche Geer, David Riesman, and Robert Weiss 1968: *Institutions and the Person*. Chicago: Aldine.

——, Michal M. McCall, and Lori V. Morris 1989: Theatres and Communities: Three Scenes. *Social Problems*, 36, 93–116.

—— and M. M. McCall (eds) 1990: *Symbolic Interaction and Cultural Studies*. Chicago: University of Chicago Press.

Benjamin, Walter 1936/68: The Work of Art in the Age of Mechanical Reproduction. In Hannah Arendt (ed.), *Illuminations*. New York: Harcourt Brace & World, 219–53.

Bennett, James 1981: *Oral History and Delinquency: The Rhetoric of Criminology*. Chicago: University of Chicago Press.

Bentz, Valerie Malhotra 1989: *Becoming Mature: Childhood Ghosts and Spirits in Adult Life*. New York: Aldine de Gruyter.

Benveniste, E. 1966/71: *Problems in General Linguistics*. Miami: University of Miami Press.

Berger, Peter and Thomas Luckmann 1967: *The Social Construction of Reality*. New York: Doubleday.

Biernacki, Patrick 1986: *Pathways from Heroin Addiction*. Philadelphia: Temple University Press.

Block, Fred 1973: Alternative Sociological Perspectives: Implications for Applied Sociology. *Catalyst*, 7, 29–41.

Blumer, Herbert 1931: Science without Concepts. *American Journal of Sociology*, 36, 515–33.

—— 1933: *Movies and Conduct*. New York: Macmillan.

—— 1935: Moulding of Mass Behavior through the Motion Picture. *Proceedings of the American Sociological Society*, 29, 115–27.

—— 1937: Social Psychology. In E. P. Schmidt (ed.), *Man and Society*, Englewood Cliffs, N. J.: Prentice-Hall, 144–98.

—— 1939/79: *Critiques of Research in the Social Sciences: An Appraisal of Thomas and Znaniecki's "The Polish Peasant in Europe and America."* New York: Social Science Research Council. Reprinted with a new introduction by the author, New Brunswick, N.J.: Transaction Books, 1979.

—— 1948: Public Opinion and Public Opinion Polling. *American Sociological Review*, 13, 542–54.

—— 1955: Attitudes and the Social Act. *Social Problems*, 3 (Summer), 59–65.

—— 1958: *The Rationale of Labor–Management Relations*. Rio Piedras Puerto Rico: Labor Relations Institute, University of Puerto Rico.

—— 1958/88: Race Prejudice as a Sense of Group Position. *Pacific Sociological Review*, 1, 3–7. Reprinted in Lyman and Vidich 1988: 196–206.

—— 1959: Suggestions for the Study of Mass-Media Effects. In E. Burdick and A. J. Brodbeck (eds), *American Voting Behavior*, Glencoe, Ill.: Free Press, 197–208.

—— 1962: Society as Symbolic Interaction. In A. Rose (ed.), 1962: 179–92.

—— 1966: Sociological Implications of the Thought of George Herbert Mead. *American Journal of Sociology*, 71, 535–48.

—— 1967: Reply to Woelfel, Stone, and Farberman. *American Journal of Sociology*, 72, 411–12.

—— 1969: *Symbolic Interactionism*. Englewood Cliffs, N.J.: Prentice-Hall.

—— 1973: Comment on "Symbolic Interaction as a Pragmatic Perspective: The Bias of Emergent Theory." *American Sociological Review*, 38, 797–8.

—— 1977: Comment on Lewis's "The Classic American Pragmatists as Forerunners to Symbolic Interaction." *Sociological Quarterly*, 18, 285–9.

—— 1978: Social Unrest and Collective Protest. *Studies in Symbolic Interaction*, 1–54.

—— 1979: *Critiques of Research in the Social Sciences: An Appraisal of Thomas and Znaniecki's "The Polish Peasant in Europe and America."* New Brunswick, N.J.: Transaction Books.

—— 1980: Mead and Blumer: The Convergent Methodological Perspectives of Social Behaviorism and Symbolic Interactionism. *American Sociological Review*, 45, 409–19.

—— 1981: George Herbert Mead. In B. Rhea (ed.), *The Future of the Sociological Classics*, Boston: George Allen & Unwin, 136–69.

—— 1983: Going Astray with a Logical Scheme. *Symbolic Interaction*, 6, 123–37.

—— 1990: *Industrialization as an Agent of Social Change. A Critical Analysis*, edited with an Introduction by D. R. Maines and T. J. Morrione. New York: Aldine de Gruyter.

—— and Philip M. Hauser 1933: *Movies, Delinquency, and Crime*. New York: Macmillan.

Bourdieu, Pierre 1984: *Distinction: A Social Critique of the Judgment of Taste*. Cambridge, Mass.: Harvard University Press.

Brissett, Dennis and Charles Edgley (eds) 1990: *Life as Theater: A Dramaturgical Sourcebook*, 2nd edn. New York: Aldine de Gruyter.

Brittan, Arthur 1973: *Meanings and Situations*. London: Routledge.

Brown, Richard Harvey 1987: *Society as Text*. Chicago: University of Chicago Press.

—— 1989: *Social Science as Civic Discourse*. Chicago: University of Chicago Press.

Buban, Steven L. 1986: Studying Social Process: The Chicago and Iowa Schools Revisited. *Studies in Symbolic Interaction, Supplement 2: The Iowa School* (Part A), 25–38.

Bulmer, Martin 1984: *The Chicago School of Sociology*. Chicago: University of Chicago Press.

Burgess, Ernest 1930/66: Discussion. In Shaw 1966: 185–97.

Burke, Kenneth 1962: *A Grammar of Motives and a Rhetoric of Motives*. Cleveland: World.

Busch, Lawrence 1982: History, Negotiation, and Structure in Agricultural Research. *Urban Life*, 11, 368–84.

Cagel, Van M. 1989: The Language of Cultural Studies: An Analysis of British Subculture Theory. *Studies in Symbolic Interaction*, 10, 301–13.

Cahill, Spencer 1989: Fashioning Males and Females: Appearance Management and the Social Reproduction of Gender. *Symbolic Interaction*, 12, 281–98.

Carey, James T. 1975: *Sociology and Public Affairs: The Chicago School*. Beverly Hills, Ca.: Sage.

Carey, James W. 1988: Introduction to J. W. Carey (ed.), *Media, Myths, and Narratives: Television and the Press*, Newbury Park, Ca.: Sage, 8–18.

—— 1989: *Communication as Culture*. Boston: Unwin Hyman.

—— and John J. Quirk 1989: The History of the Future. In Carey 1989: 173–200.

Certeau, Michel de 1984: *The Practice of Everyday Life*. Berkeley: University of California Press.

Charters, W. W. 1933: Chairman's Preface. In Blumer 1933, vii–ix.

Charmaz, Kathy 1991: *Good Days, Bad Days: The Self in Chronic Illness and Time*. New Brunswick, N. J.: Rutgers University Press.

Cheal, David 1991: *Family and the State of Theory*. New York: Guilford.

Cho, Jo-Hyun 1990: *Ressentiment and the Battered Korean Wife*. New York: Aldine de Gruyter.

Cicourel, Aaron V. 1968: *The Social Organization of Juvenile Justice*. New York: Wiley.

Clifford, James 1986: Partial Truths. In Clifford and Marcus (eds) 1986: 1–26.

—— 1988: *The Predicament of Culture: Twentieth-Century Ethnography, Literature and Art*. Cambridge, Mass.: Harvard University Press.

—— and George Marcus (eds) 1986: *Writing Culture*. Berkeley: University of California Press.

Clough, Patricia Ticineto 1987: Feminist Theory and Social Psychology. *Studies in Symbolic Interaction*, 8, 3–22.

—— 1988: The Movies and Social Observation: Reading Blumer's *Movies and Conduct*. *Symbolic Interaction*, 11, 85–97.

—— 1989: Letters from Pamela: Reading Howard S. Becker's *Writing(s) for Social Scientists*. *Symbolic Interaction*, 12, 159–70.

—— 1991: *The End(s) of Ethnography*. Newbury Park, Calif.: Sage.

Cohen, Joseph 1989: About Steaks Liking to be Eaten: The Conflicting Views of Symbolic Interactionists and Talcott Parsons Concerning the Nature of Relations between Person and Nonhuman Objects. *Symbolic Interaction*, 12, 191–213.

Collins, Randall 1975: *Conflict Sociology*. New York: Academic Press.

—— 1986: Is 1980s Sociology in the Doldrums? *American Journal of Sociology*, 91, 1336–55.

—— 1989a: Sociology: Proscience or Antiscience? *American Sociological Review*, 54, 124–39.

—— 1989b: Toward a Neo-Meadian Sociology of Mind. *Symbolic Interaction*, 12, 1–32.

Conrad, Peter and Joseph W. Schneider 1980: *Deviance and Medicalization: From Badness to Sickness*. St Louis: C. V. Mosby.

Conwell, Chic and Edwin Sutherland 1937: *The Professional Thief*. Chicago: University of Chicago Press.

Cook, David A. 1981: *A History of Narrative Film*. New York: Norton.

Cooley, Charles Horton 1902/22/56: *Human Nature and the Social Order*. New York: Scribner's/Free Press.

—— 1909/56: *Social Organization*. New York: Scribners/Free Press.

Coser, Lewis A. 1976: Two Methods in Search of a Substance. *American Sociological Review*, 40, 691–700.

Couch, Carl J. 1984a: *Constructing Civilizations*. Greenwich, Conn.: JAI Press.

—— 1984b: Symbolic Interaction and Generic Sociological Principles. *Symbolic Interaction*, 7, 1–14.

—— 1986: Questionnaires, Naturalistic Observation and Recordings. *Studies in Symbolic Interaction, Supplement 2: The Iowa School* (Part A), 45–69.

—— 1987: *Researching Social Processes in the Laboratory*. Greenwich, Conn.: JAI Press.

—— 1989: Towards the Isolation of Elements of Social Structures. *Studies in Symbolic Interaction*, 10, 445–69.

—— 1990: Mass Communications and State Structures. *Social Science Journal*, 27, 111–28.

—— and Shing-Ling Chen 1988: Orality, Literacy and Social Structure. In Maines and Couch (eds) 1988: 155–71.

—— and Robert A. Hintz, Jr (eds) 1975: *Constructing Social Life: Readings in Behavioral Sociology from the Iowa School*. Champaign, Ill.: Stipes Publishing Company.

—— Stanley L. Saxton, and Michael A. Katovich (eds) 1986a: Introduction to Couch *et al.* (eds) 1986b; xvii–xxv.

—— 1986b: *Studies in Symbolic Interaction: The Iowa School, Parts A and B*. Greenwich, Conn.: JAI Press.

Coward, R. and J. Ellis 1977: *Language and Materialism: Developments in Semiology and the Theory of the Subject*. London and Boston: Routledge & Kegan Paul.

Cowley, Malcolm 1950: Naturalism in American Literature. In S. Parsons (ed.), *Evolutionary Thought in America*, New Haven, Conn.: Yale University Press, 300–35.

Cressey, Paul G. and Frederick M. Thrasher 1933: *Boys, Movies and*

City Streets. New York: Macmillan.

Davis, Ed 1990: Everyday People Make Sense of the News. Unpublished doctoral dissertation, Department of Geography, University of Illinois at Urbana–Champaign.

Davis, Fred 1981: On the "Symbolic" in Symbolic Interaction. *Symbolic Interaction*, 5, 111–26.

Day, Robert and Jo Anne Day 1977: A Review of the Current State of Negotiated Order Theory. *Sociological Quarterly*, 19, 126–42.

Deegan, Mary Jo 1987: Symbolic Interaction and the Study of Women: An Introduction. In Deegan and Hill (eds) 1987: 3–18.

—— and Michael R. Hill (eds.) 1987: *Women and Symbolic Interaction*. Boston: Allen & Unwin.

Deleuze, Giles and Felix Guattari 1977: *Anti-Oedipus*. New York: Viking.

Denzin, Norman K. 1969: Symbolic Interactionism and Ethnomethodology: A Proposed Synthesis. *American Sociological Review*, 34, 922–34.

—— 1977a: *Childhood Socialization: Studies in the Development of Language, Social Behavior, and Identity*. San Francisco: Jossey-Bass.

—— 1977b: Notes on the Criminogenic Hypothesis: A Case Study of the American Liquor Industry. *American Sociological Review*, 42, 905–20.

—— 1978: Crime and the American Liquor Industry. *Studies in Symbolic Interaction*, 1, 887–918.

—— 1983: Interpretive Interactionism. In G. Morgan (ed.), *Beyond Method*, Beverly Hills, Calif.: Sage, 129–46.

—— 1984a: On Interpreting and Interpretation. *American Journal of Sociology*, 89, 1426–33.

—— 1984b: *On Understanding Emotion*. San Francisco: Jossey-Bass

—— 1985a: On the Phenomenology of Sexuality, Desire, and Violence. *Current Perspectives in Social Theory*, 6, 39–56.

—— 1985b: Reflections on the Social Psychologist's Camera. *Studies in Visual Communication*, 11, 78–82.

—— 1985c: Review-Essay, Robert S. Perinbanayagam, Signifying Acts. *American Journal of Sociology*, 91, 432–4.

—— 1985d: Towards an Interpretation of Semiotics and History. *Semiotica*, 5, 335–50.

—— 1986a: Foreword to Couch *et al.* 1986: xiii–xv.

—— 1986b: On a Semiotic Approach to Mass Culture. *American Journal of Sociology*, 92, 678–83.

—— 1986c: Postmodern Social Theory. *Sociological Theory*, 4, 194–204.

—— 1987a: *The Alcoholic Self*. Beverly Hills, Calif.: Sage.

—— 1987b: The Death of Sociology in the 1980s. *American Journal of Sociology*, 93, 175–80.

—— 1987c: On Semiotics and Symbolic Interaction. *Symbolic Interaction*, 10, 1–20.

—— 1987d: *The Recovering Alcoholic*. Beverly Hills, Calif.: Sage.

—— 1987e: Thoughts on "Critique and Renewal" in Symbolic Interactionism. *Studies in Symbolic Interaction*, 7, 3–9.

—— 1988: Act, Language and Self in Symbolic Interactionist Thought. *Studies in Symbolic Interaction*, 9, 51–80.

—— 1989a: *Interpretive Biography*. Newbury Park, Calif.: Sage.

—— 1989b: *Interpretive Interactionism*. Newbury Park, Calif.: Sage.

—— 1989c: Reading Tender Mercies: Two Interpretations. *Sociological Quarterly*, 30, 37–57.

—— 1989d: Reading/Writing Culture: Interpreting the Postmodern Project. *Cultural Dynamics*, 11, 9–27.

—— 1989e: *The Research Act*, 3rd edn. Englewood Cliffs, N. J.: Prentice-Hall.

—— 1990a: Harold and Agnes: A Feminist, Narrative Undoing. *Sociological Theory*, 11, 199–216.

—— 1990b: The Long Good-bye: Farewell to Rational Choice Theory. *Rationality & Society*, 2, 504–7.

—— 1990c: Presidential Address: The Sociological Imagination Reconsidered. *Sociological Quarterly*, 31, 1–23.

—— 1990d: Reading Cultural Texts. *American Journal of Sociology*, 95, 1577–80.

—— 1990e: Reading Rational Choice Theory. *Rationality & Society*, 2, 172–89.

—— 1990f: The Spaces of Postmodernism: Reading Plummer on Blumer. *Symbolic Interaction*, 13, 145–54.

—— 1991a: Empiricist Cultural Studies in America: A Deconstructive Reading. *Current Perspectives in Social Theory*, 11, 17–39.

—— 1991b: *Hollywood Shot by Shot: Alcoholism in American Cinema*. New York: Aldine de Gruyter.

—— 1991c: Postmodernism and Deconstructionism. Forthcoming in Dickens and Fontana (eds) 1991.

—— 1991d: *Images of Postmodern Society: Social Theory and Contemporary Cinema*. London: Sage.

—— 1991e: Sexuality and Gender: An Interactionist/Poststructural Reading. Forthcoming in P. England (ed.), *Theory on Gender/Feminism on Theory*, New York: Aldine de Gruyter.

—— and Charles Keller 1981: Frame Analysis Reconsidered. *Contemporary Sociology*, 10, 52–60.

Derrida, Jacques 1967/73: *Speech and Phenomena*. Evanston, Ill.: Northwestern University Press.

—— 1967/76: *Of Grammatology*. Baltimore, Md.: Johns Hopkins University Press.

—— 1967/78: *Writing and Difference*. Chicago: University of Chicago Press.

—— 1972: Structure, Sign and Play in the Discourse of the Human Sciences. In Richard Macksey and Eugene Donato (eds), *The Structuralist Controversy: The Languages of Criticism and the Sciences of Man*, Baltimore, Md.: Johns Hopkins University Press, 247–65. Reprinted in Derrida 1967/78: 247–64.

—— 1972/81a: *Dissemination*. Chicago: University of Chicago Press.

—— 1972/81b: *Positions*. Chicago: University of Chicago Press.

—— 1987/89: *Of Spirit: Heidegger and the Question*. Chicago: University of Chicago Press.

Deutscher, Irwin 1974: *What We Say: What We Do*. Glenview, Ill.: Scott, Foresman.

Dewey, John 1896: The Reflex Arc Concept in Psychology. *Psychological Review*, 3, 357–70.

—— 1922: *Human Nature and Conduct*. New York: Holt, Rinehart & Winston.

—— 1927: *The Public and its Problems*. New York: Henry Holt.

—— 1934: *Art as Experience*. New York: G. P. Putnam's.

—— 1934/86a: Character Training for Youth. *Rotarian*, 45 (September), 6–8, 58–9. Reprinted in *John Dewey: The Later Works*, Vol. 9: 1933–1934, 186–93.

—— 1934/86b: Radio's Influence on the Mind. *School and Society*, 60 (15 Dec.), 805. Reprinted in *Dewey: Later Works*, Vol 9, 309.

—— 1938: *The Theory of Inquiry*. New York: Henry Holt.

—— 1939: *Intelligence in the Modern World: John Dewey's Philosophy*, edited with an Introduction by Joseph Ratner. New York: Random House.

Dickens, David and Andrea Fontana (eds) 1991, *Postmodernism and Sociology*. Chicago: University of Chicago Press.

DiMaggio, Paul 1977: Market Structure, The Creative Process, and Popular Culture: Toward an Organizational Reinterpretation of Mass Culture Theory. *Journal of Popular Culture*, 11, 436–52.

Dollard, John 1935: *Criteria for the Life History*. New Haven, Conn.: Yale University Press.

Douglas, Jack 1976: *Investigative Social Research*. Beverly Hills, Calif.: Sage.

—— 1985: *Creative Interviewing*. Beverly Hills, Calif.: Sage.

—— (ed.) 1971: *Understanding Everyday Life*. Chicago: Aldine.

—— and John Johnson (eds) 1977: *Existential Sociology*. New York: Cambridge University Press.

—— Patricia A. Adler, Peter Adler, Andrea Fontana, C. Robert Freeman, and Joseph A. Kotarbara (eds) 1980: *Introduction to the Sociologies of Everyday Life*. Boston: Allyn & Bacon.

Downing, David B. 1987: Deconstruction's Scruples: The Politics of Enlightened Critique. *Diacritics*, 17, 66–81.

Duncan, Hugh Dalziel 1962: *Communication and Social Order*. New York: Bedminster Press.

Dykhuizen, George 1973: *The Life and Mind of John Dewey*. Carbondale, Ill: Southern Illinois University Press.

Eagleton, Terry 1990: *The Ideology of the Aesthetic*. Oxford: Blackwell.

Elbaz, Robert 1987: *The Changing Nature of the Self: A Critical Study of Autobiographical Discourse*. Iowa City: University of Iowa Press.

Ellis, Carolyn 1991: Emotional Sociology. *Symbolic Interaction*, 14, 23–50.

Ericson, Richard V., Patricia M. Baranek, and Janet B. L. Chan 1987: *Visualizing Deviance: A Study of News Organization*. Toronto: University of Toronto Press.

Farberman, Harvey 1975: A Criminogenic Market Structure: The Automobile Industry. *Sociological Quarterly*, 16, 438–57.

—— 1979: The Chicago School: Continuities in Urban Sociology. *Studies in Symbolic Interaction*, 2, 3–20.

—— 1980: Fantasy in Everyday Life: Some Aspects of the Interaction between Social Psychology and Political Economy. *Symbolic Interaction*, 3, 9–22.

—— 1989: The Sociology of Emotions. In Franks and McCarthy (eds) 1989: 271–88.

—— 1990: From the Authenticity of Lived Experience to the Justification of Theoretical Constructs. Distinguished Lecture delivered to the 1990 Annual Meeting of the Society for the Study of Symbolic Interaction, Washington D.C., 13 Aug. 1990.

—— 1991: Symbolic Interactionism and Postmodernism: Close Encounters of a Dubious Kind. *Symbolic Interaction*, 14, 471–488.

—— and R. S. Perinbanayagam (eds) 1985: *Studies in Symbolic Interaction: Supplement 1: Foundations of Interpretive Sociology: Original Essays in Symbolic Interaction*. Greenwich, Conn.: JAI Press.

Farias, Victor 1987/89: *Heidegger and Nazism*. Philadelphia: Temple University Press.

Faris, R. E. L. 1952: *Social Psychology*. New York: Ronald Press.

—— 1970: *Chicago Sociology*. Chicago: University of Chicago Press.

Faulkner, Robert 1983: *Music on Demand*. New Brunswick, N.J.: Transaction Books.

Ferraro, Kathleen and John M. Johnson 1983: How Women Experience Battering. *Social Problems*, 30, 325–39.

Fiedler, Leslie A. 1966: *Love and Death in the American Novel*. New York: Stein and Day, rev. edn.

Fine, Gary Alan 1983a: *Shared Fantasy: Role-Playing Games as Social Worlds*. Chicago: University of Chicago Press.

—— 1983b: Symbolic Interaction and Social Organization: Introduction to the Special Feature. *Symbolic Interaction*, 6, 69–70.

—— 1987: *With the Boys*. Chicago: University of Chicago Press.

—— 1990: Symbolic Interactionism in the Post-Blumerian Age. In George Ritzer (ed.), *Frontiers of Social Theory*, New York: Columbia University Press, 117–57.

—— and Sheryl Kleinman 1983: Network and Meaning. An Interactionist Approach to Structure. *Symbolic Interaction*, 6, 97–110.

—— and Sheryl Kleinman 1986: Interpreting the Sociological Classics: Can there be a "True" Meaning of Mead? *Symbolic Interaction*, 9, 129–46.

—— and Kent L. Sandstrom 1988: *Knowing Children: Participant Observation with Minors*. Newbury Park, Calif.: Sage.

Fish, Stanley 1981: *Is there a Text in this Class: The Authority of Interpretive Communities*. Cambridge, Mass.: Harvard University Press.

Fisher, Berenice M. and Anselm L. Strauss 1978: Interactionism. In T. Bottomore and R. Nisbet (eds), *A History of Sociological Analysis*, New York: Basic Books, 457–98.

Flaherty, Michael G. 1988: Review Essay: "Studies in Symbolic Interaction: The Iowa School." *Symbolic Interaction*, 11, 145–60.

—— 1989: The Depiction of Symbolic Interactionism in Theory Textbooks. *Studies in Symbolic Interaction*, 10, 25–41.

Forman, Henry James 1933: *Our Movie Made Children*. New York: Macmillan.

Foucault, Michel 1966/70: *The Order of Things*. New York: Vintage.

—— 1977: *Discipline and Punishment*. New York: Pantheon.

—— 1980: *Power/Knowledge*. New York: Pantheon.

—— 1982: Afterword: The Subject and Power. In H. Dreyfus and P. Rabinow, *Michel Foucault: Beyond Structuralism and Hermeneutics*, Chicago: University of Chicago Press, 208–26.

Frank, Arthur W. 1985: Out of Ethnomethodology. In H. J. Helle and S. N. Eisenstadt (eds.), *Micro-Sociological Theory*, Newbury Park, Calif.: Sage, 101–16.

—— 1989: Review-Essay: Habermas's Interactionism: The Micro-Macro Link to Politics. *Symbolic Interaction*, 12, 353–60.

—— 1990: The Self at the Funeral: An Ethnography on the Limits of Postmodernism. *Studies in Symbolic Interaction*, 11, 191–206.

Franks, David D. and E. Doyle McCarthy (eds) 1989: *The Sociology of Emotions: Original Essays and Research Papers*. Greenwich, Conn.: JAI Press.

Fraser, Nancy 1989: *Unruly Practices*. Minneapolis: University of Minnesota Press.

Gans, Herbert J. 1962: Urbanism and Suburbanism as Ways of Life: A Reevaluation of Definitions. In A. Rose (ed.) 1962: 625–48.

—— 1974: *Popular Culture and High Culture*. New York: Basic Books.

—— 1979: *Deciding What's News*. New York: Vintage.

Garfinkel, Harold 1967a: Passing and the Managed Achievement of Sex Status in an Intersexed Person. In Garfinkel 1967b: 116–85.

—— 1967b: *Studies in Ethnomethodology*. Englewood Cliffs, N. J.: Prentice-Hall.

—— 1988: Evidence for Locally Produced, Naturally Accountable Phenomena of Order*, Logic, Reason, Meaning, Method, etc., in and as of the Essential Quiddity of Immortal Ordinary Society, (I of IV): An Announcement of Studies, *Sociological Theory*, 6, 103–9.

——, M. Lynch, and E. Livingston 1981: The Work of Discovering Science Construed with Materials from the Optically Discovered Pulsar. *Philosophy of the Social Sciences*, 11, 131–58.

Geertz, Clifford 1973: *The Interpretation of Cultures*. New York: Basic Books.

—— 1983: *Local Knowledge*: New York: Basic Books.

—— 1988: *Works and Lives: The Anthropologist as Author*. Stanford, Calif.: Stanford University Press.

Gerth, Hans and C. Wright Mills 1953: *Character and Social Structure*. New York: Harcourt.

Giddens, Anthony 1979: *Central Problems in Social Theory: Action, Structure and Contradiction in Social Analysis*. Berkeley: University of California Press.

—— 1984: *The Constitution of Society*. Berkeley: University of California Press.

—— 1987: Structuralism, Post-structuralism and the Production of Culture. In A. Giddens and J. Turner (eds), *Social Theory Today*, Stanford, Calif.: Stanford University Press, 195–223.

Glaser, Barney and Anselm L. Strauss 1965: *Awareness of Dying*. Chicago: Aldine.

—— 1967: *The Discovery of Grounded Theory*. Chicago: Aldine.

Goffman, Erving 1959: *The Presentation of Self in Everyday Life*. Garden City, N.Y.: Doubleday.

—— 1961a: *Asylums*. New York: Doubleday.

—— 1961b: *Encounters*. Indianapolis: Bobbs–Merrill.

—— 1963a: *Behavior in Public Places*. New York: Free Press.

—— 1963b: *Stigma*. Englewood Cliffs, N.J.: Prentice-Hall.

—— 1967: *Interaction Ritual*. New York: Doubleday.

—— 1971: *Relations in Public*. New York: Basic Books.

—— 1974: *Frame Analysis*. New York: Harper.

—— 1977: The Arrangement between the Sexes. *Theory and Society*, 4, 301–31.

—— 1979: *Gender Advertisements*. New York: Harper & Row.

—— 1981: *Forms of Talk*. Philadelphia: University of Pennsylvania Press.

—— 1983a: Felicity's Condition. *American Journal of Sociology*, 89, 1–53.

—— 1983b: The Interaction Order. *American Sociological Review*, 48, 1–17.

Goodman, Ellen 1989: Kitty Dukakis Shows New Act to Morality Play. *The Champaign-Urbana News Gazette*, 14 Feb., A–4.

Gottdiener, M. 1985: Hegemony and Mass Culture: A Semiotic Approach. *American Journal of Sociology*, 90, 979–1001.

—— 1986: Reply to Denzin. *American Journal of Sociology*, 92, 683–90.

Gouldner, Alvin 1968: The Sociologist as Partisan: Sociology and the Welfare State. *American Sociologist*, 3, 103–16.

—— 1970: *The Coming Crisis in Western Sociology*. New York: Basic Books.

Griswold, Wendy 1987: The Fabrication of Meaning: Literary Interpretation in the United States, Great Britain, and the West Indies. *American Journal of Sociology*, 92, 1077–1117.

—— 1990: Provisional, Provincial Positivism: Response to Denzin. *American Journal of Sociology*, 95, 1580–3.

Gronbeck, Bruce E. 1988: Symbolic Interactionism and Communication Studies: A Prolegomena to Future Research. In Maines and Couch (eds) 1988: 323–40.

Grossberg, Lawrence 1982: Experience, Signification and Reality: The Boundaries of Cultural Semiotics. *Semiotica*, 41, 73–106.

—— 1984: Strategies of Marxist Cultural Interpretation. *Critical Studies in Mass Communication*, 1, 392–421.

—— 1988a: *It's a Sin*. Sidney: Power Publications.

—— 1988b: Putting the Pop Back into Postmodernism. In A. Ross (ed.),

Universal Abandon, Minneapolis: University of Minnesota Press, 167–90.

—— 1989a: Cultural Studies Now and in the Future. Unpublished Manuscript.

—— 1989b: The Formations of Cultural Studies: An American in Birmingham. *Strategies,* 2 (Fall), 114–49.

Guba, Egon G. and Yvonne S. Lincoln 1989: *Fourth Generation Evaluation.* Newbury Park, Calif.: Sage.

Gubrium, Jaber 1988: *Analyzing Field Reality.* Newbury Park, Calif.: Sage.

Gurevitch, Z. D. 1990: Being Other: On Otherness in the Dialogue of the Self. *Studies in Symbolic Interaction,* 11, 285–307.

Gusfield, Joseph 1981: *The Culture of Public Problems.* Chicago: University of Chicago Press.

Habermas, Jürgen 1981/83: Modernity – An Incomplete Project. *New German Critique,* 22, 1–12. Reprinted in H. Foster (ed.), *The Anti-Aesthetic: Essays on Postmodern Culture,* Port Townsend, Wash.: Bay Press, 3–15.

—— 1985: Neoconservative Cultural Criticism in the United States and West Germany: An Intellectual Movement in Two Political Cultures. In R. J. Bernstein (ed.), *Habermas and Modernity,* Cambridge Mass.: MIT Press, 78–94.

—— 1987: *The Theory of Communicative Action,* Vol. 2. Boston: Beacon Press.

Hall, G. Stanley 1898: Some Aspects of the Early Sense of Self. *American Journal of Psychology,* 9, 351–95.

Hall, Peter M. 1972: A Symbolic Interactionist Analysis of Politics. *Sociological Inquiry,* 42, 35–75.

—— 1979: The Presidency and Impression Management. *Studies in Symbolic Interaction,* 2, 283–305.

—— 1985: Asymmetric Relationships and Processes of Power. *Studies in Symbolic Interaction, Supplement 1,* 309–44.

—— 1987: Presidential Address: Interactionism and the Study of Social Organization. *Sociological Quarterly,* 28, 1–22.

—— 1988: Asymmetry, Information Control, and Information Technology. In Maines and Couch (eds). 1988: 341–56.

—— and Dee Ann Spencer–Hall 1982: The Social Conditions of the Negotiated Order. *Urban Life,* 11, 328–49.

Hall, Stuart 1980a: Cultural Studies and the Centre: Some Problematics and Problems. In S. Hall, D. Hobson A. Lowe, and P. Willis (eds), *Culture, Media and Language: Working Papers in Cultural Studies, 1972–1979,* London: Hutchinson, 17–47.

—— 1980b: Cultural Studies: Two Paradigms: *Media, Culture and*

Society, 2, 57–72.

—— 1980c: Encoding/Decoding. In Hall et al, *Culture, Media and Language*, 128–38.

—— 1986a: Gramsci's Relevance for the Study of Race and Ethnicity. *Journal of Communication Inquiry*, 10, 5–27.

—— 1986b: On Postmodernism and Articulation: An Interview with Stuart Hall (edited by Lawrence Grossberg). *Journal of Communication Inquiry*, 10, 45–60.

—— 1986c: The Problem of Ideology – Marxism without Guarantees. *Journal of Communication Inquiry*, 10, 28–44.

—— 1988a: *The Hard Road to Renewal*. London: Verso.

—— 1988b: Questions and Answers. In Nelson and Grossberg (eds.) 1988: 58–73.

Hammersley, Martyn 1989: The Problem of the Concept: Herbert Blumer on the Relationship between Concepts and Date. *Journal of Contemporary Ethnography*, 18, 133–59.

—— and Paul Atkinson 1983: *Ethnography: Principles in Practice*. London: Tavistock.

Harman, Lesley D. 1986: Sign, Symbol and Metalanguage: Against the Integration of Semiotics and Symbolic Interactionism. *Symbolic Interaction*, 9, 147–60.

Harvey, David 1989: *The Condition of Postmodernity*. New York: Blackwell.

Harvey, Irene E. 1986: *Derrida and the Economy of Différence*. Bloomington: Indiana University Press.

Hegel, G. W. F. 1807/1931: *The Phenomenology of Mind*. London: Allen & Unwin.

Heidegger, Martin 1962: *Being and Time*. New York: Harper & Row.

—— 1977: *Basic Writings from Being and Time (1927) to the Task of Thinking (1964)*. New York: Harper & Row.

—— 1982: *The Basic Problems in Phenomenology*. Bloomington: Indiana University Press.

Heritage, John 1983: Accounts in Action. In G. N. Gilbert and P. Abell (eds.), *Accounts and Action*, Farnborough, England: Gower, 117–31.

—— 1984: *Garfinkel and Ethnomethodology*. Cambridge: Polity Press.

Hewitt, John P. 1989: *Dilemmas of the American Self*. Philadelphia: Temple University Press.

Heyl, Barbara Sherman 1979: *The Madam as Entrepreneur: Career Management in House Prostitution*. New Brunswick N.J.: Transaction Books.

Hickman, C. Addison and Manford H. Kuhn 1956: *Individuals, Groups and Economic Behavior*. New York: Dryden.

Hochschild, Arlie 1983: *The Managed Heart*. Berkeley: University of

California Press.
—— 1989: *The Second Shift*. New York: Knopf.
Hoggart, Richard 1957: *The Uses of Literacy*. London: Essential Books.
Horkheimer, Max and T. W. Adorno 1972: *Dialectic of Enlightenment*. New York: Herder and Herder.
Huber, Joan 1973a: Reply to Blumer: But who will Scrutinize the Scrutinizers? *American Sociological Review*, 38, 798–800.
—— 1973b: Symbolic Interaction as Pragmatic Perspective: The Bias of Emergent Theory. *American Sociological Review*, 38, 274–84.
—— 1974: The Emergency of Emergent Theory. *American Sociological Review*, 39, 463–6.
Hughes, Everett 1958: *Men and their Work*. New York: Free Press.
—— 1971: *The Sociological Eye*. Chicago: Aldine.
Hughes, Helen 1940: *News and the Human Interest Story*. Chicago: University of Chicago Press.
Hughes, Robert 1989: Review of Jean Baudrillard, *America*. *New York Review of Books*, 1 June, 29–32.
Huyssen, Andreas 1984/90: Mapping the Postmodern. In Linda J. Nicholson (ed.), *Feminism/Postmodernism*, New York: Routledge, 234–80.
Innis, Harold A. 1972: *Empire and Communications*. Toronto: University of Toronto Press.
Jacobs, Glenn 1979: Economy and Totality: Cooley's Theory of Pecuniary Valuation. *Studies in Symbolic Interaction*, 2, 39–84.
Jakobson, Roman 1956: Two Aspects of Language and Two Types of Aphasic Disturbances. In *idem, Fundamentals of Language*, The Hague: Mouton, 55–82.
—— 1962: *Selected Writings*. The Hague: Mouton.
James, W. 1890/1950: *The Principles of Psychology*, 2 vols. New York: Holt.
—— 1899: *Talk to Teachers on Psychology: and to Students on some of Life's Ideals*. New York: Henry Holt.
—— 1907: *Pragmatism*. New York: Longmans, Green, and Co.
Jameson, Fredric 1975–6: The Ideology of the Text. *Salmagundi*, 31/2, 204–46.
—— 1984: Postmodernism and the Logic of Late Capitalism. *New Left Review*, 146, 30–72.
—— 1990: *Signatures of the Visible*. New York: Routledge.
—— 1991: *Postmodernism, or, the Cultural Logic of Late Capitalism*. Durham, N. C.: Duke University Press.
Jansen, Sue Curry 1988: *Censorship: The Knot that binds Power and Knowledge*. New York: Oxford University Press.

Joas, Hans 1985: *G. H. Mead*. Cambridge: Polity Press.

—— 1987: Symbolic Interactionism. In A. Giddens and J. H. Turner (eds), *Social Theory Today*, Stanford, Calif.: Stanford University Press, 82–115.

Joffe, Carole 1977: *The Friendly Intruders*. Berkeley: University of California Press.

Johnson, C. S. 1934: *Shadow of the Plantation*. Chicago: University of Chicago Press.

Johnson, G. David and Peggy A. Shifflet 1981: George Herbert Who? A Critique of the Objectivist Reading of Mead. *Symbolic Interaction*, 4, 143–55.

Johnson, John M. 1975: *Doing Field Research*. New York: Free Press.

—— 1987: The Third Generation of Field Research Conduct. *Journal of Contemporary Ethnography*, 16, 94–110.

—— 1989: Lessons of Burography. *Journal of Applied Behaviorial Science*, 25, 439–50.

—— and David L. Altheide 1990: Reflexive Accountability. *Studies in Symbolic Interaction*, 11, 25–33.

—— and K. J. Ferraro 1984: The Victimized Self. In Kotarba and Fontana (eds.) 1984: 119–30.

Johnson, Richard 1986/7: What is Cultural Studies Anyway? *Social Text*, 16 (Winter), 38–80.

Jorgensen, Danny 1989: *Participant Observation*. Newbury Park, Calif.: Sage.

Kanter, Rosabeth Moss 1972: Symbolic Interactionism and Politics in Systematic Perspective. *Sociological Inquiry*, 42, 77–92.

Kariel, Henry S. 1989: *The Desperate Politics of Postmodernism*. Amherst, Mass.: University of Massachussetts Press.

Karpf, Fay Berger 1932: *American Social Psychology*. New York: McGraw-Hill.

Katovich, Michael 1987: Durkheim's Macrofoundations of Time: Assessment and Critique. *Sociological Quarterly*, 28, 367–85.

——, Stanley L. Saxton, and Joel O. Powell 1986: Naturalism in the Laboratory. *Studies in Symbolic Interaction, Supplement 2: The Iowa School (Part A)*, 79–88.

Katz, Jack 1988: *Seductions of Crime*. New York: Basic Books.

Kellner, Douglas 1989: *Critical Theory, Marxism and Modernity*. Baltimore, Md.: Johns Hopkins University Press.

Kemper, Theodore D. (ed.) 1990: *Research Agendas in the Sociology of Emotions*. Albany, N.Y.: SUNY Press.

Killian, Lewis M. 1985: The Stigma of Race: Who Now Bears the Mark of Cain? *Symbolic Interaction*, 8, 1–14.

Klepp, L. S. 1990: Everyman a Philosopher King. *New York Times Magazine*, 2 Dec., 57, 117–18, 122, 124.

Kohout, Frank J. 1975: Moving Forward: A Reconstruction of G. H. Mead's Epistemology and Comments on Interactionist Orthodoxy. Paper read at the Annual Symposium of the Society for the Study of Symbolic Interaction, Iowa City, Iowa.

Kojeve, Alexandre 1947/1969/1980: *Introduction to the Reading of Hegel: Lectures on the Phenomenology of Spirit*. Ithaca, N.Y.: Cornell University Press.

Kotarba, Joseph A. 1990: Ethnography and AIDS: Returning to the Streets. *Journal of Contemporary Ethnography*, 19, 259–70.

—— 1991: A Critique of Postmodernist Views of Heavy Metal Rock Music. *Social Science Journal*, in press.

—— and Andrea Fontana (eds) 1984: *The Existential Self in Society*. Chicago: University of Chicago Press.

Krieger, Susan 1984: Fiction and Social Science. *Studies in Symbolic Interaction*, 5, 269–86.

Kristeva J. 1969: *Semiotike*. Paris: Editions du Seuil.

—— 1975: The Subject in Signifying Practice. *Semiotext(e)*, 13, 44–5.

Kroker, Arthur, Marilouise Kroker, and David Cook 1990: Panic USA: Hypermodernism as America's Postmodernism. *Social Problems*, 37, 443–59.

Krueger, E. T. and Walter C. Reckless 1930: *Social Psychology*. New York: Longmans, Green and Co.

Krug, Gary J. and Laurel D. Graham 1989: Symbolic Interactionism: Pragmatism for the Postmodern Age. *Studies in Symbolic Interaction*, 10, 61–71.

Kuhn, Manford H. 1962: The Interview and the Professional Relationship. In A. M. Rose (ed.) 1962: 193–207.

—— 1964a/72: Major Trends in Symbolic Interaction Theory in the Past Twenty-five Years. *Sociological Quarterly*, 5, 61–84. Reprinted in Manis and Meltzer (eds) 1972: 57–75.

—— 1964b/72: The Reference Group Reconsidered. *Sociological Quarterly*, 5, 6–21. Reprinted in Manis and Meltzer (eds) 1972: 171–84.

Lacan, Jacques 1949: The Mirror Stage as Formative of the Function of the I as Revealed in Psychoanalytic Experience. In Lacan 1966, 1–7.

—— 1957: The Agency of the Letter in the Unconscious or Reason since Freud. In Lacan 1966: 146–78.

—— 1966. *Ecrits*. Paris: Edition du Seuil.

—— 1968: *Speech and Language in Psychoanalysis*. Baltimore: Johns Hopkins University Press.

—— 1978: *The Four Fundamental Concepts of Psycho-Analysis*. New

York: Norton.

—— 1982: *Feminine Sexuality*. New York: Norton.

Laclau, Ernesto and Chantal Mouffe 1985: *Hegemony and Socialist Strategy: towards a Radical Democratic Politics*. London: Verso.

Lal, Barbara Ballis 1982: "So Near and Yet So Far": The "Chicago School" of Symbolic Interactionism and its Relationship to Developments in the Sociology of Sociology and Ethnomethodology. *Symbolic Interaction*, 4, 151–70.

Lamont, Michele 1987: How to Become a Dominant French Philosopher. The Case of Jacques Derrida. *American Journal of Sociology*, 93, 584–622.

Lash, Scott 1988: Discourse or Figure? Postmodernism as a "Regime of Signification." *Theory, Culture & Society*, 5, 311–35.

Lauretis, Teresa de 1987: *Technologies of Gender*. Bloomington: Indiana University Press.

Leavitt, Robin L. and Martha Bauman Power 1989: Emotional Socialization in the Postmodern Era: Children in Day Care. *Social Psychology Quarterly*, 52, 35–43.

Lee, Grace Chin 1949: *George Herbert Mead*. New York: King's Crown Press.

Lefebvre, Henri 1971/84: *Everyday Life in the Modern World*. New Brunswick, N. J.: Transaction Books.

Lemert, Charles 1979a: *Sociology and the Twilight of Man: Homocentrism and Discourse in Sociological Theory*. Carbondale: Southern Illinois University Press.

—— 1979b: Structuralist Semiotics and the Decentering of Sociology. In S. G. McNall (ed.), *Theoretical Perspectives in Sociology*, New York: St Martin's Press, 96–111.

—— 1986: Whole Life Social Theory. *Theory and Society*, 15, 431–42.

Lewis, David 1979: A Social Behaviorist Interpretation of the Meadian "I." *American Journal of Sociology*, 85, 261–87.

—— and R. L. Smith 1980: *American Sociology and Pragmatism*. Chicago: University of Chicago Press.

Lichtman, Richard T. 1970: Symbolic Interactionism and Social Reality: Some Marxist Queries. *Berkeley Journal of Sociology*, 15, 75–94.

Lindesmith, Alfred 1947: *Opiate Addiction*. Bloomington, Ind.: Principia Press.

—— 1968: *Addiction and Opiates*. Chicago, Aldine.

—— and Anselm L. Strauss 1949: *Social Psychology*. New York: Dryden.

——, A. Strauss, and N. Denzin 1978: *Social Psychology*, 5th edn. New York: Holt, Rinehart & Winston.

——, 1991: *Social Psychology*, 7th edn. Englewood Cliffs, N.J.: Prentice-Hall.

Lindsay, Vachel 1915: *The Art of the Moving Picture*. New York: Macmillan.

Lofland, John 1970: Interactionist Imagery and Analytic Interruptus. In Shibutani (ed.) 1970: 35–45.

—— 1971: *Analyzing Social Settings*. Belmont, Calif.: Wadsworth.

—— 1976: *Doing Social Life*. New York: Wiley.

—— 1977: *Doomsday Cult*, enlarged edn. New York: Irvington Press.

—— 1981: Collective Behavior: The Elementary Forms. In M. Rosenberg and R. Turner (eds), *Social Psychology*, New York: Basic Books, 411–46.

—— 1987: Reflections on a Thrice-Named Journal. *Journal of Contemporary Ethnography*, 16, 25–40.

—— (ed.) 1978: *Interaction in Everyday Life: Social Strategies*. Beverly Hills, Calif.: Sage.

—— and Lyn H. Lofland 1984: *Analyzing Social Settings*, 2nd edn. Belmont, Calif.: Wadsworth.

Lofland, Lyn 1980: The 1969 Blumer–Hughes Talk. *Urban Life and Culture*, 8, 248–60.

Loseke, Donileen R. 1987: Lived Realities and the Construction of Social Problems: The Case of Wife Abuse. *Symbolic Interaction*, 10, 229–43.

—— 1989: Evaluation Research and the Practice of Social Services: A Case for Qualitative Methodology. *Journal of Contemporary Ethnography*, 18, 202–29.

Luckmann, Thomas (ed.) 1978: *Phenomenology and Sociology*. New York: Penguin.

Luker, K. 1984: *Abortion and the Politics of Motherhood*. Berkeley: University of California Press.

Lyman, Stanford 1990a: Anhedonia: Gender and the Decline of Emotions in American Film, 1930–1988. *Sociological Inquiry*, 60, 1–19.

—— 1990b: *Civilization: Contents, Discontents, Malcontents and Other Essays in Social Theory*. Fayetteville: University of Arkansas Press.

—— 1990c: Park and Realpolitik: Race, Culture and Modern Warfare. *International Journal of Politics, Culture and Society*, 3, 565–86.

—— 1991: *Militarism, Imperialism and Racial Accommodation: An Analysis and Interpretation of the Early Writings of Robert E. Park*. Fayetteville: University of Arkansas Press.

—— and Arthur J. Vidich 1988: *Social Order and the Public Philosophy: The Analysis and Interpretation of the Work of Herbert Blumer*. Fayetteville: University of Arkansas Press.

—— and Marvin Scott 1989: *A Sociology of the Absurd*, 2nd edn. Dix

Hills, N.Y.: General Hall.
Lyotard, Jean 1979/84: *The Postmodern Condition*. Minneapolis: University of Minnesota Press.
MacKinnon, Catharine A. 1983: Feminism, Marxism, Method, and the State: Toward a Feminist Jurisprudence. *Signs*, 8, 635–59.
Maines, David R. 1977: Social Organization and Social Structure in Symbolic Interactionist Thought. *Annual Review of Sociology*, 3, 235–59.
—— 1982: In Search of Mesostructure: Studies in the Negotiated Order. *Urban Life*, 11, 267–79.
—— 1988: Myth, Text, and Interactionist Complicity in the Neglect of Blumer's Macrosociology. *Symbolic Interaction*, 11, 43–57.
—— 1989a: Herbert Blumer on the Possibility of Science in the Practice of Sociology. *Journal of Contemporary Ethnography*, 18, 160–77.
—— 1989b: Repackaging Blumer: The Myth of Herbert Blumer's Astructural Bias. *Studies in Symbolic Interaction*, 10, 383–413.
—— and Carl J. Couch (eds) 1988: *Communication and Social Structure*. Springfield, Ill.: Charles C. Thomas.
—— and Thomas J. Morrione (eds) 1990: *Industrialization as an Agent of Social Change: A Critical Analysis by Herbert Blumer*. New York: Aldine de Gruyter.
——, Noreen M. Sugrue, and Michael A. Katovich 1983: The Sociological Import of G. H. Mead's Theory of the Past. *American Sociological Review*, 484: 161–73.
Manis, Jerome G. and Bernard N. Meltzer (eds) 1967: *Symbolic Interaction: A Reader in Social Psychology*, 1st edn. Boston: Allyn and Bacon.
—— (eds) 1972: *Symbolic Interaction: A Reader in Social Psychology*, 2nd edn. Boston: Allyn and Bacon.
Manning, Peter K 1985: Limits upon the Semiotic Structuralist Perspective on Organizational Analysis. *Studies in Symbolic Interaction*, 5, 79–111.
—— 1987: *Semiotics and Fieldwork*. Newbury Park, Calif.: Sage.
—— 1988a: Semiotics and Social Psychology. *Studies in Symbolic Interaction*, 8, 40–67.
—— 1988b: *Symbolic Communication*. Cambridge, Mass.: MIT Press.
Marcus, George E. and Michael M. J. Fischer 1986: *Anthropology as Cultural Critique*. Chicago: University of Chicago Press.
Martindale, Don 1960: *The Nature and Types of Sociological Theory*, 1st edn. Boston: Houghton Mifflin.
——1981: *The Nature and Types of Sociological Theory*, 2nd edn. Boston: Houghton Mifflin.

Marx, Karl 1852/1983: From the Eighteenth Brumaire of Louis Bonaparte. In E. Kamenka (ed.), *The Portable Karl Marx*, New York: Penguin, 287–323.

Maryl, William W. 1973: Ethnomethodology: Sociology without Society. *Catalyst*, 7, 15–28.

Mascia-Lees, Frances E., Colleen B. Cohen, and Patricia Sharpe 1987–88: The Post-Modernist Turn in Anthropology: Cautions from a Feminist Perspective. *Journal of the Steward Anthropological Society*, 17, 251–82.

Mast, Gerald 1976: *A Short History of the Movies*. Indianapolis, Ind.: Bobbs-Merrill.

Matza, David 1969: *Becoming Deviant*. Englewood Cliffs N.J.: Prentice-Hall.

Maynard, Douglas M. 1987: Language and Social Interaction. *Social Psychological Quarterly*, 50, v–vi.

McCall, George J. and J. L. Simmons 1966/78: *Identities and Interactions*, rev. edn. New York: Free Press.

McCall, Michal M. 1990: The Significance of Storytelling. *Studies in Symbolic Interaction*, 11, 145–61.

—— and Judith Wittner 1990: The Good News about Life History. In H. S. Becker and M. M. McCall (eds), *Symbolic Interaction and Cultural Studies*, Chicago: University of Chicago Press, 46–89.

McCarthy, E. Doyle 1984: Toward a Sociology of the Physical World: George Herbert Mead on Physical Objects. *Studies in Symbolic Interaction*, 5, 105–21.

McLuhan, Marshall 1965: *Understanding Media*, New York: McGraw-Hill.

McPhail, Clark 1989: Meadian versus Neo-Meadian Theories of Mind. *Symbolic Interaction*, 12, 43–51.

—— 1991: *Far from the Madding Crowd*. New York: Aldine de Gruyter.

—— and Cynthia Rexroat 1979: Mead vs. Blumer. The Divergent Methodological Perspectives of Social Behaviorism and Symbolic Interactionism. *American Sociological Review*, 44, 449–67.

—— —— 1980: Ex Cathedra Blumer or Ex Libris Mead? *American Sociological Review*, 45, 420–30.

Mead, George Herbert 1900: Suggestions toward a Theory of the Philosophical Disciplines. *Philosophical Review*, 9, 1–17.

—— 1904: The Relations of Psychology and Philology. *Psychological Bulletin*, 1, 375–91.

—— 1907: Concerning Animal Perception. *Psychological Review*, 14, 383–90.

—— 1910/64: What Social Objects must Psychology Presuppose?

Journal of Philosophy, Psychology, and Scientific Methods, 7, 174–80. Reprinted in Reck (ed.), *Mead: Selected Writings*, 105–13.

—— 1912: The Mechanism of Social Consciousness. *Journal of Philosophy, Psychology, and Scientific Methods*, 9, 401–6.

—— 1925–6/64: The Nature of Aesthetic Experience. In Reck (ed.), *Mead: Selected Writings*, 294–305.

—— 1929–30/64: The Philosophies of Royce, James, and Dewey in their American Setting. In Reck (ed.), *Mead: Selected Writings*, 371–91.

—— 1930/64: Philanthropy from the Point of View of Ethics. In A. Reck (ed.), *George Herbert Mead: Selected Writings*, Indianapolis, Ind.: Bobbs-Merrill, 392–407.

—— 1932: *The Philosophy of the Present*. Chicago: University of Chicago Press.

—— 1934: Mind, Self and Society. Chicago: University of Chicago Press.

—— 1936: *Movements of Thought in the Nineteenth Century*. Chicago: University of Chicago Press.

—— 1938: *The Philosophy of the Act*. Chicago: University of Chicago Press.

—— 1964: *Selected Writings: George Herbert Mead*, edited with an Introduction by A. J. Reck. Indianapolis Ind.: Bobbs-Merrill.

—— 1982: *The Individual and the Social Self: Unpublished Work of George Herbert Mead*, edited with an Introduction by D. L. Miller. Chicago: University of Chicago Press.

Meltzer, Bernard N. 1959/72: The Social Psychology of George Herbert Mead. Kalamazoo: Center for Sociological Research, Western Michigan University. Reprinted in Manis and Meltzer 1972, 4–22.

—— and Nancy J. Herman 1990: Epilogue: Human Emotion, Social Structure and Symbolic Interactionism. In Reynolds 1990: 181–225.

——, John W. Petras, and Larry T. Reynolds 1975: *Symbolic Interactionism: Genesis, Varieties and Criticism*. Boston: Routledge.

Merleau-Ponty, M. 1964: *Sense and Non-Sense*. Evanston, Ill.: Northwestern University Press.

—— 1969: *Humanism and Terror*. Boston: Beacon Press.

—— 1973: *The Prose of the World*, ed. C. Lefrot, tr. J. O'Neill. Evanston, Ill.: Northwestern University Press.

Merrill, Frances E. 1970: *Le Group des Batignolles*: A Study in the Sociology of Art. In Shibutani (ed.) 1970: 250–9.

Merton, Robert K. 1957: *Social Theory and Social Structure*. New York: Free Press.

Metz, Christian 1982: *The Imaginary Signifier: Psychoanalysis and the Cinema*. Bloomington: Indiana University Press.

Meyrowitz, Joshua 1985: *No Sense of Place*. New York: Oxford

University Press.

Mills, C. Wright 1942/63: Pragmatism, Politics and Religion. Reprinted in Wright Mills 1963: 159–69.

—— 1943/63: The Professional Ideology of Social Pathologists. *American Journal of Sociology*, 49, 165–80. Reprinted in *Wright Mills* 1963: 525–52.

—— 1948: *The New Men of Power: America's Labor Leaders*. New York: Harcourt.

—— 1950/63: Mass Media and Public Opinion. In *Wright Mills* 1963: 577–98.

—— 1951: *White Collar*. New York: Oxford University Press.

—— 1956: *The Power Elite*. New York: Oxford University Press.

—— 1959: *The Sociological Imagination*. New York: Oxford University Press.

—— 1963: *Power, Politics and People: The Collected Essays of C. Wright Mills*, edited with an Introduction by Irving Louis Horowitz. New York: Ballantine.

—— 1964: *Sociology and Pragmatism*. New York: Oxford University Press.

—— and Hazel Gaudet 1946: What the People Think: Review of Selected Opinion Polls. *Labor and Nation*, 11 (Nov.–Dec.), 11–13.

Mitchell, Juliet 1982: Introduction — I. In J. Mitchell and J. Rose (eds), *Feminine Sexuality: Jacques Lacan and the école freudienne*, New York: Pantheon, 1–26.

Molseed, Mari J. 1989: Gender, Silence, and Group Structure. *Studies in Symbolic Interaction*, 10, 145–65.

Monaco, James 1981: *How to Read a Film*, rev. edn. New York: Oxford University Press.

Morrione, Thomas J. 1985: Situated Interaction. In Farberman and Perinbanayagam (eds) 1985: 161–92.

—— 1988: Herbert Blumer (1900–1987): A Legacy of Concepts, Criticisms, and Contributions. *Symbolic Interaction*, 11, 1–12.

—— and Harvey A. Farberman 1981a: Conversation with Herbert Blumer: I. *Symbolic Interaction*, 4, 113–28.

—— 1981b. Conversation with Herbert Blumer: II. *Symbolic Interaction*, 4, 273–95.

Morris, Charles 1938: *Foundations of the Theory of Signs*. Chicago: University of Chicago Press.

Morris, Meaghan 1988a: At Henry Parkes Motel. *Cultural Studies*, 2, 1–47.

—— 1988b: Introduction: Feminism, Reading, Postmodernism. In Morris 1988c: 1–18.

—— 1988c: *The Pirate's Fiancée: Feminism, Reading, Postmodernism.* London: Verso.

Mukerji, Chandra and Michael Schudson 1986: Popular Culture. *Annual Review of Sociology*, 12, 47–66.

Mullins, Nicholas C. (with the assistance of Carolyn J. Mullins) 1973: *Theories and Theory Groups in Contemporary American Sociology.* New York: Harper & Row.

Mulvey, Laura 1982: Visual Pleasure and Narrative Cinema. *Screen*, Autumn, 412–28.

Munch, Richard and Neil J. Smelser 1987: Relating the Micro and Macro. In J. C. Alexander *et al.* (eds), *The Micro-Macro Link*, Berkeley: University of California Press, 356–87.

Munsterberg, Hugo 1916: *The Film: A Psychological Study.* New York: Dover.

Natanson, Maurice 1956: *The Social Dynamics of George H. Mead.* Washington, D.C.: Public Affairs Press.

Nelson, Cary and Lawrence Grossberg (eds) 1988: *Marxism and the Interpretation of Culture.* Urbana: University of Illinois Press.

Norris, Christopher 1983: *The Deconstructive Turn: Essays in the Rhetoric of Philosophy.* New York: Methuen.

—— 1985: *The Contest of Faculties: Philosophy and Theory after Deconstruction.* New York: Methuen.

Novack, George 1975: *Pragmatism versus Marxism: An Appraisal of John Dewey's Philosophy.* New York: Pathfinder Press.

Park, Robert E. 1925/67: Community Organization and Juvenile Delinquency. In R. E. Park and E. W. Burgess (eds), *The City*, Chicago: University of Chicago Press, 99–112.

—— 1926/50: Behind our Masks. Reprinted in Park 1950: 244–55.

—— 1926/67: The Urban Community as a Spatial Pattern and a Moral Order. In Ernest W. Burgess (ed.), *The Urban Community*, Chicago: University of Chicago Press, 3–18. Reprinted in Turner (ed.), *Park on Social Control*, 55–68.

—— 1934/50: The Negro and his Plantation Heritage. Introduction to C. S. Johnson 1964: xi–xxiv. Reprinted in Park 1950: 66–78.

—— 1938/50: Reflections on Communications and Culture. *American Journal of Sociology*, 44, 187–205. Reprinted in Park 1950: 36–54.

—— 1940/67: News as a Form of Knowledge. *American Journal of Sociology*, 45, 669–86. Reprinted in Turner (ed.), in *Park on Social Control*, 33–52.

—— 1950: *Race and Culture.* New York: Free Press.

—— 1967: *Robert E. Park on Social Control and Collective Behavior*, edited with an Introduction by Ralph H. Turner. Chicago: University of Chicago Press.

—— and Ernest W. Burgess (eds) 1921: *Introduction to the Science of Sociology*. Chicago: University of Chicago Press.

Parsons, Talcott 1961: The Point of View of the Author. In Max Black (ed.), *The Social Theories of Talcott Parsons*, Englewood Cliffs, N.J.: Prentice-Hall, 311–63.

Peirce, C. S. 1934: *Collected Papers of Charles Sanders Peirce*, Vols 5 and 6, ed. C. Hartshone, tr. P. Weiss. Cambridge, Mass.: Harvard University Press (Belknap).

—— 1958: *Collected Papers of Charles Sanders Peirce*, vols 7 and 8, ed. C. Hartshone, tr. P. Weiss. Cambridge, Mass.: Harvard University Press (Belknap).

People Weekly 1988: no. 15, 18 Apr.

Perinbanayagam, Robert 1985: *Signifying Acts*. Carbondale, Ill.: Southern Illinois University Press.

—— 1991: *Discursive Acts*. New York: Aldine de Gruyter.

Peterson, Richard A. (ed.) 1976: *The Production of Culture*. Beverly Hills, Calif.: Sage.

Peterson, R. C. and L. L. Thurstone 1933: *Motion Pictures and the Social Attitudes of Children*. New York: Macmillan.

Pfeutze, Paul E. 1954: *The Social Self*. New York: Bookman Associates. Reprinted in 1961 as *Self, Society, and Existence*. New York: Harper.

Plummer, Ken 1983: *Documents of Life*. London: George Allen & Unwin.

—— 1990: Herbert Blumer and the Life History Tradition. *Symbolic Interaction*, 13, 125–44.

—— (ed.) 1991: *Symbolic Interactionism*, Volume I and II: *Classic and Contemporary Issues*. Hants, England: Edward Elgar.

Power, Martha Bauman 1985: The Ritualization of Emotional Conduct in Early Childhood. *Studies in Symbolic Interaction*, 6, 213–27.

Prendergast, Christopher and John David Knottnerus 1990: The Astructural Bias and Presuppositional Reform in Symbolic Interactionism: A Noninteractionist Evaluation of the New Studies in Social Organization. In Reynolds 1990: 158–80.

Prus, Robert 1987: Generic Social Processes: Maximizing Conceptual Development in Ethnographic Research. *Journal of Contemporary Ethnography*, 16, 250–93.

Racevskis, Karlis 1983: *Michel Foucault and the Subversion of Intellect*. Ithaca, N.Y.: Cornell University Press.

Ragland-Sullivan, Ellie 1986: *Jacques Lacan and the Philosophy of Psychoanalysis*. Urbana: University of Illinois Press.

Rawls, Anne 1987: The Interaction Order Sui Generis: Goffman's

Contribution to Social Theory. *Sociological Theory*, 5, 136–49.

Ray, Robert 1985: *A Certain Tendency in Hollywood Cinema: 1930–1980*. Princeton: Princeton University Press.

Reck, Andrew J. 1964: Introduction to A. Reck (ed.), *George Herbert Mead: Selected Writings*, Indianapolis, Ind.: Bobbs-Merrill, xiii–lxii.

Reese, William A. II, and Michael A. Katovich 1989: Untimely Acts: Extending the Interactionist Conception of Deviance. *Sociological Quarterly*, 30, 159–84.

Reisner, Ann E. 1990: The Bounded Constraints of Rules: A Model of Rule-Use using a Newsroom Example. *Studies in Symbolic Interaction*, 11, 373–409.

Reynolds, Larry T. 1990: *Interactionism: Exposition and Critique*, 2nd edn. Dix Hills, N.Y.: General Hall.

—— and Janice M. Reynolds 1973: The Origins of Divergent Methodological Stances in Symbolic Interactionism. *Sociological Quarterly*, 14, 189–99.

Rice, Stuart C. (ed.) 1931: *Methods of Social Science: A Case Book*. Chicago: University of Chicago Press.

Richardson, Laurel 1988: The Collective Story: Postmodernism and the Writing of Sociology. *Sociological Focus*, 21, 199–208.

—— 1990: *Writing Strategies*, Newbury Park, Calif.: Sage.

—— 1991a: The Poetic Representation of Lives: Writing a Postmodernist Sociology. *Studies in Symbolic Interaction*, 13, in press.

—— 1991b: Speakers Whose Voices Matter: Toward a Feminist Postmodernist Sociological Praxis. *Studies in Symbolic Interaction*, 12, in press.

Rochberg-Halton, Eugene 1986: *Meaning and Modernity: Social Theory in the Pragmatic Attitude*. Chicago: University of Chicago Press.

—— 1989: Review-Essay: Jürgen Habermas's Theory of Communicative Etherealization. *Symbolic Interaction*, 12, 333–60.

Rock, Paul 1979: *The Making of Symbolic Interactionism*. London: Macmillan.

Roffman, Peter and Jim Purdy 1981: *The Hollywood Social Problem Film*. Bloomington: Indiana University Press.

Ropers, Richard 1973: Mead, Marx and Social Psychology. *Catalyst*, 7, 42–61.

Rorty, Richard 1979: *Philosophy and the Mirror of Nature*. Princeton: Princeton University Press.

—— 1982: *Consequences of Pragmatism*. Minneapolis: University of Minnesota Press.

—— 1985: Habermas and Lyotard on Postmodernity. In R. J. Bernstein (ed.), *Habermas and Modernity*, Cambridge, Mass.: MIT Press,

161–76.

—— 1989: *Contingency, Irony, and Solidarity*. New York: Cambridge University Press.

Rose, Arnold M. (ed.) 1962: *Human Behavior and Social Processes*. Boston: Houghton Mifflin.

Rose, Dan 1987–8: Ethnography as a Form of Life: The Written Word and the Work of the World. *Journal of the Steward Anthropological Society*, 17, 219–50.

—— 1990: *Living the Ethnographic Life*. Newbury Park, Calif.: Sage.

Rose, Jacqueline 1982: Introduction – II. In J. Mitchell and J. Rose (eds), *Feminine Sexuality: Jacques Lacan and the école freudienne*, New York: Pantheon, 27–58.

Ross, Andrew 1989: *No Respect: Intellectuals & Popular Culture*. New York: Routledge.

Ross, E. A. 1928: *In World Drift*. New York: Macmillan.

Russell, Bertrand 1945: *A History of Western Philosophy*. New York: Simon and Schuster.

Ryan, Michael and Douglas Kellner 1988: *Camera Politica*. Bloomington: Indiana University Press.

Rytina, Joan Huber and Charles P. Loomis 1970: Marxist Dialectic and Pragmatism: Power as Knowledge. *American Sociological Review*, 35, 308–18.

Said, Edward 1978: *Orientalism*. New York: Pantheon.

Sartre, Jean-Paul 1943/56: *Being and Nothingness*. New York: Philosophical Library.

—— 1957: *The Transcendence of the Ego*. New York: Noonday Press.

—— 1963: *Search for a Method*. New York: Knopf.

—— 1974: *Between Existentialism and Marxism*. New York: Morrow Quill.

—— 1976: *Critique of Dialectical Reason*. London: NLP.

—— 1981: *The Family Idiot: Gustave Flaubert*, Vol. 1, *1821–1857*. Chicago: University of Chicago Press.

Saussure, F. de 1959. *The Course in General Linguistics*. New York: Philosophical Library.

Saxton, Stanley L. 1989: Reading Recent Interactionist Work. *Studies in Symbolic Interaction*, 10, 9–24.

Schatz, Thomas 1981: *Hollywood Genres: Formulas, Film-making, and the Studio System*. New York: Random House.

Scheff, Thomas 1979: *Catharsis in Healing, Ritual and Drama*. Berkeley: University of California Press.

Schmitt, Tiffani Mari and Raymond L. Schmitt 1990: Constructing AIDS Policy in the Public Schools: A Multimethod Case Study. *Journal of*

Contemporary Ethnography, 19, 295–321.

Schmitt, Raymond L. 1974: SI and Emergent Theory: A Re-examination. *American Sociological Review*, 39, 453–6.

Schutz, Alfred 1932/67: *The Phenomenology of the Social World*. Evanston, Ill.: Northwestern University Press.

Sciulli, David 1989: Reconsidering Blumer's Corrective against the Excesses of Functionalism. *Symbolic Interaction*, 11, 69–84.

Searle, John 1990: The Storm over the University: Review-Essay. *New York Review of Books*, 37 (6 Dec.), 34–42.

Shalin, Dmitri N. 1984: The Romantic Antecedents of Meadian Social Psychology. *Symbolic Interaction*, 7, 44–66.

—— 1986: Pragmatism and Social Interactionism. *American Sociological Review*, 51, 9–29.

—— 1987a: G. H. Mead, Socialism, and the Progressive Agenda. *American Journal of Sociology*, 93, 913–51.

—— 1987b: Socialism, Democracy and Reform: A Letter and an Article by George H. Mead. *Symbolic Interaction*, 10, 267–78.

—— 1991: The Pragmatic Origins of Symbolic Interactionism and the Crisis of Classical Science. *Studies in Symbolic Interaction*, 12, in press.

Shaskolsky, Leon 1970: The Development of Sociological Theory in America: A Sociology of Knowledge Interpretation. In L. T. Reynolds and J. M. Reynolds (eds), *The Sociology of Sociology*, New York: McKay, 6–30.

Shaw, Clifford R. 1930/66: *The Jack-Roller: A Delinquent Boy's Own Story*. Chicago: University of Chicago Press.

Shibutani, Tamotsu (ed.) 1961: *Society and Personality*. Englewood Cliffs, N. J.: Prentice-Hall.

—— 1970: *Human Nature and Collective Behavior: Papers in Honor of Herbert Blumer*. Englewood Cliffs N.J.: Prentice-Hall.

—— and Kian Kwan 1965: *Ethnic Stratification*. Englewood Cliffs, N.J.: Prentice-Hall.

Shils, Edward 1948: *The Present State of American Sociology*. Glencoe, Ill.: Free Press.

—— 1961: The Calling of Sociology. In T. Parsons *et al.* (eds), *Theories of Society*, New York: Free Press, 1405–48.

Simmel, Georg 1908/21: The Sociological Significance of the Stranger. In Simmel, *Soziologie*, Leipzig: Duncker and Humbolt, 1908: 685–91. Reprinted in Park and Burgess (eds.) 1921: 322–27.

—— 1909: The Problem of Sociology. *American Journal of Sociology*, 15, 289–320.

Sklar, Robert 1975: *Movie-Made America*. New York: Random House.

Smedley, Charles 1985: Mead's Problematics. Unpublished doctoral dissertation, Department of Sociology, University of Illinois at Urbana–Champaign.

Smelser, Neil J. 1984: *Sociology: Alternate Edition.* Englewood Cliffs, N.J.: Prentice-Hall.

—— 1988: Social Structure. In Neil J. Smelser (ed.), *Handbook of Sociology*, Newbury Park, Calif.: Sage, 103–29.

Smith, Dorothy E. 1987: *The Everyday World as Problematic: A Feminist Sociology.* Toronto: University of Toronto Press.

Smith, Dusky Lee 1973: Symbolic Interactionism: Definitions of the Situation from H. Becker to J. Lofland. *Catalyst*, 7, 62–75.

Snodgrass, Jon 1982: *The Jack-Roller at Seventy: A Fifty-Year Follow-Up.* Lexington, Mass.: Lexington Books.

Snow, Robert 1988: Forms, Formats and Grammatical Structure in Mass Media. In Maines and Couch (eds) 1988: 201–14.

Spector, Malcolm and John I. Kitsuse 1977: *Constructing Social Problems.* Menlo Park, Calif.: Cummings.

Spivak, Gayatri Chakravorty 1974/76: Translator's Preface. In Jacques Derrida, *Of Grammatology*, tr. G. C. Spivak, Baltimore, Md.: Johns Hopkins University Press, ix–xxxvii.

Stewart, Robert L. 1981: What George Herbert Mead should have Said: Exploration of a Problem of Interpretation. *Symbolic Interaction*, 4, 157–66.

Stoller, Robert J. 1968/74: *Sex and Gender.* Vol. 1: *The Development of Masculinity and Femininity.* New York: Jason Aronson.

Stone, Gregory P. 1962: Appearance and the Self. In A. Rose (ed.) 1962: 86–118.

—— 1981: Appearance and the Self: A Slightly Revised Version. In Stone and Farberman (eds) 1981: 187–202.

—— and H. A. Farberman (eds.) 1970: *Social Psychology through Symbolic Interaction.* Waltham, Ma.: Ginn-Blaisdell.

——, —— (eds.) 1981: *Social Psychology through Symbolic Interaction*, 2nd edn. New York: Wiley.

——, D. R. Maines, H. A. Farberman, G. I. Stone, and N. K. Denzin 1974: On Methodology and Craftsmanship in the Criticism of Sociological Perspectives. *American Sociological Review*, 39, 456–63.

Strauss, Anselm 1959: *Mirrors and Masks.* New York: Free Press.

—— 1978: *Negotiations.* San Francisco: Jossey-Bass.

—— 1984: Social Worlds and their Segmentation Processes. *Studies in Symbolic Interaction*, 5, 125–39.

—— 1987: *Qualitative Analysis for Social Scientists.* New York: Cambridge University Press.

—— (ed.) 1956: *George Herbert Mead on Social Psychology*. Chicago: University of Chicago Press.

—— and Juliet Corbin 1990: *Basics of Qualitative Research*. Newbury Park, Calif.: Sage.

——, S. Fagerhaugh, B. Suczek, and B. Wiener 1985: *The Social Organization of Medical Work*. Chicago: University of Chicago Press.

Stryker, Sheldon 1980: *Symbolic Interactionism*. Menlo Park, Calif.: Benjamin/Cummings.

—— 1981: Symbolic Interactionism: Themes and Variations. In M. Rosenberg and R. Turner (eds), *Social Psychology: Sociological Perspectives*, New York: Basic Books, 3–29.

—— 1987: The Vitalization of Symbolic Interactionism. *Social Psychology Quarterly*, 50, 83–94.

—— 1988: Substance and Style: An Appraisal of the Sociological Legacy of Herbert Blumer. *Symbolic Interaction*, 11, 33–42.

Sullivan, Harry Stack 1953: *The Interpersonal Theory of Psychiatry*. New York: Norton.

Swidler, Ann 1986: Culture in Action. *American Sociological Review*, 51, 273–86.

Symbolic Interaction 1981: Commemorative Issue in Honor of George Herbert Mead, 4, entire issue.

Symbolic Interaction 1988: Special Issue on Herbert Blumer's Legacy, 11, 1–144.

Symbolic Interaction 1989: Special Issue on G. H. Mead, 12, 1–120.

Taylor, Mark S. (ed.) 1986: *Deconstruction in Context: Literature and Philosophy*. Chicago: University of Chicago Press.

Thomas, W. I. and Florian Znaniecki 1918/19/20: *The Polish Peasant in Europe and America*. Chicago: University of Chicago Press, 1918, 1919; Boston: Badger Press, 1920.

Thompson, E. P. 1963: *The Making of the English Working Class*. New York: Vintage.

Tuchman, Gaye 1978: *Making News*. New York: Free Press.

Tucker, Charles W. 1966: Some Methodological Problems of Kuhn's Self Theory. *Sociological Quarterly*, 7, 345–58.

—— 1988: Herbert Blumer: A Pilgrimage with Pragmatism. *Symbolic Interaction*, 11, 99–124.

—— and Robert L. Stewart 1989: Science, Self and Symbolic Interaction. *Studies in Symbolic Interaction*, 10, 45–60.

Turner, Ralph 1978: Role and the Person. *American Journal of Sociology*, 84, 1–23.

Turner, Victor W. and Edward M. Bruner (eds) 1986: *The Anthropology of Experience*. Urbana: University of Illinois Press.

Ulbrecht, Robert E. 1953: A Study of John Dewey's Philosophy of Art. Unpublished Master's thesis, Department of Philosophy, University of Illinois at Urbana–Champaign.

Ulmer, Gregory L. 1985: *Applied Grammatology: Post (e)-Pedagogy from Jacques Derrida to Joseph Beuys*. Baltimore, Md.: Johns Hopkins University Press.

—— 1989: *Teletheory*. New York: Routledge.

Unger, Roberto 1983: *The Critical Legal Studies Movement*. Cambridge, Mass.: Harvard University Press.

—— 1987: *Social Theory, its Situation and its Task*. Cambridge: Cambridge University Press.

Urry, John 1990: *The Tourist Gaze*. London: Sage.

Van Maanen, John 1988: *Tales of the Field*. Chicago: University of Chicago Press.

Vaughn, Ted R. and Larry T. Reynolds 1968: The Sociology of Symbolic Interactionism. *American Sociologist*, 3, 208–14.

Vidich, Arthur J. and Stanford M. Lyman 1985: *American Sociology*. New Haven, Conn.: Yale University Press.

Wagner, Helmut R. 1964: Displacement of Scope: A Problem of Relation between Small-Scale and Large-Scale Sociological Theories. *American Journal of Sociology*, 69, 571–84.

—— 1983: *Alfred Schutz: An Intellectual Biography*. Chicago: University of Chicago Press.

Warren, Carol A. B. 1988: *Gender Issues in Field Research*. Newbury Park, Calif.: Sage.

Warshay, L. 1975: *The Current State of Sociological Theory*. New York: McKay.

—— and D. Warshay 1986: The Individualizing and Subjectivizing of George Herbert Mead: A Sociology of Knowledge Interpretation. *Sociological Focus*, 19, 177–88.

Wellman, David 1988: The Politics of Herbert Blumer's Sociological Method. *Symbolic Interaction*, 11, 59–68.

West, Candace and Don Zimmerman 1987: Doing Gender. *Gender and Society*, 1, 125–51.

West, Cornel 1988: Interview with Cornel West by Anders Stephanson. In A. Ross (ed.), *Universal Abandon*, Minneapolis: University of Minnesota Press, 269–86.

—— 1989: *The American Evasion of Philosophy*. Madison: University of Wisconsin Press.

Wiener, Carolyn 1981: *The Politics of Alcoholism*. New Brunswick, N.J.: Transaction Books.

Wiley, Norbert 1979: Notes on Self-Genesis: From Me to We to I. *Studies in Symbolic Interaction*, 2, 87–105.

—— 1986: Early American Sociology and *The Polish Peasant*. *Sociological Theory*, 4, 20–40.

—— 1989: The Complementarity of Durkheim and Mead. *Symbolic Interaction*, 12, 77–9.

—— 1990: Reflexivity and Solidarity: The Mead–Durkheim Connection. Paper presented to the 1990 Annual Meeting of the American Sociological Association, Washington, D.C.

Williams, Norma 1990: *The Mexican-American Family: Tradition and Change*. Dix Hills, N.Y.: General Hall.

Williams, Raymond 1958: *Culture and Society: 1780–1950*. New York: Harper & Row.

—— 1965: *The Long Revolution*. Harmondsworth: Penguin.

Wilson, John 1988: Post-Modern Theory: Review-essay of *Social Theory Today* edited by Anthony Giddens and Jonathan Turner, and *A History and Philosophy of the Social Sciences* by Peter T. Manicas. *Contemporary Sociology*, 17, 706–11.

Woelfel, Joseph 1967: Comment on the Blumer–Bales Dialogue Concerning the Interpretation of Mead's Thought. *American Journal of Sociology*, 72, 409.

Wolf, Charlotte 1986: Legitimation and Oppression: Response and Reflexivity. *Symbolic Interaction*, 9, 217–34.

Wolff, Kurt (ed.) 1950: *The Sociology of Georg Simmel*. New York: Free Press.

Wuthnow, Robert 1987: *Meaning and Moral Order: Explorations in Cultural Analysis*. Berkeley: University of California Press.

—— 1988: On the Theory of Culture. *ASA Footnotes*, 16 (Feb.), 6.

—— and Marsha Witten 1988: New Directions in the Study of Culture. *Annual Review of Sociology*, 14, 49–67.

Young, Kimball 1935: Review of the Payne Fund Studies. *American Journal of Sociology*, 40, 255.

Zeitlin, Irving 1973: *Rethinking Sociology*. Englewood Cliffs, N.J.: Prentice-Hall.

Zorbaugh, H. 1929: *The Gold Coast and the Slum*. Chicago: University of Chicago Press.

INDEX

ACM 3751

DATE DUE